SYSTEMS
PROGRAMMING
IN PARALLEL LOGIC
LANGUAGES

SYSTEMS PROGRAMMING IN PARALLEL LOGIC LANGUAGES

IAN FOSTER
Argonne National Laboratory

PRENTICE HALL
NEW YORK   LONDON   TORONTO   SYDNEY   TOKYO

First published 1990 by
Prentice Hall International (UK) Ltd
66 Wood Lane End, Hemel Hempstead
Hertfordshire, HP2 4RG.
A division of
Simon & Schuster International Group

Printed and bound in Great Britain at the
University Press, Cambridge.

Library of Congress Cataloging-in-Publication Data

Foster, Ian, 1959–
    Systems programming in parallel logic
        languages / by Ian Foster.
        p.   cm.
    Includes bibliographical references.
    ISBN 0-13-880774-4 : $40.00
    1. Systems programming (Computer science)
    2. Parallel processing (Electronic computers)
    I. Title.
    QA76.66.F67   1990
    005.4′2—dc20   89–38590
                                              CIP

British Library Cataloguing in Publication Data

Foster, Ian, 1959–
    Systems programming in parallel logic
    languages.   1. Computer systems. Parallel
    programming. Applications of Mathematical
    logic
    I. Title
    004′.35

    ISBN 0-13-880774-4

1 2 3 4 5   94 93 92 91 90

To Angie

CONTENTS

PREFACE

Probably the greatest problem that computer scientists and software engineers have to deal with is that of complexity in large systems. They tackle this problem by identifying abstractions that reduce problem scales to manageable levels. Powerful techniques have been developed for building abstractions on uniprocessor computers. However, computers of tomorrow are likely to be highly parallel machines, consisting of hundreds or thousands of cooperating processors. We are now faced with the challenge of designing new concepts and tools that will enable us to deal with complexity in multiprocessor systems.

This book introduces a novel approach to parallel processing based on three simple concepts: lightweight process, logical variable, and task. It investigates the application of these concepts in a particular area: the design and implementation of operating systems. This demanding, inherently concurrent problem domain is of considerable interest in its own right. It also provides an excellent testbed for parallel processing ideas.

This approach to parallel processing finds an elegant expression in a computational formalism termed 'parallel logic programming'. Parallel logic languages are used throughout the book to present ideas and results. Topics covered include: design of an operating system kernel; implementation of kernel facilities; the operating system nucleus; programming environments; and multiprocessor systems. An appendix provides a tutorial introduction to parallel logic programming.

The book is suitable for use as a textbook. It not only provides useful background reading for courses in operating systems and parallel programming, but can also be used to teach a stimulating 'hands-on' operating systems class: if students have access to a parallel logic programming system then it is entirely feasible to construct a simple multiprocessor operating system during a one-semester course.

The book will otherwise be of interest to two main groups of people. The first comprises computer scientists, engineers and students with an interest in operating systems, parallel processing or logic programming. They will find novel solutions to system design problems and learn what parallel logic programming has to offer the systems programmer. The second comprises programmers using parallel logic programming systems in industry. They will read this book to gain insights into how to build large applications using parallel logic languages. Both should appreciate the first treatment of parallel logic programming that focuses on a real application rather than artificial examples.

It should be emphasized that the material in this book is not merely of academic interest. The principal ideas have already been incorporated in industrial systems. The Strand system, developed by Strand Software Technologies, Inc., provides the first practical programming tool to be used on a wide variety of architectures: workstations, networks of workstations, hypercubes, mesh architectures and shared-memory machines. The design of this system derives in part from this work. The multiprocessor operating systems being constructed by the Japanese as part of their fifth generation computer systems project are based on similar ideas. Furthermore, operating system design is representative in its concerns of a much broader class of problem. Much of the material presented here is applicable wherever designers must deal with complexity in concurrent systems: in telecommunications, programming environments, and distributed databases, for example.

The research that formed the basis for this book was performed while at Imperial College, London, and was funded by the Science and Engineering Research Council. Like all work in parallel logic programming, it has benefited substantially from the pioneering efforts of Keith Clark and Steve Gregory. I am grateful to colleagues who constructed tools that made experimental studies easier: notably Alistair Burt, Tony Kusalik, Graem Ringwood and Ken Satoh. I would like to thank them and also Jim Crammond, Andrew Davison, Chris Hogger, Yonit Kesten and Frank McCabe for fruitful discussions. Visits to other institutions have also proved beneficial to the research. I would like to thank Ehud Shapiro of the Weizmann Institute, Kazuhiro Fuchi and Koichi Furukawa of the ICOT research centre, and Ross Overbeek of Argonne National Laboratory, for making these visits possible. In the latter stages of this work, I had the good fortune to work closely with Stephen Taylor. His critical insights and intellectual rigor have been a great stimulus and inspiration. The Strand system used as a basis for the multiprocessor performance studies reported in Chapter 6 was developed jointly with him.

The parallel implementation scheme described in Chapter 5 was published in 'Parallel implementation of Parlog' [Foster, 1988a]. The uniprocessor performance studies in Chapter 6 first appeared in 'Flat Parlog: a basis for comparison' [Foster and Taylor, 1988]. The task management performance studies in Chapter 6 have been reported in 'Efficient metacontrol in parallel logic languages' [Foster, 1987b]. The programming environment design in Chapter 8 was published in 'A declarative state transition system' [Foster, 1988b]. The implementation scheme in Chapter 8 was published in 'Implementation of a declarative state transition system' [Foster, 1989]; a revised version of this material is reprinted here by permission of John Wiley and Sons.

1

INTRODUCTION

A primary focus of research in operating system (OS) design is the development of conceptual tools for constructing abstractions. The process, which represents a thread of control capable of executing a single program, and the monitor, used to encapsulate and control access to shared resources, are examples of tools of this kind.

Unfortunately, techniques developed in the context of uniprocessor machines are not necessarily appropriate for highly parallel computers. These techniques generally incorporate assumptions about computer architecture, such as sequential execution and shared memory, that may not be true of multiprocessors. In consequence, programs developed using these techniques are not easily ported to parallel machines. For example, a program structured as a small number of sequential processes has to be restructured to exploit a larger number of processors. A system that uses shared memory for inter-process communication must be rewritten to run on a message-passing architecture.

A promising approach to this problem is to define a small set of abstract, architecture-independent concepts as a basis for system design and implementation. These concepts must be capable of expressing the complexities of real systems. They must also permit efficient implementation on both uniprocessors and a range of parallel computers.

This book proposes the *lightweight process, logical variable*, and *task* as a possible basis for the design and implementation of operating systems. As will be seen, these three abstract concepts find an elegant expression in a computational formalism called *parallel logic programming*. In addition, parallel logic languages provide a useful notation based on guarded clauses for expressing these ideas.

1.1 EXAMPLE: A SIMPLE TERMINAL SYSTEM

A simple example is used to provide a brief and informal introduction to the key concepts explored in this book. The example concerns a terminal system which is to provide a number of users with access to a set of resources.

An implementation of the terminal system must perform three distinct tasks: handle interaction with users, manage resources, and route requests from users to resources. It can hence be constructed using three types of entity: terminals, resources, and distributor. Each of these components can be viewed as a distinct thread of control or process (see Figure 1.1). The arrows in this figure indicate how processes interact: commands processed at terminals (T1–T4) cause requests to flow to resources (R1–R3) via the distributor. Results then flow back to terminals as represented by dashed lines.

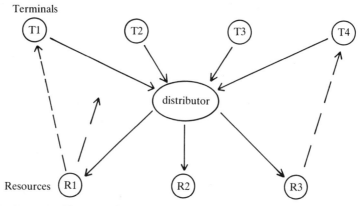

Figure 1.1 Terminal system process network.

The functionality of each component can be defined in terms of further, simpler processes. For example, zooming in on a terminal may reveal that it consists of one component that reads characters from a keyboard, another that parses these characters to form commands, and a third that interprets these commands. The terminal component is itself composed of three simpler processes, as shown in Figure 1.2.

These simple processes can be defined in terms of yet simpler processes. For example, the parser may be composed of processes that identify a character, parse an integer, etc. In fact, this decomposition can be continued until only primitive operations, such as arithmetic, remain. Some of these processes, such as the distributor, appear long-lived; others are created to perform a specific task and then disappear.

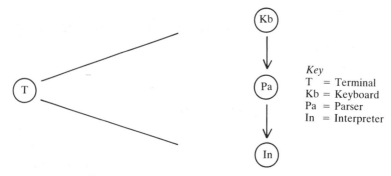

Key
T = Terminal
Kb = Keyboard
Pa = Parser
In = Interpreter

Figure 1.2 Decomposition of terminal.

This view of computation as an activity performed by a large, dynamically-varying number of small, cooperating processes is referred to as a *lightweight process model*. In most computational models, a process is a complex entity. Creating or destroying such a process may require thousands of processor cycles; switching from one process to another can also be expensive. In contrast, it may be possible to create, destroy or schedule a lightweight process in only a few cycles.

An important advantage of a lightweight process model is that concurrency in an application is immediately manifest. This means that applications need not be rewritten to take advantage of additional processors. For example, the definition of a terminal in terms of concurrent keyboard, parsing, and interpreter processes means that the terminal system can execute on a varying number of processors (see Figure 1.3). In effect, the definition of a system in terms of a large number of small processes means that the tasks of solving a problem and mapping a solution to a multiprocessor are distinct and independent. A formulation in terms of a small number of large processes does not give the same freedom.

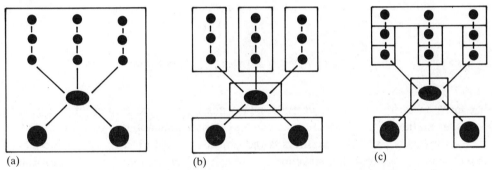

Figure 1.3 Mapping the terminal system to different architectures. (a) One processor. (b) Five processors. (c) Ten processors.

Unfortunately, simply allocating processes to processors is only half the story. In order to be able to cooperate, processes must be able to both communicate so as to exchange data and synchronize so as to sequence their activities. Communication and synchronization are generally achieved using one of two mechanisms: shared memory or message passing. The first is the more flexible but requires a global address space. The second can be implemented efficiently on message passing multiprocessors but is inflexible on single processors because references cannot generally be included in messages.

A novel communication and synchronization mechanism termed the *logical variable* combines features of both shared memory and message passing. A logical variable is a data structure with a single assignment property: its value is either defined or undefined, and once defined cannot be redefined. On a shared memory machine, logical variables act much like conventional variables: one process writes a variable which other processes read. On a message passing machine, writing a value to a logical variable shared by processes located on different processors has the effect of communicating that value to those processors. As will be seen, the single assignment property permits efficient implementation of the logical variable on both uniprocessors and multiprocessors.

The final component of the programming model to be explored in this book is the concept of *task*: a collection of lightweight processes that are to be managed as a single unit. For example, the command interpreter component of the terminal may process requests to execute user programs. Execution of these programs will create many lightweight processes which may be mapped over a large number of processors. The command interpreter must be able to manage the execution of these processes in various ways: for example, detect errors and termination, allocate processor resources, and abort their execution.

In summary, a lightweight process model provides a degree of architecture-independence by permitting separate development of programs and the mapping of programs to processors. The logical variable makes this separation of concerns possible by providing an interprocess communication mechanism that is viable on a range of architectures. Finally, the notion of task provides support for computation management. These three concepts together constitute an abstract model of computation which, it will be argued, provides a suitable basis for constructing complex concurrent systems.

1.2 OBJECT-ORIENTED OPERATING SYSTEMS

For concreteness, it has proved useful to place this work in the context of a particular OS design methodology. The approach to OS design that appears to have the most promise for highly parallel computers is the object-oriented or *client-server* model. In this methodology, systems are structured as sets of objects (servers) which encapsulate resources and to which other processes (clients) can direct requests. In multiprocessor systems, servers can readily be distributed and requests can be implemented efficiently using message passing. Figure 1.4 shows the structure of a typical object-oriented OS. A small kernel located on each processor provides very basic facilities. A small nucleus of basic services is implemented using these facilities; all other OS functions are implemented as user-level services using nucleus services and kernel facilities.

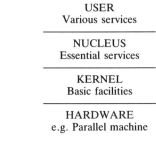

USER
Various services

NUCLEUS
Essential services

KERNEL
Basic facilities

HARDWARE
e.g. Parallel machine

Figure 1.4 Object-oriented operating system structure.

This discussion can be used to define requirements that an abstract computational model must satisfy if it is to provide a useful basis for OS design. It must support the construction of a simple kernel that incorporates solutions to OS design problems mentioned at the beginning of this chapter. Facilities provided by this kernel must be sufficient to implement essential services in the nucleus. The nucleus must also be able to provide other programs with access to these services and to protect these services against erroneous or malicious access. User-level programs must be able to construct new services from old and build comprehensive programming systems.

1.3 GOALS AND CONTRIBUTIONS

The goal of the research on which this book is based has been to determine whether dynamic lightweight processes, logical variables, and tasks provide a sufficient and effective basis for building operating systems. A particular goal has been to understand and evaluate the minimal kernel required to support systems programming using these concepts. These goals can be summarized as follows.

- To identify fundamental OS design problems.
- To investigate kernel facilities required to solve these problems using lightweight processes, logical variables and tasks.
- To determine whether these facilities can be implemented efficiently.
- To determine whether these facilities can be used to construct an operating system: that is, a nucleus and useful user-level services.

Two classes of machine have been investigated: uniprocessors and tightly-coupled multiprocessors in which processors communicate by message passing. Attention is restricted to those types of system in which interprocessor communication is inexpensive and reliable.

The main contributions of the work are as follows.

- A small set of kernel facilities that support operating systems constructed using dynamic lightweight processes, tasks, and logical variables.
- Efficient uniprocessor and multiprocessor implementation techniques for these facilities.
- A body of techniques for implementing operating systems and programming environments using the three concepts.

The utility of the kernel facilities and implementation techniques has been demonstrated in a working, single-user OS. Referring to Figure 1.4, this consists of three main components. A software emulator running on top of the Unix OS implements the necessary kernel facilities. This supports a nucleus, implemented in a parallel logic programming language. The nucleus provides basic services such as terminal and disk input/output, and task management. These services are used to construct user-level programs including a programming environment. The environment supports a high-level programming model that provides persistent data and concurrent, atomic transactions on this data. The OS executes on a uniprocessor workstation. The kernel facilities required to support multiprocessor execution have also been demonstrated and evaluated but have not been used to execute the OS.

1.4 HOW TO READ THIS BOOK

Of the remaining nine chapters of this book, the first two are introductory in nature and should be of interest to all readers. Chapter 2 reviews important OS design problems and previous solutions to these problems; Chapter 3 describes the Flat Parlog (FP) language used throughout the book as a framework for presentation and experimental evaluation of techniques.

Subsequent material is structured in much the same way as an object-oriented OS (Figure 1.4): successive chapters deal with the kernel (Chapters 4–6), nucleus (Chapter 7) and user levels (Chapter 8). The reader who is primarily interested in how parallel logic languages are used for systems programming may wish to skim Chapter 4 to learn about kernel facilities and then turn to Chapters 7 and 8 before returning to Chapters 5 and 6. The reader with an interest in the design and implementation of kernel facilities should read the book in textual order.

Chapter 4 proposes a set of kernel facilities and shows that these provide solutions to OS design problems introduced in Chapter 2. The problems of task management and processor scheduling are considered in detail. Chapter 5 describes implementation techniques for these kernel facilities on both uniprocessors and multiprocessors. Performance studies that permit evaluation of the efficiency of these techniques are presented in Chapter 6.

Chapter 7 shows that the kernel facilities described previously are sufficient to implement essential services required in any OS, to provide other programs with access to these services, and to protect services against illicit or erroneous access. It also presents implementation techniques for an OS nucleus. Chapter 8 presents a novel approach to the design and implementation of user-level programming environments.

Chapter 9 discusses how material presented in previous chapters can be applied in multiprocessors. It also describes extensions to these facilities that support more sophisticated processor scheduling algorithms.

Chapter 10 draws conclusions, reviews some related research, and notes directions for further investigation. Appendices provide a tutorial introduction to, and a formal definition of, the FP language.

2

OPERATING SYSTEM DESIGN

This chapter reviews fundamental problems in OS design and describes potential solutions. The problems considered are concurrency, communication and synchronization, nondeterminism, shared resources, protection, task management and kernel design.

A central strategy adopted to manage complexity in OS design is the definition of hierarchies of abstractions [Dijkstra, 1968a]. The solutions described here are abstractions to be introduced at the lowest levels in these hierarchies. They constitute basic design tools; the designer applies a coherent set of these tools to construct a particular OS. Criteria to be applied when selecting a tool set are discussed at the end of the chapter.

2.1 CONCURRENCY

Most computers execute machine instructions at a memory address determined by a program counter. In general, the program counter moves through memory in a well-defined way: the address of each instruction executed is determined by the previous instruction. However, interrupts can cause the contents of the program counter to change in unpredictable ways. If these *control jumps* are allowed to happen in an unstructured manner it becomes difficult to understand the actions of a computer.

Early OS designers proposed the process as a solution to this problem [Dijkstra, 1968a]. A *process* is an abstract entity capable of executing a single sequence of instructions (a *program*). An implementation of processes saves the program counter and other components of machine state when an interrupt occurs. This permits the current process to be resumed at a later time as if no interruption had occurred. A process, therefore, constitutes a *thread of control*; several threads of control can be in existence at one time, but only one can be active. A *process switch* transfers control from one process to another.

Although initially introduced as a means of dealing with interrupts, the notion of process was soon extended to support multiprogramming and multiprocessing [Brinch Hansen, 1972]. In the first case, the OS is not constrained to resume the same process following an interrupt. Several processes can thus appear to execute concurrently on the same processor. In the second, multiple processes execute in parallel on multiple processors.

2.1.1 Varieties of process

Different operating systems support different varieties of process. These may be distinguished according to whether they are static or dynamic, heavyweight or lightweight.

Some operating systems support only a *static* number of processes created when the system is initialized. A static process structure can be implemented efficiently and has proved sufficient for simple operating systems such as Brinch Hansen's influential SOLO system [Brinch Hansen, 1976]. However, modern operating systems that support multiprogramming and multiprocessing generally require the ability to create and destroy processes *dynamically*.

In most operating systems in use today (for example, Unix [Ritchie and Thompson, 1974]) processes are *heavyweight* entities that carry a great deal of status information such as accounting data and open files. This makes them expensive to create, destroy and reschedule following a process switch. A number of researchers have argued the advantages of *lightweight* processes [Cheriton *et al.*, 1979; Almes *et al.*, 1985; Berglund, 1986]. A lightweight process has little status information associated with it and can be created, destroyed and scheduled rapidly. Lightweight processes are particularly appropriate on multiprocessor architectures, where delays incurred following requests for remote data (*communication latency*) result in processes frequently becoming idle. Lightweight processes permit a processor to switch rapidly to executing another process, hence reducing the effect of latency. In systems that support lightweight processes, processes are generally grouped into *tasks* [Cheriton *et al.*, 1979]. Accounting information and so forth are associated with a task rather than individual processes.

2.1.2 Expressing concurrency

In most programming models that support multiple processes, sequential evaluation is the norm and programmers must explicitly specify concurrent evaluation. This can be achieved by direct calls to kernel mechanisms that create and destroy processes. However, research has identified a number of tools for defining processes that minimize the risk of error and simplify programs by imposing structure. Two such constructs are considered here: fork/join and parbegin/parend.

The fork statement is used to represent process creation [Conway, 1963]. A fork instruction creates a new process which starts to execute a specified program. The invoking process proceeds concurrently with the new process. The join statement permits the invoking process to synchronize with termination of the new process. Execution of this instruction delays the invoking process until a specified invoked process terminates.

fork/join is a general notation for specifying concurrent processes. It is widely used in the Unix operating system [Ritchie and Thompson, 1974]. However, its lack of structure can result in programs that are difficult to understand, particularly if fork or join statements occur in loops or conditionals.

The parbegin statement provides a more structured representation of concurrent execution [Dijkstra, 1968b]. A statement:

parbegin S_1; S_2; ...; S_n; parend;

denotes concurrent execution of the statements S_1, S_2, ..., S_n. Execution of this statement terminates only when all the S_i have terminated. The S_i can themselves be parbegin statements.

parbegin/parend can only be used to create a fixed number of processes, organized in a tree structure in which each node waits for its offspring to terminate before terminating itself. fork/join is more expressive in the sense that it can represent more complex process dependencies. However, a consequence of parbegin/parend's limitations is that programs that use this construct are easier to understand.

2.1.3 Functional concurrency

Functional programming is an abstract computational model in which concurrency is implicit rather than specified explicitly by the programmer [Backus, 1978; Henderson 1980]. Evaluation of a functional program computes the value of a function. For example, consider the following functional program:

g(X,Y) = X+Y.
h(X) = X*X.
f(X) = g(h(X),h(X)).

Each statement defines a function. A function call is evaluated by replacing it with the right-hand side of a statement that has a matching left-hand side. A function call f(3) is hence rewritten to g(h(3),h(3)), then to g(9,9), and eventually to the value 18.

Functional programs are referentially transparent: that is, evaluation of a function always gives the same result, in whatever context it is evaluated. It is therefore possible to execute functions calls in parallel without changing the result computed. This permits both *restricted* concurrency (where multiple arguments to a function are evaluated concurrently) and *stream* concurrency (concurrent evaluation of a function and its argument) [Kahn and MacQueen, 1977]. In the program above, restricted concurrency allows evaluation of the two calls to h in the call g(h(3),h(3)) to proceed in parallel. Stream concurrency permits evaluation of these calls to h to proceed in parallel with the call to g.

The functional programming model is abstract: it says nothing about processes at all. However, the concurrently executing functions f, g and h can be regarded as lightweight, dynamic processes. The function definitions f, g and h can be read as definitions of process actions. An implementation of these processes needs maintain little more than their name and arguments.

2.1.4 Parallel logic programming

Parallel logic programming is another computational model that provides an abstract specification of concurrent execution [Clark and Gregory, 1981; Takeuchi and Furukawa, 1986]. In this model, a computation is a set of lightweight, dynamic processes. Processes can communicate, terminate, change state, and create new processes. Process actions are specified by logic clauses, which have the form:

$$A_0 \leftarrow A_1, \ldots, A_N. \quad N \geq 0$$

Each clause can be read as a rewrite rule for a process network: it states that a process A_0 is to be replaced with a network of processes $A_1, \ldots, A_N$. If $N > 1$, then $N - 1$ new processes are created. If $N = 0$, the process terminates. If $N = 1$, the current process effectively continues executing with potentially changed state. Recursively-defined rules can be used to define arbitrary numbers of processes.

Actors represent another abstract, intrinsically concurrent computational model [Hewitt, 1977; Agha, 1986]. An actor system consists of a dynamically varying number of actors which cooperate to perform computation. Parallel logic programming has many similarities with the actor model and can in fact be regarded as an implementation of actors. Actors will not therefore be considered further here.

2.1.5 Summary

The process is a central abstraction in OS design. It permits programmers to disregard the effect of control jumps and to concern themselves with the behavior of individual processes. This can significantly reduce system complexity.

Many operating systems are constructed using a small (often static) number of heavyweight processes that execute more or less independently. The programmer specifies both the sequences of actions to be performed by individual processes and, as described in the next section, how these processes are to interact. However, this approach does not scale well to massively parallel multiprocessors, as potential interactions between many sequential processes become hard to handle. In addition, heavyweight processes suffer from communication latency.

Lightweight processes can reduce the effect of communication latency. However, most lightweight process models still require the programmer to explicitly specify concurrent execution. In contrast, concurrency is implicit in abstract computational models such as functional and parallel logic programming. In these models, computation is performed entirely by cooperating concurrent processes.

2.2 COMMUNICATION AND SYNCHRONIZATION

In order to cooperate, concurrent processes must be able to exchange data: that is, to communicate. They must also be able to synchronize their execution so as to order their activities [Andrews and Schneider, 1983].

Research has identified two main models for communication and synchronization. One uses *shared resources* to implement communication; the other relies on *message passing*. More specialized and abstract models have also been proposed: for example, remote procedure call, functional composition and shared logical variables.

2.2.1 Shared resources

The shared resource model assumes that processes communicate by reading and writing shared memory locations. This implies a need for synchronization mechanisms to control access to shared resources. Two types of synchronization can be distinguished. *Mutual exclusion* restricts access to a resource while a critical operation (such as reading and updating a shared variable) is performed. *Condition synchronization* delays access to a resource until some condition (such as 'buffer is full') is satisfied.

Both types of synchronization can be implemented explicitly using *busy-waiting*. Busy-waiting requires that a process wishing to perform some action wait until a particular location has a specified value. However, busy-waiting is clumsy and wastes processor cycles. More abstract synchronization operations have therefore been defined. Two are described here: semaphores and monitors.

SEMAPHORES

A semaphore [Dijkstra, 1968a] is a nonnegative-integer-valued variable on which operations commonly called P and V are defined. Given a semaphore S, P(S) delays until S is zero and then executes the operation $S := S - 1$. V(S) executes the operation $S := S + 1$. Both P's test and decrement and V's increment must be performed as indivisible operations.

Semaphores are used to implement mutual exclusion as follows. A semaphore is associated with a resource to which access is to be controlled; this is initialized to 0. Any process that wishes to access the resource must perform a P operation on this semaphore, access the resource and then perform a V operation on the same semaphore.

Semaphores are higher-level and hence easier to use than busy-waiting. Furthermore, they may be supported by an operating system kernel, which can implement P and V operations by moving processes to and from a ready queue – a queue of processes that can be executed – and suspension queues containing processes waiting to perform P operations on different semaphores. This avoids wasting processor cycles.

However, semaphores do not enforce any structure on synchronization operations. It is thus easy to misuse them. For example, a P or V operation may be omitted or applied to the wrong semaphore. Also, as P and V operations may be scattered through code that is not concerned with synchronization, programs that use semaphores can be difficult to understand.

MONITORS

Monitors were proposed by Hoare [1974] and others as a more structured way of con-

type linebuffer = monitor	% Monitor definition begins.
var buffer : line; count : integer;	% Define state variables.
sender, receiver: queue;	% Define queue variables.
procedure write(item : char)	% Write a character to buffer.
if count = N then **delay**(sender);	% Delay writer if buffer full.
buffer[count] := item; count := count + 1;	% Add item to buffer.
if count = N then **continue**(receiver);	% Resume reader if buffer full.
procedure read(text : line)	% Read line from buffer.
if count < N **delay**(receiver);	% Delay reader if buffer not full.
text := buffer; count := 0;	% Empty buffer.
continue(sender);	% Resume writer.
begin count := 0 end	% Initialize buffer to empty

Program 2.1 Printer buffer monitor in Concurrent Pascal.

trolling access to a shared resource. A monitor consists of a state and a number of procedures that define operations on that state. An implementation of monitors ensures that processes executing a monitor's procedures are mutually excluded. A monitor hence serves both to synchronize access to a resource and to hide the resource's internal structure from other processes. The data abstraction functions of a monitor are also found in the class construct of Simula 67 [Dahl, 1968]. However, the monitor's integration of data abstraction and synchronization functions has proved to be particularly powerful.

Queue variables may be defined within monitors to provide condition synchronization: that is, to delay processes that invoke monitor procedures until certain conditions are satisfied [Brinch Hansen, 1975]. Two operations are defined on these variables: *delay* delays the process which executes it until another process resumes it; *continue* resumes a process. For example, consider the problem of synchronizing access to a printer buffer to which a producer process adds characters and which a printer process periodically empties. The printer must not read the buffer before it is written and the producer must not write to the buffer when it is full. The buffer is encapsulated in a monitor that provides write and read operations which write a character and read a line respectively. Two queue variables, sender and receiver, are defined. The variable sender is used in write to delay the producer process when the buffer is full and in read to resume it once the buffer has been emptied. The state variable receiver is used in read to delay the printer process when the buffer is not full and in write to resume it when it is full. An implementation of this monitor in a simplified form of Concurrent Pascal is presented as

Program 2.1 [Brinch Hansen, 1975]. The program declares state and queue variables. It provides routines to read and write the buffer plus initialization code that sets the buffer to empty.

2.2.2 Message passing

The second model of communication and synchronization does not assume shared resources. Instead, processes communicate by sending and receiving messages. Messages are sent using a send (<destination>, <value>) command and received using a receive(<source>, <variable>) command, where <destination> and <source> designate processes. Message-passing models differ according to whether processes are named directly or indirectly and whether sources and destinations must be specified at compile-time or may be computed at run-time. Communication in these models may be synchronous or asynchronous and may be reliable or unreliable.

Direct naming requires that a process name be specified in send and receive commands. This is easy to implement but inflexible, as a process can only send to or receive from a named process, rather than *any* process, as is sometimes required. Indirect naming schemes introduce a level of indirection and hence permit many to one or many to many communication. The send and/or receive commands may designate a port or other indirect construct.

Fixing sources and destinations at compile time simplifies implementation, but precludes the programming of reconfigurable systems. For example, new user processes cannot be created at run-time; instead, a fixed number of processes must be defined and allocated to user programs as required. Alternatively, processes may be permitted to compute values for sources and destinations at run-time. The latter approach is more flexible but less efficient.

Synchronous communication means that both sender and receiver must be ready to communicate for communication to proceed [Hoare, 1978]. This can require two-phase communication protocols which ask for permission to send before sending data. Asynchronous communication permits a sender to send a message that a receiver is not ready to receive [Seitz, 1985]. As the sender can then run arbitrarily ahead of the receiver, buffering is required in a kernel that supports asynchronous communication.

An OS kernel may choose to support only unreliable communication [Tannenbaum and van Renesse, 1985]. This can be used to build reliable communication protocols. Unreliable communication simplifies kernel implementation and permits efficient communication when reliability is not vital. Reliability is more of an issue in distributed systems than in multiprocessors, however, and so reliable communication is assumed here.

REMOTE PROCEDURE CALL

A remote procedure call is a higher-level message-passing construct that represents two communications: one to request a remote service and one to return a result [Birrell and Nelson, 1984]. A process uses a call statement to communicate a request to a named process. The request invokes a named procedure in the remote process; this invocation is (generally) implicit. The request is blocking, so the process making the request is delayed until a reply is received. One advantage of the remote procedure call is that it reduces opportunity for programming errors. Another is its similarity to local procedure call; this reduces the number of new concepts introduced. However, the similarity is more apparent than real, as local and remote procedure calls rarely use the same calling conventions: local procedure calls generally use call-by-reference, but remote procedure calls must use call-by-value, as messages cannot easily contain references to data structures. Remote procedure call constitutes the basic communication mechanism in operating systems structured using the client-server model [Jones, 1978]. Lightweight processes are frequently used in these systems to avoid delays when waiting for replies from remote procedure calls.

2.2.3 Functional composition

The functional programming model provides a more abstract representation of inter-process communication. Recall that stream concurrency permits functions to be executed concurrently with their arguments. The only restriction on this concurrent execution is that a function that uses the result of another function must wait for the result to be available. If functions are viewed as processes, then function applications define communication channels and availability of data provides a synchronization mechanism. This is referred to as *dataflow synchronization*.

Henderson [1982] and Jones [1984] have explored the application of functional programming in systems programming. Their basic insight is that operating systems can be viewed as functions that map external events to side-effects in the external world. Simple systems can be defined as functions that map keyboard input to screen output. These programs represent an OS as a set of recursive functions that communicate by incrementally constructing and consuming potentially infinite data structures (usually lists) called *streams*. Lazy evaluation (a demand-driven evaluation strategy which only evaluates functions when their values are required [Henderson and Morris, 1976; Friedman and Wise, 1976]) ensures that a data item is only demanded from the keyboard as it is required to calculate an output value. Stream concurrency permits concurrent evaluation of the various functions defining the system. The underlying implementation is assumed to provide interfaces to the outside world by generating the input stream and displaying the output stream.

Program 2.2 defines a simple OS that repeatedly executes functions named by the user if they can be found in a supplied filestore Fs. Consider firstly the function lookup. This can be executed to find the value associated with a particular key in a list. (Strings beginning with capital letters denote variables; the syntax [H |T] denotes a list with head H and tail T and [ ] denotes the empty list). A function call lookup(f, [[g, defn1], [f, defn2]]) returns the value defn2. A function call lookup(h, [[g, defn1], [f, defn2]]) returns the value missing.

The function system in Program 2.2 generates an output stream consisting of either

```
lookup(Key, [ ]) = missing                                    % Not found.
lookup(Key, [ [Key1, Value] |Data] ) =                        % Next element:
  if Key = Key1                                               % same key?
  then Value                                                  %    Yes: return.
  else lookup(Key, Data).                                     %    No: recurse.

system( [Function |Kb], Fs) =                                 % Receive input.
  if lookup(Fs, Function) = missing                           % Defined?
  then [error |system(Kb, Fs)]                                %    No: ERROR.
  else append(execute(lookup(Fs, Function) ), system(Kb, Fs) ) %    Yes: execute.
```

Program 2.2 Simple functional operating system.

function output or the constant error if Fs does not contain the definition of a named function. The matching of its first argument with the data structure [Function | Kb] is assumed to return the next term Function input by the user. Kb is the remainder of the input stream. The implementation displays system's output at a terminal.

Figure 2.1 represents the execution of Program 2.2. Circles represent processes and other symbols represent screen and keyboard. Lines joining entities represent communication channels; arrows indicate the direction of dataflow along these channels. An input f results in evaluation of functions f, append and system, if f is defined in the structure Fs representing the filestore (Figure 2.1(b)). Otherwise an error value is generated (c). This program can exploit both restricted and stream concurrency: restricted concurrency permits the functions f and system to be executed concurrently; stream concurrency permits these functions to be executed concurrently with the function append.

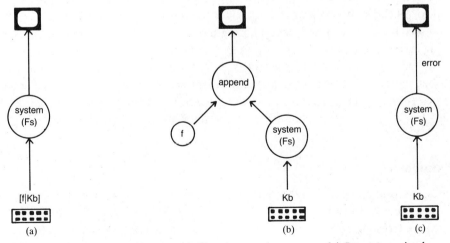

Figure 2.1 Execution of simple functional operating system. (a) Input f received. (b) f defined in Fs. (c) f not defined.

2.2.4 Shared logical variables

The parallel logic programming model also uses dataflow synchronization. However, communication channels are represented explicitly using shared logical variables rather than implicitly using function applications. This notation can be more verbose but is more expressive. The logical variable has the single assignment property: it is initially unbound, but once assigned a value (instantiated) cannot be modified. Processes synchronize and communicate by reading and writing shared logical variables. An attempt to read an unbound logical variable causes a process to suspend. For example, the process and communication network represented by the function application:

> append(execute(lookup(Fs, Name)), system(Kb, Fs))

(illustrated in Figure 2.1) is represented by the parallel logic processes:

> lookup(Fs, Name, Val), execute(Val, Os1), system(Kb, Fs, Os2), append(Os1, Os2, Os)

The shared variable Os1 defines the communication channel between the execute and append processes; Os2 defines the channel between system and append; and Val represents the channel between lookup and execute. The variable Os is the output channel. Assume that Name = f. If lookup finds a definition for f in the filestore Fs, this definition is passed to execute using the communication channel Val. The process network that results is the same as that produced by the functional program, illustrated in Figure 2.1(b).

Despite their single assignment property, logical variables can be used to implement a range of communication patterns. The most important is stream communication: a variable can be bound to a structure containing other unbound variables which can be used subsequently to communicate further values. For example, the process f may bind the variable Os1 to a list [hello |Os1a], where Os1a is an unbound variable. This has the effect of communicating the value hello to the append process. If f then binds Os1a to a further incomplete structure (say [bye |Os1b]) then a further value is communicated.

Shapiro [1984a] showed that parallel logic programs can be used to express OS structures in much the same way as functional programs. He re-expressed Henderson's simple operating systems in a parallel logic language, and emphasized the advantages of being able to include logical variables in messages. This permits communication channels to be established dynamically. For example, the process f may generate a request input(Input) to the screen service, where Input is an unbound variable. The screen service can use this variable as a communication channel to return data to the requesting process.

2.2.5 Summary

Interprocess communication and synchronization is traditionally achieved using either shared resources or message passing. Each approach has its advantages and disadvantages. Shared resources introduce complex synchronization problems. These can be partially hidden using suitable abstractions but still stretch the programmer's ability to understand interprocess interactions. Also, shared resources are difficult to implement efficiently on nonshared memory multiprocessors as the overhead of maintaining shared mutable structures consistent is likely to be high. Message passing, on the other hand, tends to suffer from restrictive 'call-by-value' semantics. Operating systems, therefore, frequently use a combination of both methods: for example, in Thoth and the V kernel, lightweight processes communicate with processes in the same task via shared memory but use message passing for other communication [Cheriton *et al.*, 1979; Berglund, 1986]. The result is a complex computational model.

Shared resource and message passing models of interprocess interaction are based on particular computer architectures: shared-memory and message-passing multiprocessors respectively. In contrast, more abstract models of interaction such as function application and shared logical variables make no assumptions about architecture. In concurrent functional programming, function applications are used to define communication channels, and dataflow constraints provide synchronization. Unfortunately, function application can only represent static communication structures.

Logical variables are an interesting tool for representing communication and synchronization as they combine features of both the shared resource and message passing models. Like shared resources, they permit references rather than values to be passed between processes. However, their single assignment property suggests that they may not share the implementation problems of shared resources on message-passing architectures. Another attractive feature is the ease with which a wide range of communication patterns can be expressed: in particular, the ability to include an unbound variable in a message provides a concise representation of a return address.

2.3 SHARED RESOURCES

An OS must be able to control access to resources so as to prevent contention when several processes attempt to access them concurrently. Access to both physical resources such as disks and keyboards, and logical resources such as file systems may need to be controlled. Two related techniques have been used to solve this problem. *Data abstraction* mechanisms hide implementation details by forcing processes to access resources using special access functions. *Synchronization* mechanisms sequence calls to access functions when required.

The monitor combines both data abstraction and synchronization by providing a set of access functions and sequencing calls to these functions. Monitors can be used to encapsulate physical as well as logical resources. Brinch Hansen [1976] used them for this purpose in his SOLO operating system. SOLO was implemented in the programming language Concurrent Pascal, which supports monitors via special language constructs. A Concurrent Pascal program creates a fixed number of concurrent processes which use monitors to access shared resources such as data structures, I/O devices and other hardware resources.

No resources are shared directly in message passing models. Any resource that may need to be accessed by more than one process must be represented as an independent process, to which other processes send requests to access or modify resource state. For example, the printer buffer described in Section 2.2.1 can be represented as a process to which a producer process sends write_char messages and a printer process sends read_line messages. Message passing models thus provide natural support for data abstraction; sequencing the processing of requests provides synchronization. Hardware resources can be encapsulated in processes in the same way as logical resources. For example, an I/O device can be represented as a process that handles read and write messages.

As functional programs can only define static communication topologies, functional programming has difficulty implementing systems in which dynamic numbers of processes communicate with a shared resource. This problem can be solved by extending the model. For example, Arvind and Brock [1982] introduce a construct called a manager that encapsulates a shared resource and handles the routing of replies to processes making requests to the resource. The logical variable provides the same functionality, as was illustrated by the input request in the example in Section 2.2.4.

2.4 NONDETERMINISM

The behavior of OS processes must often depend on the timing and ordering of external events. For example, a device manager may need to respond to input from one of several devices. The OS designer needs a way of controlling this nondeterminism by localizing its effects to specific program fragments. This is generally achieved by the use of some form of guarded command.

2.4.1 Guarded commands

A guarded command consists of one or more statements, each of which comprises a guard and a body [Dijkstra, 1975]. A guard is a conjunction of boolean expressions and is said to succeed if its boolean expressions evaluate to true. It fails if any boolean expression evaluates to false. Evaluation of a guarded command evaluates the guards of each statement. If one or more guards succeeds, a nondeterministic choice is made and the chosen statement's body is executed.

Guarded commands have been used to represent nondeterministic choice in a number of programming models and languages. In message passing models, guarded commands are extended to include input commands in the guard. A guard that includes input commands succeeds if its boolean expressions evaluate to true *and* its input commands would not delay, fails if any boolean expression evaluates to false and *delays* otherwise.

CSP AND OCCAM

The programming language occam illustrates the application of guarded commands in a message passing model. Occam [Inmos Ltd, 1984] is a programming language derived from Communicating Sequential Processes (CSP) [Hoare, 1978], a programming notation based on synchronous message passing, guarded commands and a form of parbegin statement. Occam is essentially a subset of CSP with a more readable syntax. It was designed as a systems programming language. In particular, it has been used as the machine language for the transputer [May and Shepherd, 1984], a VLSI microprocessor that has been used to construct parallel computers. The transputer effectively implements the kernel mechanisms required to support programming in occam directly in hardware.

Occam programs combine three types of command – assignment, input (receive) and output (send) – in SEQ, ALT and PAR blocks. SEQ blocks represent sequential evaluation; ALT blocks express guarded commands; PAR blocks are a type of parbegin statement.

Assignment commands assign values to variables. They have the form variable := value. Input and output commands permit concurrent processes to communicate using named communication links termed *channels*. They have the form channel ? variable and channel ! value, respectively. Message passing is synchronous: either sender or receiver delay until the other is ready to communicate.

Processes created within a PAR block communicate using channels. Predeclared channels like 'keyboard' and 'screen' provide an interface to I/O devices. When executing on several processors, occam permits the programmer to specify where processes are to be executed.

```
PROC buffer(CHAN from_writer, to_printer, from_printer) =
    VAR char, count, line [BYTE N]          % Declare local variables.
    SEQ
        count := 0                          % Initialize buffer to empty.
        WHILE TRUE                          % Repeatedly process messages ...
            ALT
                (count < N) & from_writer ? char   % Command 1: Buffer not full
                    SEQ                            %                & char received.
                        line [BYTE count] := char  %     Add to line buffer, &
                        count := count + 1         %     increment count.
                (count = N) & from_printer ? ANY   % Command 2: Buffer full
                    SEQ                            %                & line requested.
                        to_printer ! line          %     Send line to printer, &
                        count := 0:                %     reset count.
```

Program 2.3 Printer buffer in occam.

Program 2.3 illustrates programming in occam. This program implements the same buffer as Program 2.1. However, the buffer is implemented here as a process, buffer, that maintains a line buffer and character count and has channel connections from a producer process and to and from a printer process. Its two guarded commands accept a character from the producer when the buffer is *not* full, and a request for a line from the printer when the buffer *is* full, respectively.

Occam has been widely used for programming parallel algorithms and parallel computers. An attractive feature of the language is its simplicity, which has permitted efficient implementation in hardware and the development of verification rules. However, the language only supports static process structures and does not support recursion. This limits its utility. Brinch Hansen has described a language, Joyce, that removes certain of these restrictions [Brinch Hansen, 1987]. It is not clear that similar verification rules apply.

2.4.2 Nondeterministic primitives

Pure functions cannot describe time-dependent or nondeterministic behavior: a function should always return the same result regardless of the order in which its arguments are evaluated.

A number of solutions to this problem have been proposed. The simplest is to extend a functional language with a nondeterministic primitive. This can either be a merge primitive (as proposed by Henderson [1982] and Abramsky [1982]) or some lower-level operator that can be used to program merge and other operations, such as frons [Friedman and Wise, 1980] or a nondeterministic choice operator [Jones, 1984]. All of these approaches provide (or can be used to define) a merge operation which, when applied to two streams a and b, generates a stream c that is a 'nondeterministic' interleaving of the elements on a and b. The stream c contains all the elements of a and b, with the ordering of elements in a preserved, the ordering of elements in b preserved but with the elements of a and b interleaved in some arbitrary fashion. Merge is nondeterministic in the sense that the interleaving of elements in the output stream is not determined by any functional description.

Some form of nondeterminism is essential if the functional programming model is to be used for systems programming. Unfortunately, nondeterminism compromises the mathematical purity of functional programs and invalidates certain transformation and proof techniques. For example, the expression:

```
if X = X then yes else no
   where X = E
```

always gives the result yes for any expression E. On the other hand, the apparently equivalent expression:

```
if E = E then yes else no
```

may give result no if E contains nondeterministic components. This is because in the latter case E is evaluated twice; a nondeterministic choice may cause it to compute different values.

2.5 PROTECTION

An OS must be able to protect processes from other erroneous or malicious processes. This permits individual processes to execute as if no other processes were running. Processes must also be able to share resources, so it must be possible to give processes differing access rights to different resources. Access rights can range from none at all, through the ability to read, modify, etc. Protection mechanisms must be built in at the lowest level of an OS if security is to be ensured.

Two main approaches to protection can be distinguished: access list and capability. Access list mechanisms associate a list of valid users with a resource [Saltzer, 1974]. Capability mechanisms require a user to present a ticket called a capability when attempting to access a resource [Dennis and van Horn, 1966]. The former approach has a number of drawbacks, particularly in distributed systems. Each user must have a globally unique identifier and a centralized manager must maintain a record of these identifiers. In contrast, capabilities can be generated and validated by individual services. They also permit more flexible access patterns. For example, they can be used to define a database resource that provides controlled access to sensitive data on behalf of users who do not themselves have the right to access that data. This degree of control is hard to provide using access lists.

Both access list and capability systems must ensure that processes cannot forge authorization to access a resource. This can be achieved using hardware support, compile-time verification and encryption. For example, hardware support for memory management can ensure that an untrusted program does not access memory locations outside a restricted address space; a special supervisor call instruction must be used to request a privileged program to perform accesses on its behalf. Hardware support for capabilities may prevent modification of memory locations containing capabilities. If user programs are expressed in a high-level language, it can be possible to verify at compile-time that only a restricted set of valid operations is performed and that special kernel mechanisms are invoked to perform privileged operations such as creating, copying, or modifying capabilities [Cohen and Jefferson, 1975]. An alternative approach to protecting capabilities is to encrypt them or to choose them from a large address space [Tannenbaum et al., 1986]. This is appropriate in distributed systems, in which remote kernels or communication links may not be trusted.

In summary, capabilities appear superior to access lists in distributed systems and are probably to be preferred in multiprocessors. High-level languages provide the most elegant form of protection; alternatives include hardware support and encryption.

2.6 TASK MANAGEMENT

A task is a computation initiated to perform some particular action. In a conventional uniprocessor OS, a task may correspond to a process. In systems based on lightweight processes a task may be a set of processes [Cheriton *et al.*, 1979].

An OS must be able to monitor and control tasks. Control functions include aborting execution and allocating processor resources; monitoring functions include detecting termination and run-time errors. These facilities are easy to provide if a task executes on a single processor. If, however, a task is a pool of processes or a taskforce distributed over several processors then functions such as termination detection become more complex [Francez, 1980; Dijkstra *et al.*, 1983].

Processor scheduling refers to the allocation of processor resources to tasks. This is a complex problem, particularly on multiprocessors [Wang and Morris, 1985]. There it comprises both the *global* scheduling problem – allocating processors to tasks – and the *local* scheduling problem – allocating processor resources to tasks executing on the same processor.

Most operating systems constrain both single and multi-process tasks to execute on a single processor. This is appropriate in small multiprocessors used for multiprogramming: the aim here is to maximize throughput by allocating a large number of tasks to a small number of processors. It is not suitable on massively parallel machines, however, as it does not permit parallel execution. Effective support for the creation, monitoring and control of tasks executing on several processors will certainly be required in future systems. Medusa addresses these problems to some extent [Ousterhout, 1982]. This OS attempts to maximize throughput when multiprogramming parallel programs by coscheduling teams of processes on several processors.

Many researchers have considered the problem of computing optimal schedules for multiprocessors, but few general results have been developed. This emphasizes the importance of being able to migrate processes and hence redistribute load at run-time [Powell and Miller, 1983; Douglis and Ousterhout, 1987]. Ideally, process migration should be under programmer control [Hudak, 1986; Taylor *et al.*, 1987a]. In a functional programming framework, Hudak proposes mapping notations that permit programmers to indicate on which processor expressions are to be evaluated. For example, the notation f on p may be used to indicate the evaluation of function f on processor p. Notations such as f on left(self) can be used to express relative mappings on topologies that support the notion of left and right self evaluates to the identifier of the processor on which it is evaluated. For example, using mapping notations, Program 2.2 may be reexpressed as follows:

```
system([Function |Kb], Fs) =
    if lookup(Fs, Function) = missing
    then [error |system(Kb, Fs) ]
    else merge( execute(lookup(Fs, Function)), system(Kb, Fs) on left(self))
```

This program specifies that upon receiving a valid input, the function named by the user shall start executing on the current processor while the OS (system) continues executing on an adjacent processor. Note the use of merge rather than append as in Program 2.2; this intermingles rather than concatenates the output of the user function and subsequent function evaluations. The modified program allows several function evaluations to proceed in parallel, each executing on a different processor.

2.7 KERNEL DESIGN

Recall that an OS kernel (Figure 1.4) provides basic facilities which are used to implement other OS components. The kernel can provide implementations of complex functions such as device control, exception handling, and resource management. Alternatively, it can provide simpler mechanisms that permit these functions to be implemented at a higher level. Fundamental design problems associated with the kernel include: which facilities to provide in the kernel; how OS programs are to invoke these facilities; and how to inform OS programs of events detected by the kernel.

2.7.1 Kernel functionality

Kernel design must resolve four conflicting requirements: functionality, efficiency, flexibility, and simplicity. A kernel must provide all facilities required to implement OS services. Functions are more efficient when implemented in the kernel. However, as the kernel is difficult to modify, they are generally less flexible. A kernel is typically resident on every processor in a multiprocessor and may be implemented in machine language for efficiency. A simple (and hence compact) kernel therefore increases the proportion of high-level language code and minimizes the amount of code that must be duplicated on each processor. It is also likely to be more reliable.

Wulf *et al.* [1981] propose that the performance/flexibility conflict be resolved by implementing *mechanisms* in the kernel while providing higher-level programs with the ability to define the *policies* that determine how these mechanisms are used. For example, a kernel may implement memory management functions but allow OS programs to specify paging policies. Of course, absolute policy/mechanism separation is not achievable: the mechanisms implemented determine the policies that can be supported. Also, generality may conflict with the need for compactness. The kernel of Wulf *et al.*'s [1981] Hydra OS, for example, provides a high degree of policy/mechanism separation. However, it is large: about 130,000 words of object code.

OS programs must be provided with access to mechanisms implemented in the kernel. This can always be achieved by providing primitive operations that invoke the appropriate kernel mechanism. If, however, existing facilities are extended to fulfill this function, the number of new concepts is reduced. For example, an I/O device can be implemented as a monitor [Brinch Hansen, 1976]. In a message passing OS, messages sent to certain reserved destinations can be interpreted as instructions to the kernel.

2.7.2 Exceptions

An exception is an unexpected occurrence that requires special attention, such as floating point overflow and memory parity errors. Exceptions are typically detected by hardware which translate them into interrupts that are trapped by the OS kernel. It is generally desirable for the kernel to inform OS programs of exceptional conditions, so that exception handling can be performed under programmer control. Goodenough [1975] identifies four central issues in exception handling:

1. *Exception handlers*. Programmers must be able to associate exception handlers with operations.
2. *Control flow*. It must be possible to specify whether an operation should terminate or continue following an exception.
3. *Defaults*. An exception handling mechanism should provide a uniform treatment of defaults.
4. *Hierarchies*. Exceptions that cannot be handled at one level in a hierarchy of operations must be handled at a higher level.

Two main approaches to exception handling can be distinguished: synchronous and asynchronous. In systems that use synchronous exception handling, the programmer is permitted to associate exception handlers with program blocks or processes. When an exception occurs, control passes to a local exception handler. If no exception handler has been defined, the exception may be passed to a parent process or to the exception handler associated with an enclosing block. Programs can frequently generate exceptions using special primitives; this permits the programmer to modify control flow in potentially useful ways. In Multilisp, for example, *catch* and *throw* primitives are used to bind exception handlers to a subcomputation, and to signal exceptions within the subcomputation, respectively [Halstead and Loaiza, 1985]. In Unix, exceptions are translated into signals, which may be trapped either by the process in which the exception occurred or by the process' parent [Ritchie and Thompson, 1974].

In systems that use asynchronous exception handling, exceptions are signalled by an exception message sent to a process's parent or to a special exception handling process, potentially nominated by the programmer. In the V kernel, for example, the kernel signals an exception by sending a message to an exception server [Berglund, 1986]. The programmer can register an exception handling process with this server.

Asynchronous exception handling is more appropriate in message passing models and on multiprocessors. If exception handling is performed on a remote processor, it may not be desirable to suspend execution of a task in which an exception occurred while exception handling is performed. Exception messages can permit computation to proceed while exception handling is performed.

2.8 OTHER ISSUES

Memory management, although an important OS design issue, will not be studied in detail in this book. Memory management is concerned with controlling and optimizing the use of fast storage. Most modern computer systems support memory management mechanisms that permit programs to address a storage space much bigger than the physical memory of the computer. Effective control of this *virtual memory* requires both suitable hardware support and well-tuned paging algorithms [Peterson and Silberschatz, 1983]. Memory management mechanisms must typically be implemented in the kernel for efficiency, though OS programs can be given considerable control over the policies applied to control their use [Wulf *et al.*, 1981].

A number of less central OS design issues are also not considered here. One is *fault tolerance*. A system is reliable, or fault tolerant, if it is able to deliver a minimum level of service in the face of hardware and software failure [Tanenbaum and van Renesse, 1985]. Reliability may be achieved by redundancy and by implementing atomic actions. Redundancy duplicates critical services and data. Atomic actions ensure that hardware failure does not lead to inconsistent states.

Another problem area not considered is *distributed systems* [Tannenbaum and van Renesse, 1985; Sloman and Kramer, 1986]. These have particular requirements that are not necessarily encountered in tightly coupled systems. Communication links and processors may be unreliable or untrustworthy. Heterogeneous hardware may require the use of special communication protocols, and expensive interprocessor communication may require the use of specialized communication mechanisms.

2.9 SUMMARY

This chapter has reviewed representative solutions to fundamental OS design problems. The OS designer can select from among these and similar solutions to build a *solution set* that is appropriate for a particular OS and machine. A solution set determines the computational model that will be used to structure the remainder of the OS. It is often (but by no means necessarily) expressed in terms of a high-level language that supports the chosen facilities via appropriate constructs.

Five criteria can be used to judge a potential solution set: abstractive power, sufficiency, minimality, efficiency, and utility. *Abstractive power* refers to the extent to which a facility hides implementation decisions or hardware details from other system components. Details that can usefully be hidden range from the concrete (such as the existence of interrupts and the number and configuration of processors) to the more abstract (such as the existence of other processes). A set of tools must clearly be *sufficient*: that is, it must provide solutions to the problems that are important for a particular OS design. It is also desirable that a tool set be *minimal*: a small set of facilities will generally result in a simpler design and more reliable implementation. It is important that it be possible to implement the abstraction *efficiently* on potential target architectures. Finally, the solution set must be *useful*: that is, it must support the construction of comprehensive operating systems.

Several solution sets have been introduced in this chapter. The programming language Concurrent Pascal represents a simple solution set suitable for uniprocessors and shared-memory multiprocessors [Brinch Hansen, 1976; Joseph *et al.*, 1984]. This provides static process structures, communication via shared resources, monitors, and compile-time protection. This solution set uses a small number of simple concepts: in Brinch Hansen's SOLO system, it is supported by a kernel of only 4K words of assembler.

Hydra represents a more ambitious solution set. Hydra is an OS for a shared memory multiprocessor called C.mmp [Wulf *et al.*, 1975]. It uses dynamic heavyweight processes and represents resources as typed objects. Communication is by shared resources, synchronization is achieved using semaphores and capabilities are used to control access to objects. An interesting feature of Hydra is its emphasis on separation of policy and mechanism. This, and its capability-based protection scheme, permits a more flexible structure than most contemporary systems. Most traditional OS facilities (such as file systems and schedulers) are implemented by user-level programs. Disadvantages of Hydra from the perspective of this study are the complexity of its kernel and the reliance placed on shared resources, which limits portability. Hydra's designers suggest that the design would benefit from a more widespread use of processes [Wulf *et al.*, 1981].

The programming language occam represents a solution set designed for message-passing multiprocessors. It provides static process structures, synchronous message passing and guarded commands. Advantages of this solution set are its simplicity and the efficiency with which its facilities can be implemented: in fact, it has proved possible to implement occam in hardware. However, its lack of support for dynamic process structures limits its utility.

Functional programming represents a machine-independent solution set. It provides dynamic, lightweight processes and static, asynchronous communication. Functions are used to define dynamic process networks, function application to define communication channels and dataflow constraints to provide synchronization. Unfortunately, these abstractions do not provide an adequate basis for OS design: dynamic communication structures and nondeterminism require ad hoc extensions to the basic model.

Parallel logic programming provides another machine-independent solution set. This model combines dynamic lightweight processes with the more flexible communication facilities represented by the logical variable. It also supports nondeterminism via a form of guarded command. Subsequent chapters describe a comprehensive solution set based on these concepts and evaluate its sufficiency, efficiency, and utility.

3

FLAT PARLOG

The programming language Flat Parlog (FP) is used in this book as a framework for investigations in OS design [Foster and Taylor, 1988]. This chapter provides a brief introduction to the language. A tutorial introduction to FP and a formal definition of its operational model are presented in Appendices I and II. Readers unfamilar with parallel logic programming will probably want to refer to these appendices before attempting to read FP programs.

3.1 CONCEPTS

The parallel logic programming language FP is based on a small number of simple concepts. These are reviewed here, and the language's syntax is introduced.

Concurrent processes. The state of an FP computation is a set of processes: a *process pool*. A process is characterized by a name, indicating the procedure that is to be used to reduce it, and a tuple of arguments. A process may be represented as: $P(T_1, \ldots, T_k)$, $k \geq 0$, where P is the name and $T_1, \ldots, T_k$ are the arguments. If $k = 0$, the parentheses are omitted.

Computation proceeds by repeatedly selecting processes from the process pool and attempting to reduce these processes using program clauses. Process reduction can occur in any order or in parallel. The only restriction on reduction order is that any process which is continuously capable of being reduced must eventually be selected for reduction.

Guarded reduction. An FP program is a finite set of guarded clauses. A guarded clause has the form:

$$H \leftarrow G_1, \ldots, G_m : B_1, \ldots, B_n. \qquad m, n \geq 0$$

H is called the clause's head, $G_1, \ldots, G_m$ its guard and $B_1, \ldots, B_n$ its body. '←' is an implies operator, and ':' a commit operator. (In other parallel logic languages, such as Strand and FCP, these are written ':–' and '|', respectively.) If the guard is empty ($m = 0$), the commit operator is omitted; if the body is also empty the clause is written simply as *H*. The head *H* and each of the $G_1, \ldots, G_m$ and $B_1, \ldots, B_n$ are processes. Clauses with the same name and arity are grouped together into procedures.

The guard contains only predefined guard processes. These can perform simple tests such as term comparison, type tests, etc., on process arguments. Body processes can execute both other procedures and predefined body primitives. Body primitives perform arithmetic, type conversion, term manipulation, etc.

Process reduction involves replacing a process in the process pool by the body processes of a program clause. A clause's head and guard represent preconditions on process arguments that must be satisfied before a clause can be used to reduce a process. Non-variable head arguments define matching operations on corresponding process arguments; guard processes define further tests. It can happen that several clauses in a procedure are capable of reducing a process. In this case, one clause is nondeterministically selected.

Recursively-defined data structures. FP, like other symbolic languages such as Lisp, defines complex data structures recursively from a small set of primitive elements. A *term* is a variable, constant or structured term. A *structured term* is like a record in other languages, and is constructed from one or more terms.

A *variable* is represented by an alphanumeric sequence beginning with a capital letter. The symbol '_' represents an *anonymous variable*. A *constant* is a number such as 0, 3.16 and −19 or a string. A *string* is any character sequence; if it could be confused with other types of term, it is enclosed in single quotes. A structured term may be written using tuple notation:

$$\{T_1, \ldots, T_j\}, j \geq 1$$

where the $T_1, \ldots, T_j$ are terms. If T_1 is a string F, it may also be written as $F(T_2, \ldots, T_j)$, and F is termed the *function name*.

A special syntax is used for the type of structured term known as *lists*. The notation [H | T] is used to denote the list with head H and tail T. A nested list term [X | [Y |Z]] may be abbreviated as [X, Y |Z] or, if Z is the empty list or *nil* (denoted by the symbol [ ]), as [X, Y].

Logical variables. Process arguments are terms and may contain variables. Processes that share variables can communicate by reading and writing these variables. FP's so-called *logical variable* has the single assignment property: a variable's value is either undefined or defined, and once defined cannot be redefined.

Processes write variables using a unification primitive '='. A call $X = Y$ attempts to equate two terms X and Y, binding variables in either term if necessary. In practice, the unification primitive is generally used to bind one variable (by convention, the left-hand term, X) to another variable or nonvariable term. It is used in this way in all the programs in this book. A variable that is bound to a nonvariable term is said to be *instan-*

tiated. Second and subsequent attempts to instantiate a variable are signalled as run-time errors.

Dataflow synchronization. Nonvariable head arguments and guard tests define read operations on process arguments: they test whether a process argument has a particular value. If the process argument is a variable the test, and hence the attempt to reduce the process using that clause, suspends. The test can proceed when the variable is given a value by another process. This is FP's process synchronization mechanism.

3.2 AN EXAMPLE PROGRAM

Program 3.1 is used to illustrate FP's computational model. This program defines a simple database that maintains a state subject to change over time. The database can be viewed as a process which evaluates a list of requests Rs to read and write named items. It achieves this by maintaining a database Db as a list of {Key, Value} pairs. The first clause of the program initializes the database to an initially empty list (C1). (In discussions of this and subsequent programs, clause numbers (C*i*) refer to the program text.) The second and third clauses process read and write requests respectively.

When a message of the form read(Key, Value) is received, a lookup process is created to search the database for the appropriate key and retrieve the associated value (C2). Meanwhile, database recurses to process further requests. The lookup process inspects

```
database_init(Rs) ← database(Rs, [ ]).        % Initialize empty database        (C1)

database([read(Key, Value) | Rs], Db) ←       % Receive read request.            (C2)
    lookup(Key, Db, Value),                    %    Look up Key in Db for Value;
    database(Rs, Db).                          %    Recurse.
database([write(Key, Value) | Rs], Db) ←       % Receive write request.           (C3)
    database(Rs, [{Key, Value} | Db]).         %    Recurse with new item.
database([ ], Db).                             % No more requests: terminate.     (C4)

lookup(Key, [ ], Value) ← Value = missing.     % Not found & end of database.     (C5)
lookup(Key, [{Key1,Value1}| Db], Value) ←      % Found: return value              (C6)
    Key == Key1 :
        Value = Value1.
lookup(Key, [{Key1, _}| Db], Value) ←          % Not found.                       (C7)
    Key =\= Key1 :                             %    Check Key;
    lookup(Key, Db, Value).                    %    Continue.
```

Program 3.1 Simple database.

the database Db recursively (C6,C7). If the key is found the associated value is returned (C6). If it is not present the lookup process returns the value missing (C5). When a message write(Key, Value) is received, the database simply recurses with an augmented database as its second argument (C3).

The database/2 procedure illustrates dataflow constraints. The first argument of each of its clauses is a nonvariable term: evaluation of a database process hence suspends until this argument is instantiated; that is, until a request is received from another process.

The lookup/3 procedure illustrates clause selection. Its first clause is selected if the database is empty. Its second clause is selected if the database is not empty and the guard test $==$ succeeds, indicating that the Key specified in the message (the first argument) matches that of the first entry in the database. Its third clause is selected if the guard test $=\backslash=$ succeeds, indicating that they do *not* match.

The lookup process also illustrates the use of unification. The first argument of a read request is assumed to be a valid key, and the second argument a variable. If an entry with the appropriate key is found in the database, the read request's variable argument is bound to the associated value (C6). This has the effect of passing this value back to the process which generated the original request, if it is waiting for the value.

3.3 AN EXAMPLE EXECUTION

Consider the following process:

    database_init([write(10,99), read(X,Y), read(10,X)]).

This creates a database and passes it three requests. To execute this process, repeated attempts are made to reduce processes created by its execution, until either no processes remain (the computation has *succeeded*), a process fails (the computation has *failed*) or no processes can be reduced (the computation is *deadlocked*).

Figure 3.1 illustrates execution of this process, showing the process pool and operation performed at each step. Operations are characterized as either *reduction* using a program clause, or *unification* of two terms. It is assumed here that the first process (textually) in the process pool is selected at each step. Dataflow constraints may prevent a selected process from being reduced: this is the case in step 4(a), where the process lookup(X, [{10,99}], Y) cannot be reduced because its first argument is variable. (This prevents the guard tests Key $==$ Key1 and Key $=\backslash=$ Key1 in clauses C6 and C7 from proceeding.) This process is placed here at the end of the process pool; in an FP implementation, it would be recorded in a separate area, to avoid reselection before the variable for which it requires a value becomes instantiated. The process is subsequently reduced using clause C7 in step 7, at which time its first argument has been instantiated.

Note that the process pool frequently contains several processes. Any of these could have been selected for reduction. The execution path shown here is hence not the only

1. Reduction (C1)

⟨database_init([write(10, 99), read(X, Y), read(10, X)])⟩

⟨database([write(10, 99), read(X, Y), read(10, X)], [ ])⟩

2. Reduction (C3)

⟨database([read(X, Y), read(10, X)], [{10, 99}])⟩

3. Reduction (C2)

⟨lookup(X, [{10, 99}], Y) database([read(10, X)], [{10, 99}])⟩

4(a) Suspension ...
4(b) Reduction (C2)

⟨lookup(10, [{10, 99}], X) database([ ], [{10, 99}]) lookup(X, [{10,99}], Y)⟩

5. Reduction (C6)

⟨X = 99 database([ ], [{10, 99}]) lookup(X, [{10, 99}], Y)⟩

6. Unification

⟨database([ ], [{10, 99}]) lookup(99, [{10, 99}], Y)⟩

7. Reduction (C4)

⟨lookup(99, [{10, 99}], Y)⟩

8. Reduction (C7)

⟨lookup(99, [ ], Y)⟩

9. Reduction (C5)

⟨Y = missing⟩

10. Unification

⟨ ⟩

Figure 3.1 Execution of database process.

one possible. In a parallel machine, all processes in the process pool could be reduced in parallel.

3.4 PARALLEL LOGIC PROGRAMMING LANGUAGES

FP is one of a family of programming languages based on four simple concepts: dynamic lightweight processes, logical variables, dataflow synchronization, and guarded commands. Languages in this family differ according to whether they can construct process hierarchies, how they express synchronization, and how they assign values to variables. The resulting syntactic and semantic differences are relatively minor and need not concern the average programmer. The interested reader is referred to [Clark and Gregory, 1981; 1986; Shapiro, 1986; Ueda, 1986; Gregory, 1987; Foster and Taylor, 1988; Foster and Taylor, 1989] for descriptions of representative languages.

Concurrent Prolog, Parlog and Guarded Horn Clauses were the first parallel logic programming languages. These differed from FP in permitting calls to user-defined procedures in clause guards. Research showed that this feature provided little added expressive power and significantly complicated language implementation; interest has hence focused subsequently on *flat* forms of these languages such as Flat Concurrent Prolog (FCP) [Mierowsky *et al.*, 1985] and FP [Foster and Taylor, 1988] in which guards can only contain primitive operations.

3.5 DECLARATIVE CONTENT OF PARALLEL LOGIC PROGRAMS

Declarative programming seeks to separate the description of a problem from the computation of solutions to that problem. Declarative programs specify knowledge using some suitable abstract formalism; a declarative programming language incorporates an evaluation strategy which, when applied to a program, can compute problem solutions from the knowledge incorporated in the program.

In logic programming languages, knowledge is represented as sets of logical axioms. Computation seeks to prove an existentially quantified goal from these axioms, in the process constructing bindings for variables in the goal [Kowalski, 1974, 1979]. These bindings are the output of the computation and, if the logic programming language's evaluation strategy is correct, represent a member of the relation defined by the program invoked by the goal.

Guarded clauses have been presented in this chapter as rewrite rules for process networks. This *process* reading of parallel logic programs is generally the most useful. Parallel logic programs also have a *declarative* reading as sets of logical axioms. A clause:

$$H \leftarrow G_1, \ldots, G_m : B_1, \ldots, B_n.$$

can be read declaratively as *H* is true if the *G*s and *B*s are true. This permits procedures to be read as descriptions of relations between entities in a problem domain. For example, in Program 3.1, database(Rs) can be read as a relation over lists of requests, with the logical reading: Rs is a valid list of requests. Or, more precisely: Rs is a list of terms read(_,_), and write(_,_), in which each term read(K,V) is preceded by a term write(K,V), with no write(K,V1) such that V ≠ V1 intervening. database([write(1,john), read(1,john)]) is a member of this relation; database([write(1,john),read(1,mary)]) is not.

The evaluation strategies used by parallel logic languages are generally *correct*: any solution they compute from a program is a solution according to the program's declarative semantics. The nondeterministic choices made when selecting clauses to reduce processes mean, however, that parallel logic languages are *incomplete*. Each time evaluation commits to a single clause, it irrevocably abandons other potential solutions. In consequence, the set of solutions that can be computed is in general a subset of the set of solutions implied by the declarative reading of a program. The declarative reading of a parallel logic program is thus of little formal value. In addition, it says nothing about issues such as liveness or termination, which are of central importance in concurrent systems [Pnueli, 1986]. It does, however, provide a useful check on program correctness and is hence generally viewed as a valuable feature of these languages.

4

KERNEL SUPPORT

Recall that the kernel of an OS is the component that provides the most basic facilities and that is resident on every processor.

USER
Various services

NUCLEUS
Essential services

KERNEL
Basic facilities

HARDWARE
e.g. Parallel machine

Effective kernel support for dynamic lightweight processes, logical variables, and tasks is required if these concepts are to be used to construct operating systems. This support must provide solutions to OS design problems identified in Chapter 2 and should also be simple, flexible, and efficient.

As lightweight processes and logical variables are simple and fundamental concepts it is proposed that these be supported directly in an OS kernel. The FP language is used as a definition for this support. The task (a group of lightweight processes to be managed as a unit) is a more complex concept. This chapter is primarily concerned with the facilities required to support tasks. In particular it:

- Describes kernel facilities that support *task management*.
- Shows how these facilities can be used to provide task management functions on uniprocessors and multiprocessors.
- Describes kernel facilities to support local and global *processor scheduling*.

Note that the focus of this chapter is the nature of the kernel facilities required to support systems programming in a lightweight process model. The implementation of these facilities is considered in Chapter 5.

4.1 BACKGROUND

The specification of operating systems using networks of lightweight processes has been explored by Henderson [1982], Jones [1984], Shapiro [1984a], and Kusalik [1986]. These authors define kernel support for their systems in terms of high-level implementation languages that express process management and interprocess communication. However, they do not consider the two fundamental problems of task management and processor scheduling (Section 2.6).

Clark and Gregory [1984] propose a simple solution to task management problems. They propose that a kernel support the creation of tasks, termination detection in tasks, and the suspension, resumption, and abortion of tasks. They suggest a linguistic construct termed a *control call* as a means of making these facilities available to programmers in a logic programming language. A control call has the general form:

call(Processes, Status, Control)

This creates a task that initially contains a set of supplied Processes. Other processes can abort, suspend, and resume the execution of this task by binding the Control variable to appropriate control messages; the kernel reports task termination by binding the Status variable. Unfortunately, Clark and Gregory do not show how the apparently complex control functions represented by the control call can be implemented in a kernel. Hirsch *et al.* [1987] propose an approach to implementation that requires no kernel support. They use program transformations to augment the processes comprising a task with code that reports changes in status and permits control. However, they report that this approach incurs substantial run-time overhead.

It seems likely that any OS constructed using a lightweight process model will require kernel support for the detection of task termination and quiescence. A task is *terminated* when all its processes have terminated. It is *quiescent* when unavailability of data prevents any of its processes from continuing execution. In systems programming, the chief utility of these functions is to permit the release of resources allocated to idle tasks. Both are complex functions in multiprocessors as they require global information about a distributed state.

A well-known quiescence detection algorithm for synchronous multiprocessor systems is due to Dijkstra *et al.* [1983]. This algorithm detects global quiescence by repeatedly visiting processors on which a computation is active until it has verified that all are simultaneously *inactive*. Taylor [1989] and Nobuyuki Ichiyoshi [personal communication, 1987] have proposed extensions to Dijkstra's algorithm that permit quiescence detection in asynchronous systems. A count of messages sent and messages received is maintained at each processor on which a task is executing. The algorithm then visits each such processor, checking that the task is inactive and summing messages sent and received. If all processors are found to be simultaneously inactive *and* the total number of messages sent is equal to the total number of messages received, then quiescence has been detected. The message counts indicate that no messages are in transit.

As noted in Section 2.6, the processor scheduling problem can be divided into local and global components. The local scheduling problem has received the most attention to date and many algorithms have been proposed [Peterson and Silberschatz, 1983]. Modula and Hydra are interesting examples of two different approaches to kernel support for local scheduling. The Modula language uses a simple round-robin scheduler implemented in the kernel: this is sufficient for the process control applications for which the language was designed [Wirth, 1977]. In the Hydra OS, the principle of separation of policy and mechanism is applied, and user programs are able to set both short-term and long-term scheduling parameters [Wulf et al., 1981]. The resulting kernel is, however, complex.

General techniques for global scheduling have yet to be developed. Previous work in the use of lightweight processes for systems programming has assumed a static mapping of processes to processors [Jones, 1984]. This is not an adequate solution, as it prevents on-the-fly reconfiguration of an OS. Automatic distribution of processes to processors by kernel mechanisms is not the answer either: this is too inflexible [Hudak and Goldberg, 1985; Sato et al., 1987b]. Taylor et al. [1987a] take a more promising approach. They argue that as scheduling is a difficult problem, it should be performed under programmer control. They show how programmer control can be achieved with little kernel support. It is assumed that the kernel creates an initial set of bootstrap processes, one per processor, plus a set of communication channels between these processes. Subsequent process migration is implemented using message passing between the bootstrap processes and other processes that they create. The uniform address space supported by the parallel logic programming model makes process migration straightforward. Migration is complex in other models [Douglis and Ousterhout, 1987].

This chapter presents a set of kernel facilities that support the construction of operating systems using lightweight processes, logical variables and tasks. It describes a small set of task management facilities and shows that these can be used to implement more complex functions. A variant of Dijkstra's algorithm is used for multiprocessor termination and quiescence detection. This variant supports quiescence detection in asynchronous systems without the global counts required in the Taylor/Ichiyoshi algorithm. Kernel facilities that permit the programmer to specify local scheduling policies are described. It is assumed that global scheduling is to be performed under programmer control, as proposed by Taylor et al. Kernel facilities that support this approach to global scheduling are described.

4.2 TASK MANAGEMENT FACILITIES

A task is a unit of computation to be managed as a unit. In a computational model based on lightweight processes, a task is naturally viewed as a group of processes. The processes comprising a task may execute on a single processor or may be distributed over many processors. It must be possible to monitor and control both uniprocessor and multiprocessor tasks.

The design of kernel facilities to support multiprocessor task management is problematic, for three reasons:

1. The monitoring and control of multiprocessor tasks can require the use of complex algorithms.
2. Different programmers are likely to require different task management functions. For example, one may need to detect task termination; another task quiescence. Different mechanisms and costs are associated with these two functions.
3. The efficiency of task management functions is central to the efficiency of operating systems that use these functions.

One approach to multiprocessor task management is to decide on a set of functions and support these directly in the kernel. This is essentially what is proposed by Clark and Gregory [1984]. Such a direct implementation is likely to be highly efficient. However, it leads to a complex kernel (because of (1)) and is furthermore inflexible (because of (2)). An alternative approach is adopted here: only a small set of simple mechanisms is supported in the kernel. Each kernel mechanism supports just one primitive function: this simplifies kernel design and increases flexibility. Kernel mechanisms can be used to implement a range of more complex task management facilities.

4.2.1 Concepts

The design of the kernel's task management facilities utilizes the following concepts:

- *Uniprocessor tasks*. Kernel facilities only provide direct support for management of tasks executing on a single processor.
- *Status variable*. A status variable is associated with a task, as in Clark and Gregory's control call. This is a logical variable which the kernel binds to inform monitoring processes of changes in task status. The same communication mechanism is hence used for both kernel-OS and interprocess communication.
- *Exceptions*. Exceptions that occur during process execution are signalled by messages placed on the appropriate task's status stream. An exception message includes a continuation variable which can be used to specify how the process in which the exception occurred is to continue executing.
- *Task record*. The kernel facility which creates a task constructs a representation of the new task termed a *task record*. Other tasks can control a task by applying kernel-supported functions to its task record.
- *Code management*. An OS must be able to move code between memory and disk or between processors, and also provide and control access to code. Both these functions are complex, particularly in a multiprocessor. Rather than support them directly in the kernel, two simpler facilities are provided that permit more complex code management functions to be specified at a higher level. First, as in languages such as Smalltalk

[Krasner, 1983] and FCP [Mierowsky *et al.*, 1985], object code modules are defined to be first class language objects. A module consists of executable versions of one or more procedures plus a dictionary data structure which can be used to access particular procedures by name. The dictionary associated with a module need not contain all of the module's procedures: this supports information-hiding. Second, two kernel functions are provided that can be used to initiate execution of a process using procedures defined in a module. These are presented in the next section.

4.2.2 Task management primitives

A number of distinct and generally orthogonal task management functions can be distinguished:

- Creation of a task.
- Detection of run-time errors in a task.
- Detection of task termination (the process pool is empty).
- Detection of task quiescence (no process is able to proceed).
- Suspension, resumption and termination of a task.
- Execution of code in a particular module.

The kernel facilities developed to support these functions are defined here as a set of FP primitives. The annotations on primitive arguments indicate whether they are to be supplied when the function is invoked ($\downarrow$) or are generated by the primitive ($\uparrow$).

- 'TASK'(S $\uparrow$, TR $\uparrow$, T $\downarrow$, P $\downarrow$): creates a uniprocessor task with status variable S. The task contains a new process P which executes in the current module. P is supplied at compile-time. The TASK primitive generates a *task record*, TR. This is a term representing the new task, to which other primitives can be applied to control the task. A call to this primitive succeeds immediately; once created, a task executes independently of the task that created it. Status messages include succeeded, stopped and exception/3. The purpose of the type argument T is described subsequently.
- 'SUSPEND'(TR $\downarrow$, Done $\uparrow$), 'CONTINUE'(TR $\downarrow$, Done $\uparrow$), 'STOP'(TR $\downarrow$, Done $\uparrow$): suspends, resumes, or stops the task represented by the task record TR respectively and binds the variable Done to the constant ok when completed.
- Module $\downarrow$ @Process $\downarrow$: accesses the dictionary associated with Module to find the code associated with Process and creates a process to execute that code.
- 'CALL'(Process $\downarrow$): accesses the dictionary associated with the current module (the module in which the process that calls this primitive is located) to find the code associated with Process and creates a process to execute that code.
- raise_exception(T $\downarrow$, P $\downarrow$): signals an exception of type T involving process P on the status stream of the current task.

The following observations can be made about these primitives:

- They do not support nested tasks. However, management of nested tasks can be achieved using these facilities.
- Process and unification failure are signalled as exceptions rather than as task failure. This permits programmers to provide exception handlers and debuggers that deal with failure.
- The primitives only support the creation, monitoring and control of uniprocessor tasks. Multiprocessor task management functions must be constructed using these facilities.

4.2.3 Status messages

The kernel may both bind a status variable associated with a task to a stream of exception messages and terminate this stream with constants succeeded and stopped. The following are hence all valid bindings for a status variable:

```
S = succeeded
S = [exception(_,_,_), exception(_,_,_) | stopped]
S = [exception(_,_,_) | S1]
```

The constant succeeded indicates that the task in question has terminated: that is, that its process pool is empty. The constant stopped signals that the task has been aborted using the STOP primitive. Exception messages have the general form:

```
exception(Type, Process, Cont).
```

An exception message indicates that an exception of a particular Type occurred when evaluating the process represented by the term Process. Cont is a *continuation variable* [Foster, 1987a]. A continuation variable is so called because a monitoring process can use it to specify how the process in which the exception occurred is to continue execution. Evaluation of the erroneous process is suspended until its continuation variable is bound to a term representing a new process. It is important to note that the generation of an exception message does not affect other processes in the task: these can continue executing. Note also that the exception message exploits two features of the parallel logic programming model. The continuation variable included in an exception message provides a *return address*. Evaluation of the process represented by this variable *suspends* until the variable is assigned a value.

Figure 4.1 illustrates a possible sequence of events following a call to an undefined procedure proc in the application task. It is assumed that a *monitoring process* is monitoring the status stream of an *application task:*

1. An exception message is generated to signal an exception of type undefined.
2. The erroneous process is replaced in the task by the continuation variable Cont.
3. The monitoring process instantiates the continuation variable Cont to the dummy process true.

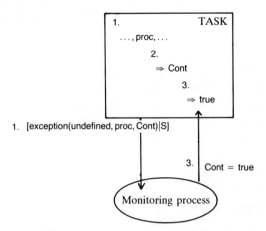

Figure 4.1 The exception message.

The instantiation of the continuation variable has the effect of passing a process – in this case the process true – to the task in which the exception occurred. The process true terminates immediately, so the exception is effectively ignored. Alternatively, the monitoring process could have instantiated Cont to a call to an exception handler.

The raise_exception primitive permits programs to generate exceptions explicitly. A call:

raise_exception(Type, Process)

causes the exception message exception(Type, Process, Cont) to be signalled on the status stream of the task that made the call.

The call to the raise_exception primitive is replaced by a continuation variable, Cont, included in the exception message.

The exception handling mechanism described here addresses each of the four issues listed by Goodenough [1975] in his analysis of exception handling (cited in Section 2.7.3). *Exception handlers* can be associated with the invocation of an operation: the operation is invoked as a task, and a handler is created as a process that monitors the task's status stream. The continuation variable permits an elegant treatment of *control flow* issues: a handler can instantiate this variable to signify whether evaluation of an erroneous process should terminate or continue following an exception. *Defaults* and exception handling in *hierarchies* are not supported directly but can be programmed if required.

4.2.4 Task types

In addition to signalling exceptions and termination, the kernel can also be requested to signal task quiescence. This is achieved using the TASK primitive's Type argument, which indicates what termination and quiescence detection functions are to be provided for a task by the kernel. When quiescence detection is enabled, the status message quiescent(P) indicates quiescence, where P is the number of processes in the quiescent task. Communication with the outside world or with other tasks can permit a quiescent task subsequently to become active. This is reported by an active status message.

Quiescence detection is made optional because a significant cost is associated with this feature in multiprocessors, and many computations do not require it. The reason for its high cost will be made clear in Chapter 5; for the moment, it suffices to identify the four types of task that can be specified using the TASK primitive:

Local	Purely local
GlobalT	Global termination
LocalQ	Local quiescence
GlobalQ	Global quiescence

Briefly, the type *Local* should be used when only termination detection is required and a task does not share data with processes executing on other processors. If it can share data, the type *GlobalT* should be used.

Types *LocalQ* and *GlobalQ* support quiescence detection. The former type is used when quiescence needs to be signalled in a single uniprocessor task. The latter permits quiescence detection in multiprocessor tasks constructed from several uniprocessor tasks. The use of this type is discussed in Section 4.5.

4.2.5 Task management through transformation

Hirsch *et al.* [1987] propose an alternative approach to task management based on *source-to-source transformations* rather than kernel support. They describe program transformations that extend programs with additional code that reports termination, permits control, etc. This approach is illustrated using a simple example. Performance studies that quantify costs associated with Hirsch *et al.*'s transformations and the kernel facilities described in this chapter are presented in Chapter 6.

Program 4.1 is Program 3.1 transformed to report termination and to permit control. The database procedures are augmented with two additional arguments, Done and Stop; the lookup procedure called by database also has additional arguments. The augmented program executes in the same way as the original program, but in addition it reports termination by binding the variable Done to the constant succeeded and halts if the variable Stop is bound to the constant halt. Note the additional clauses introduced to cause the process to terminate if the Stop variable is bound (C2, C6), the additional guard test var added to recursive clauses to ensure that they are not selected in this case (C3, C4, C8), and the binding of the Done variable upon termination (C2, C5–C7, C9). A call var(X) succeeds if its argument is a variable and fails otherwise.

This approach has the advantage of simplicity. However, it appears to be less expressive than kernel facilities. For example, it has yet to be shown that program transformation can provide efficient support for quiescence detection.

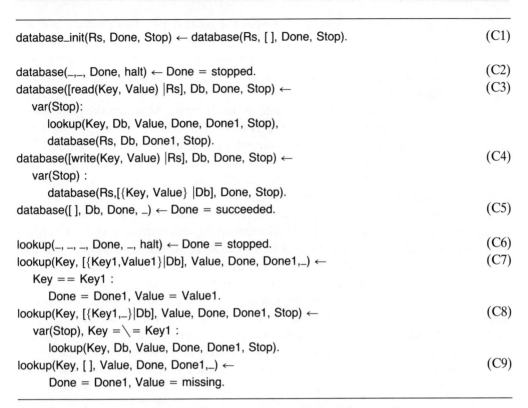

```
database_init(Rs, Done, Stop) ← database(Rs, [ ], Done, Stop).                (C1)

database(_,_, Done, halt) ← Done = stopped.                                   (C2)
database([read(Key, Value) |Rs], Db, Done, Stop) ←                            (C3)
    var(Stop):
        lookup(Key, Db, Value, Done, Done1, Stop),
        database(Rs, Db, Done1, Stop).
database([write(Key, Value) |Rs], Db, Done, Stop) ←                           (C4)
    var(Stop) :
        database(Rs,[{Key, Value} |Db], Done, Stop).
database([ ], Db, Done, _) ← Done = succeeded.                                (C5)

lookup(_, _, _, Done, _, halt) ← Done = stopped.                              (C6)
lookup(Key, [{Key1,Value1}|Db], Value, Done, Done1,_) ←                       (C7)
    Key == Key1 :
        Done = Done1, Value = Value1.
lookup(Key, [{Key1,_}|Db], Value, Done, Done1, Stop) ←                        (C8)
    var(Stop), Key =\= Key1 :
        lookup(Key, Db, Value, Done, Done1, Stop).
lookup(Key, [ ], Value, Done, Done1,_) ←                                      (C9)
    Done = Done1, Value = missing.
```

Program 4.1 Database augmented to permit control.

4.3 UNIPROCESSOR TASK MANAGEMENT

The kernel facilities described in the previous section can be used to provide a range of task management functions. This is achieved by providing *monitor processes* that encapsulate tasks and process both task status messages generated by the kernel and control requests generated by other processes. An FP program that implements a monitor process is presented to illustrate the approach. This program defines a *control call* with the general form:

    call(Module, Process, Status, Control)

The arguments are a module, an initial process, and status and control variables. A control call initiates a task to execute Process using Module. It then reports termination and exceptions in the new task by binding the Status variable. It also permits other processes to abort the task's execution by binding the Control variable. The control call thus provides a higher-level interface to task management functions than is provided by the primitives described in the previous section.

The procedure call/4 in Program 4.2 defines the control call. This program uses the TASK primitive to create the new task and creates a monitor process to manage the task's execution (C1). The new task executes the process run(Module, Process). This process immediately uses the @ primitive to execute the specified Process using the supplied Module (C2).

The task record and status variable made available by the TASK primitive are passed to the concurrently executing monitor process (C1). This takes as arguments the task's status variable Si, the status and control variables provided with the call, S and C, and the task record TR. The monitoring process is defined by the procedure monitor/4. Each monitor clause can be read in isolation as a specification of how to handle a particular event. Two kinds of event are handled: control messages from other processes, and task status messages generated by the kernel. Task termination – signalled by the status succeeded – causes the monitor to signal termination and terminate (C3). Exception messages are output on the control call's status stream (C5). A stop message received on the control variable C is handled by calling the STOP primitive with the task record as an argument (C4). The constant stopped is used to terminate the status stream only *after* the corresponding control function has been performed: the procedure await_stop uses the value generated by the STOP primitive to detect when it has completed (C6).

Figure 4.2 illustrates the action of this control call. A single task exists before a call to call/4. After the call, two tasks exist. The 'parent' task (TR1) contains a monitor process which possesses references to the task record representing the second task, TR2, and to its status variable, Si. The monitor process monitors both this status variable, Si, and the control variable C. It generates a filtered status stream S and translates a stop control message into a call to the STOP task management primitive.

```
call(Module, Process, Status, Control) ←        % Control Call.                    (C1)
    'TASK'(Si, TR, 'Local', run(Module, Process) ),  %     Create task.
    monitor(Si, Status, Control, TR).            %     Monitor its execution.

run(Module, Process) ← Module@Process.           % Execute specified code.           (C2)

monitor(succeeded, S, _, _) ← S = succeeded.     % Termination.                      (C3)
monitor(_, S, stop, TR) ←                        % Stop request received:            (C4)
    'STOP'(TR, D),                               %     Abort execution.
    await_stop(D, S).                            %     Signal termination.
monitor([M |Si], S, C, TR) ←                     % Exception message:                (C5)
    S = [M |S1],                                 %     Forward on status var.
    monitor(Si, S1, C, TR).                      %     Recurse.

await_stop(ok, S) ← S = stopped.                 % Signal termination.               (C6)
```

Program 4.2 Uniprocessor task management.

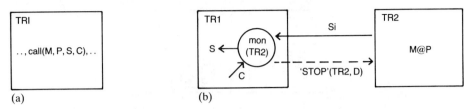

Figure 4.2 Implementation of the control call. (a) Before. (b) After.

Many similar facilities can be provided using kernel task management facilities. These can be implemented by *extending* or *restricting* the monitor process presented here or by *composing* this process with other processes. For example:

- An extended facility can support requests to *suspend* and *resume* a task.
- A restricted facility can report termination and exceptions but not permit a task to be aborted.
- An extended facility can abort a task following any exception.
- An extended facility can monitor and control *nested* tasks.

4.4 MULTIPROCESSOR TASK MANAGEMENT

The kernel facilities used to provide uniprocessor task management functions can also be used to provide these functions on a multiprocessor. The same basic approach is taken: a monitor is defined which handles control requests and signals changes in task status. However, this monitor is implemented as not one process but a network of communicating processes, one or more per processor on which a multiprocessor task is active. These processes exchange control and status information about the task in order to manage its execution. As in the uniprocessor case, a range of task management functions can be implemented by extending or restricting the functionality of simple processes.

Recall that the kernel supports interprocessor communication but not process migration. (Process migration is programmed in FP). In consequence, processes cannot exist in transit between processors, which means that the process pool representing a multiprocessor task can be viewed as a number of subpools, one per processor. Each subpool can be executed as a separate uniprocessor task. For example, Figure 4.3 shows a multiprocessor task *T* executing on three processors *n1, n2* and *n3*. This consists of three subtasks *T1, T2* and *T3*.

Each uniprocessor task can be managed using kernel facilities, so if additional processes are provided that coordinate the management of these tasks, the multiprocessor task itself can be monitored and controlled. For example, to control the task *T* in Figure 4.3, the subtasks *T1, T2* and *T3* must be controlled; to detect termination of *T*, it is necessary to determine that *T1, T2* and *T3* have terminated.

Figure 4.4 illustrates the sort of process network that is used to manage the execution

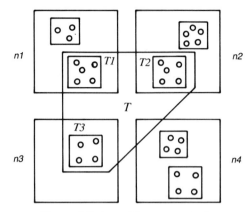

Figure 4.3 A multiprocessor task.

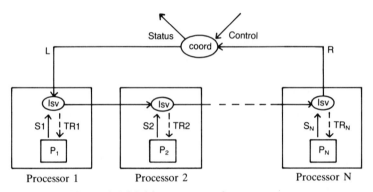

Figure 4.4 Multiprocessor task management.

of a multiprocessor task. This consists of a central *coordinator* process (coord) and one *local supervisor* (lsv) per uniprocessor task. The coordinator and supervisors are linked in a circuit using shared stream variables; this circuit is used to pass status and control information between processes.

The procedure dcall/4 (Program 4.3) defines the process network illustrated in Figure 4.4. This program is intended to manage the execution of a multiprocessor task consisting of N processes, $P_1, P_2, \ldots, P_N$. A call to dcall/4 has the general form:

dcall(M, [P_1, ..., P_N], S, C)

where M is a module containing the code to be executed by the P_i.

The procedure dcall/4 uses the TASK primitive to request the kernel to execute each of the processes $P_1, P_2, \ldots, P_N$ as a separate uniprocessor task (C2). Note that the tasks created are given type *GlobalT*: this requests the kernel to perform housekeeping functions required for termination detection in a multiprocessor. The procedure also creates N local supervisor processes, one per uniprocessor task, and a single coordinator process. If each {task, lsv} pair is made to execute on a different processor in a multiprocessor, then a call to dcall/4 creates the process network illustrated in Figure 4.4. This

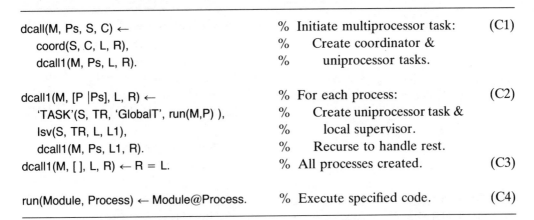

dcall(M, Ps, S, C) ←
   coord(S, C, L, R),
   dcall1(M, Ps, L, R).
	% Initiate multiprocessor task: (C1)
	% Create coordinator &
	% uniprocessor tasks.

dcall1(M, [P |Ps], L, R) ←
   'TASK'(S, TR, 'GlobalT', run(M,P)),
   lsv(S, TR, L, L1),
   dcall1(M, Ps, L1, R).
dcall1(M, [ ], L, R) ← R = L.
	% For each process: (C2)
	% Create uniprocessor task &
	% local supervisor.
	% Recurse to handle rest.
	% All processes created. (C3)

run(Module, Process) ← Module@Process.	% Execute specified code. (C4)

Program 4.3 Multiprocessor task management: top level.

distribution can be achieved by migrating the TASK and lsv processes to other processors using message passing, as will be described in Section 4.7.

The local supervisor processes created by dcall/4 communicate using shared variables. Each of the N local supervisors lsv_i, $1 < i < N$, shares variables with supervisors lsv_{i-1} and lsv_{i+1}. These shared variables implement a *circuit* that encompasses all the local supervisors, as illustrated in Figure 4.4. Streams to lsv_1 and lsv_N (L and R respectively) provide the coordinator with access to the left and right sides of this circuit. The coordinator also maintains references to the task's status and control streams S and C.

Program 4.4 implements a local supervisor and coordinator. This program uses the circuit linking the local supervisors for three purposes: to control evaluation, to notify the coordinator of exceptions and to detect global termination. Briefly, a task is controlled by passing a stop request around the circuit. Each local supervisor receiving a stop request terminates its task and then forwards the request. Exceptions are passed around the circuit to the coordinator, which outputs them on the status stream. Each local supervisor closes its portion of the circuit when its task terminates; global termination can hence be signalled when the entire circuit is closed.

- *Control.* The coordinator places stop requests received on the control variable on the left-hand side of the circuit (C1). A local supervisor receiving such a message controls its task (using the task management primitive STOP) and calls await_stop to await completion of the stop request (C5). It then forwards the message and terminates (C9). When the stop message placed on the left-hand side of the circuit arrives on the right-hand side (C2), the coordinator hence knows that all subtasks have terminated. It can then terminate the status stream with the constant stopped (C2).
- *Exceptions.* A local supervisor generates messages on its output (right-hand) stream when it detects exceptions in its task (C8). It also forwards any exception messages received from its neighbor (C6). The coordinator echoes exception messages received on the right-hand side of the circuit on the status stream (C4).

```
coord(S, stop, L, R) ←              % Stop request received:              (C1)
    L = [stop |L1],                 %     Request task termination.
        coord(S,_, L1, R).          %     Await termination.
coord(S,_,_, [stop |_]) ← S = stopped.   % Task termination complete.     (C2)
coord(S,_, L, R) ← L == R : S = succeeded.   % Circuit closed = success.  (C3)
coord(S, C, L, [M |R]) ←            % Exception signalled in task.        (C4)
    M = \= stop :                   %
        S = [M |S1],                %     Output on status stream.
        coord(S1, C, L, R).         %     Recurse.


lsv(S, TR, [stop |L], R) ←          % Stop request from coordinator       (C5)
    'STOP'(TR, D),                  %     Abort task.
    await_stop(D, L, R).            %     Await termination.
lsv(S, TR, [exception(T,P,C) |L], R) ←   % Exception signalled by nbor    (C6)
    R = [exception(T,P,C) |R1],     %     Forward exception.
    lsv(S, TR, L, R1).              %     Recurse.
lsv(succeeded, TR, L, R) ← R = L.   % Termination: close circuit.         (C7)
lsv([exception(T,P,C) |S], TR, L, R) ←   % Local exception detected:      (C8)
    R = [exception(T,P,C) |R1],     %     Forward exception.
    lsv(S, TR, L, R1).              %     Recurse.


await_stop(ok, L, R) ← R = [stop |L].   % Stopped: close circuit.         (C9)
```

Program 4.4 Multiprocessor task management.

■ *Termination*. A local supervisor unifies its left- and right-hand streams when it detects termination of its task (C8). This 'closes' its part of the circuit. The coordinator has references to both the left and right ends of the circuit. These will be identical variables (C3) when all supervisors have detected termination of their task. (A call to the FP primitive == succeeds when its two arguments are identical constants or variables or are structures of the same arity and with identical subterms.) This programming technique, known as a *short circuit*, is due to Takeuchi [1983].

The local supervisor and coordinator presented here support the same task management functions for a multiprocessor task as did Program 4.2 for a uniprocessor task. A task comprising N processes, $P_1, P_2, \ldots, P_N$, can hence be executed as a *uniprocessor* task using the uniprocessor control call defined by the procedure call/4 (Program 4.2).

    call(M,(P_1, ..., P_N), S, C)

(where M is a module containing the code to be executed by the P_i) and can also be executed as a *multiprocessor* task using the procedure dcall/4 (Program 4.3):

    dcall(M,[P_1, ..., P_N], S, C)

The call dcall(M,[P$_1$, ..., P$_N$], S, C) results in the same computation and can be managed in the same way as the call call(M,(P$_1$, ..., P$_N$), S, C). However, its evaluation can be distributed over N processors.

4.5 TERMINATION AND QUIESCENCE DETECTION

A programmer may wish to detect both when all processes comprising a task have terminated and when these processes have become quiescent. Termination and quiescence detection are straightforward on a uniprocessor and can hence be implemented directly in the kernel. (Recall that they are supported by the succeeded and quiescent task statuses.) These functions are more complex on a multiprocessor, for two reasons: (1) they require global knowledge about a distributed state, which is not immediately available, and (2) messages can exist in transit between processors.

Global knowledge can be gathered by visiting each processor on which a task is executing in turn or by causing each processor to report changes in state to a central monitor. However, this information is only valid if subsequent communication cannot change the state of a task once its status has been determined.

A multiprocessor termination detection algorithm was presented in the previous section. Termination of a uniprocessor component of a multiprocessor task is signalled by closing a portion of a short circuit; the closing of the entire circuit signals termination of the multiprocessor task. This technique is effective because a uniprocessor task cannot resume execution once it has terminated. In addition, the kernel facility invoked by the TASK primitive ensures that termination of each uniprocessor task is only signalled when it is known that all interprocessor communications that could generate exceptions have been acknowledged. (This is the function of the task type *GlobalT*.)

Multiprocessor quiescence detection is more complex. Dijkstra *et al*. [1983] describe a quiescence detection algorithm for synchronous systems. This detects global quiescence by repeatedly visiting processors on which a computation is active until it has verified that all are simultaneously *inactive*. The algorithm requires that: (1) inactive processors cannot generate messages, (2) inactive tasks cannot become active except by receiving messages, and (3) communication is synchronous.

Each processor is assumed to maintain a state: black or white. A processor is initially black, may be set to white when visited by the algorithm and reverts to black if any other communication is received. The algorithm visits each processor in turn, setting its state to white if it is inactive. If all processors are inactive when visited, it then revisits all processors. If all are still white, then it is known that no processor has generated or received a communication since the last visit. All processors are hence known to be simultaneouly inactive.

Dijkstra's algorithm can be used in asynchronous systems if acknowledgement messages are introduced at the application level and messages and acknowledgements are counted at each processor. This permits the use of Dijkstra's algorithm to verify both that all processors are simultaneously inactive and that no processor has outstanding communications. (A processor has no outstanding messages if has received as many acknowledgements as it has generated messages.) As it is then known that no messages exist in transit, quiescence can be confirmed. This approach is adopted here: the task type *GlobalQ* requests that the kernel generate acknowledgements required for quiescence detection. Quiescence can hence be detected in multiprocessor tasks constructed entirely of uniprocessor tasks of this type.

The use of kernel facilities to implement multiprocessor quiescence detection is illustrated using an FP program. Program 4.5 exploits the quiescent(_) and active status messages provided by the kernel to implement a variant of Dijkstra's algorithm. This only advances from one processor to the next when a processor is inactive. It can hence be used to detect quiescence but not to verify whether or not a task is quiescent. If a processor never becomes inactive, the algorithm never advances.

It is assumed that a multiprocessor task is expressed in terms of a number of uniprocessor tasks and supervisor processes as in Progam 4.3 and that each such task has type *GlobalQ*. Program 4.5 specifies a coordinator and local supervisor similar to those

coord(S, L, R) ←   % Initiate check with 'yes' token.   (C1)
    L = [yes |L1], coord1(S, L1, R).

coord1(S, _, [yes |R]) ← S = quiescent.   % Quiescence confirmed: stop.   (C2)
coord1(S, L, [no |R]) ← coord(S, L, R).   % Not confirmed: repeat.   (C3)

lsv(S, L, R) ← lsv(active, S, L, R).   % Each subtask initially active.   (C4)

lsv(active, [quiescent(_) |S], L, R) ←   % Enter quiescent state.   (C5)
    lsv(quiescent, S, L, R).
lsv(wait, [quiescent(_) |S], L,R) ←   % Enter white state.   (C6)
    R = [no |R1], lsv(white, S, L, R1).
lsv(Any, [active |S], L, R) ←   % Enter active state.   (C7)
    lsv(active, S, L, R).
lsv(active, S, [Any |L], R) ← lsv(wait, S, L, R).   % Enter wait state.   (C8)
lsv(quiescent, S, [Any |L], R) ←   % Enter white state.   (C9)
    R = [no | R1], lsv(white, S, L, R1).
lsv(white, S, [Any |L], R) ←   % Forward token.   (C10)
    var(S) :
    R = [Any |R1], lsv(white, S, L, R1).
lsv(active, succeeded, L,R) ← R = L.   % Termination.   (C11)
lsv(wait, succeeded, L,R) ← R = [no | L].   % Termination.   (C12)

Program 4.5 Multiprocessor quiescence detection.

provided in Program 4.4. To simplify presentation, these do not provide task manage-ment functions other than quiescence detection. (They can easily be extended along the lines of Program 4.4 to provide other functions.) The coordinator takes as arguments a status variable, to be bound if quiescence is detected, and the left- and right-hand sides of a circuit linking the supervisors. The supervisor takes as arguments a state, the status variable of its task and its portion of the circuit.

Each local supervisor records the state of its task: *quiescent, active, wait,* or *white*. A task is initially active (C4). If a quiescent(_) message is received on its status stream it becomes quiescent (C5) until an active status message is received – in which case it becomes active (C7) – or (as described below) a token is received, in which case it becomes white (C9). A task also becomes quiescent if it terminates (C11). The state white can only change to active. This happens if an active status message is received (C7).

To check for quiescence, a *yes* token is injected into the left side of the circuit (C1). Each local supervisor forwards a token received on its left stream if it itself is white (C10); changes its state to white and forwards a *no* token if it is quiescent (C9); or changes its state to wait if it is active (C8). A supervisor in wait state forwards a *no* token and sets its state to white if its task becomes quiescent (C6) or terminates (C12). A token thus circulates round all the supervisors until either a *yes* or *no* token appears on the right side of the circuit. If a *yes* token appears, quiescence has been confirmed (C2); otherwise, the process is repeated (C3). Note the use of the var test in C10. By checking that its task's status stream is a variable, a supervisor ensures that there are no pending active messages and hence that its task is currently quiescent.

For quiescence to be confirmed, every task must be white (and hence continuously quiescent with no unreceived messages) for a complete circuit of the token. This implies that all tasks, and hence the task as a whole, are simultaneously quiescent. At least two circuits of the token are required to confirm quiescence in a multiprocessor task. How-ever, each circuit only requires $O(N)$ communications and process reductions, where N is the number of processors on which the multiprocessor task is executing.

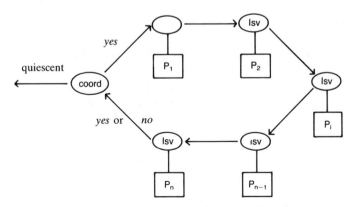

Figure 4.5 Multiprocessor quiescence detection.

Figure 4.5 illustrates the application of this algorithm. Note that for simplicity the quiescent status message generated by Program 4.5 does not indicate the number of processes in the quiescent task. This information can be accumulated by the *yes* token as it visits each processor.

4.6 LOCAL SCHEDULING

A computational model based on lightweight processes and tasks permits two different approaches to the allocation of processor resources. Processes can be scheduled independently of tasks. Alternatively, processor resources can be allocated firstly to tasks and then to processes within tasks. The latter approach is adopted here: the task is treated as a unit of computation to which resources can be allocated and for which programmers can specify scheduling policies. Tasks may be scheduled in several different ways:

1. A fixed algorithm such as round-robin can be implemented in the kernel.
2. Programmers can specify policies that control the application of a fixed algorithm.
3. Programmers may be allowed to provide their own schedulers. These can implement any scheduling algorithm they desire.

The first and second approaches have been adopted in the systems constructed in this study [Foster, 1987b; Gregory *et al.*, 1989]. A scheduler based on the second approach is described here. This is incorporated in the kernel but is sensitive to task priorities specified by programmers. This gives programmers control over scheduling policy.

Each time this scheduler is invoked, it selects as the *current task* the highest priority task that requires processor resources. If several tasks have the same highest priority, the task that has been waiting the longest time is selected. This current task is scheduled for a fixed *task timeslice*. The scheduler is invoked when a timeslice ends, when the current task no longer requires processor resources, or when a task with priority higher than the current task requires processor resources.

Programmers specify task priorities using a kernel mechanism that sets a priority field in a task record. This may be represented as a PRIORITY primitive.

- 'PRIORITY'(TR ↓, P ↓, Done ↑): associates an integer-valued priority P with the task represented by the task record TR and binds the variable Done to the constant ok when completed.

Programmers could be provided with more control over scheduler policy, for example by permitting specification of the timeslice which is allocated to different tasks. However, this added complexity has not been found necessary in the systems constructed to date.

4.7 GLOBAL SCHEDULING

Recall that only minimal kernel support is provided for global scheduling. The nature of this support is defined here and its application is illustrated.

4.7.1 Bootstrap, and code and process mapping

The kernel is assumed to create an initial process network used for bootstrap purposes. This initial network consists of a single *mapping server* process on each processor plus a central *bootstrap* process, with shared logical variables providing a stream connection from the bootstrap process to each mapping server. The bootstrap and mapping server process can then communicate to perform the process and code migration required to bootstrap an OS.

Program 4.6 defines a simple mapping server. This process accepts process and task messages which request it to create new processes and tasks respectively. Each message includes an object code module and a term representing a process. The central bootstrap process can thus create the services required to bootstrap an OS by sending process messages to the appropriate mapping servers. Shared variables in these messages provide the OS's communication streams.

The problem of creating a multiprocessor task is used to illustrate the use of mapping servers. Recall that multiprocessor task management functions are provided by a network of coordinator and supervisor processes (Figure 4.4). Each supervisor manages the execution of a uniprocessor task. To create a multiprocessor task, both this process network and the uniprocessor tasks must be created.

The mapping server processes a message task(M,P,L,R) by creating both a local supervisor process and a task to evaluate process P. (The procedure call/4, defined in Program 4.2, is used for the latter purpose). L and R are the left- and right-hand sides of a circuit. A multiprocessor task can hence be created by sending task messages to several mapping servers, with shared variables providing the communication channels required to implement the circuit. Figure 4.6 illustrates the message passing required to create the process network illustrated in Figure 4.4.

Assume that a central distributor process has the responsibility of deciding which

```
mserver([process(M, P) |Rs]) ←        % Create process and recurse.
    M@P, mserver(Rs).
mserver([task(M, P, L, R) |Rs]) ←
    call(M, P, S, C),                  % Create uniprocessor task (Program 4.1)
    lsv(S, C, L, R),                   %     and a local supervisor (Program 4.3).
    mserver(Rs).                       %     Recurse.
```

Program 4.6 Mapping server.

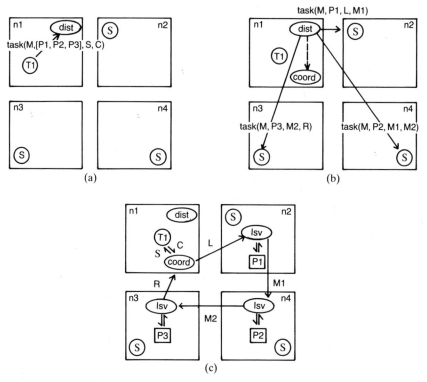

Figure 4.6 Creating a multiprocessor task.

processors to allocate to a particular task. Other processes communicate with the distributor to request the creation of multiprocessor tasks. In Figure 4.6(a), the distributor receives a request task(M,[P1, P2, P3],S, C) which it interprets as a request to initiate multiprocessor execution of the processes (P1, P2, P3). In (b), it determines that it can allocate three processors to the task – n2, n3 and n4 – and generates messages to mapping servers (S) on these processors: task(M, P1, L, M1), task(M, P2, M1, M2), task(M, P3, M2, R). It also creates a coordinator: coord(S,C,L,R). In (c), the task messages are received and processed by the mapping servers. The process network illustrated in Figure 4.4 has been created. The shared variables L, M1, M2 and R in the original messages implement the circuit linking the supervisors and the coordinator. The process that requested the distributor to create this task can now manage its execution using the status and control streams S and C provided in the original request.

4.7.2 Scheduling and task management

The previous section showed how the process migration required to support global scheduling can be implemented with message passing. Similar techniques can be used to implement scheduling within an application. An initital network of mapping processes is created in a suitable topology. Process migration in the application is then implemented using message passing between these processes. The reader is referred to Taylor, [1989] and Foster and Taylor [1989] for a description of these programming techniques; this section is concerned only to show that the implementation of process migration using message passing does not prevent the use of task management mechanisms described previously.

The process topologies that are used for process mapping are frequently circular in structure, with each mapping process receiving requests from one or more neighbors. In consequence, these processes do not terminate when their application terminates; instead, they continue waiting for process migration requests. This means that if the processes created to provide process mapping are executed in the same task as the application (as is generally convenient), that task will never terminate but will only become quiescent. The task management program presented previously does not therefore immediately provide termination detection. Recall however that the quiescent exception message has a process count associated with it. Observe that when the application program terminates, tasks at each processor will be quiescent and the total process count will be equal to the number of mapping processes created for the application. The quiescence detection algorithm described in Section 4.5 can detect this situation and report it as termination. For example, if three mapping processes are created for an application, then a status message quiescent(3) denotes termination of the application task; quiescent(N), $N > 3$, denotes normal quiescence.

The task management mechanisms described previously can thus be applied when process migration is implemented using message passing. However, termination detection must be achieved in a slightly different way.

4.8 SUMMARY

This chapter has described kernel facilities to support systems programming using lightweight processes, logical variables, and tasks. A kernel that provides these facilities has been implemented on a network of workstations. The techniques used to implement this kernel are described in the following chapter.

The kernel supports lightweight processes and logical variables directly: it is capable of executing FP programs. This support provides immediate solutions to three of the OS design problems listed in Chapter 2: concurrency, communication and synchronization, and nondeterminism. In fact, it also provides solutions to the problems of shared resources and protection: lightweight processes provide a natural mechanism for encapsulating shared resources, and shared logical variables can be used to implement capability-based protection schemes. Detailed discussion of these two issues is however postponed until Chapter 7.

Task management is problematic because of the range and complexity of management functions that may be required. This complexity is reduced by providing only a sparse set of kernel facilities. These are used to provide a range of more complex task management functions by defining processes or, in multiprocessors, process networks that implement the desired functionality. A simple local scheduler is incorporated in the kernel; OS programs specify scheduling policies by setting task priorities. Global scheduling is not supported directly but is instead programmed using message passing.

The kernel design presented in this chapter has been motivated by a desire for minimality. It is believed that minimality has been achieved, subject to necessary tradeoffs between functionality, simplicity, flexibility, and efficiency. Some task management functions supported by kernel facilities can also be implemented by source-to-source transformations. However, it has yet to be shown that the latter approach supports quiescence detection or processor scheduling; these functions were identified as necessary for operating systems and have been incorporated in the kernel described here. If systems do not require these functions, transformation becomes a viable alternative. The relative efficiency of kernel support and transformation may then be a deciding factor. Performance studies reported in Chapter 6 permit an evaluation of the efficiency of the two approaches.

5

KERNEL IMPLEMENTATION TECHNIQUES

The kernel facilities presented in the previous chapter define the interface between the kernel and the rest of the OS.

USER
Various services

NUCLEUS
Essential services

KERNEL
Basic facilities

HARDWARE
e.g. Parallel machine

Kernel facilities were defined in terms of the FP language plus a set of task management primitives. This chapter presents techniques that permit efficient implementation of these facilities. These techniques fall naturally into four groups.

Uniprocessor process management and interprocess communication.
Interprocessor communication.
Uniprocessor task management and processor scheduling.
Multiprocessor task management.

The techniques are sufficiently abstract to permit implementation in machine code, microcode, or hardware. They have been incorporated in emulators of the kernel that have been used for performance studies.

5.1 BACKGROUND

The kernel's process management and communication facilities have been defined in terms of the parallel logic programming language FP. Recall that the parallel logic

programming model permits processes to synchronize, communicate, change state, terminate, and create new processes. Guarded clauses provide succinct descriptions of
these actions. Run-time support for process reduction can be provided by an *interpreter*
that selects and attempts to reduce processes using program clauses. For efficiency it is,
however, preferable to *compile* programs. In essence, compilation translates clauses
defining process actions into code which, when executed, attempts to perform these
actions. For example, consider the following clause:

consumer([X |Xs]) ← X = sync, consumer(Xs).

This can be compiled to a program for executing consumer processes. The code that is
generated must:

- check whether a process's argument is a list, and if so
- unify the list head with the string sync, and
- generate a new consumer process, with the list tail as an argument.

Rather than compile high-level language programs directly to the machine code of
a particular physical machine, it is frequently useful to define an intermediate *abstract
machine* as a compilation target. This abstract machine may then be implemented by an
emulator written in another language, by microcode, or by hardware. Alternatively,
abstract machine instructions can be further compiled to the machine code of a physical
machine. The O-code used in the implementation of BCPL represents an early use of an
abstract machine [Richards, 1971]. An abstract machine provides data structures that
represent the state of a computation plus an instruction set that encodes basic operations
on this state. For example, the FP abstract machine introduced in this chapter provides
registers to contain process arguments and includes instructions such as *load*, which
copies process arguments to machine registers, *test_list*, which tests whether a register
contains a reference to a list, and *execute*, which encodes process reduction.

Warren [1977] was the first to investigate compilation and abstract machine design
for logic programming languages. He showed that this class of languages can be executed
efficiently on conventional processors. He also designed an influential abstract machine
for the sequential logic programming language Prolog [Warren, 1983].

In parallel logic languages, the state of a computation consists of a set of processes
and their data. Operations on this state include creating and destroying processes and
reading and writing data. Early attempts to design abstract machines for parallel logic
languages include a proposal by Crammond and Miller [1984] and the Sequential Parlog
Machine (SPM) [Foster *et al.*, 1986; Gregory *et al.*, 1989]. In the SPM, processes are
represented by data structures called *process records*. These process records are linked
in a *process tree*; this provides support for the management of nested processes. Processes are also linked into a *scheduling structure* which records potentially reducible
processes and associates suspended processes with the variables for which they require
data. This structure avoids the overhead of repeatedly attempting to reduce suspended

processes (busy waiting). Another important optimization is the use of *tail recursion* to avoid searching for a reducible process at every reduction. Tail recursion would permit the consumer program given previously to continue executing the new consumer process created by the recursive call.

Researchers at the Weizmann Institute have developed an alternative approach to parallel logic language implementation. They adopted a *flat* computational model similar to that described in Chapter 3 and have designed data and control structures to support this model. These are significantly simpler than equivalent SPM structures, because they do not need to maintain a process tree. These stuctures have been incorporated in an interpreter for the parallel logic language Flat Concurrent Prolog (FCP) [Mierowsky *et al.*, 1985] and subsequently in compilers for the same language [Houri and Shapiro, 1987; Taylor, 1989].

Multiprocessor implementation of parallel logic languages requires that processes located on different processors be able to communicate by reading and writing shared logical variables. This implies a need for kernel support for some form of global address space. Taylor *et al.* [1987b] were the first to investigate seriously the algorithms and run-time support required to implement this communication. They developed an implementation scheme based on the use of *remote references* to represent multiple occurrences of variables and *distributed unification* algorithms which translate read and write operations on remote references into interprocessor communications. In addition, Taylor [1989] showed that the communication necessary for distributed unification can be incorporated in the compilation process by appropriate extensions to an abstract machine instruction set. Ichiyoshi *et al.* [1987; 1988] have developed similar algorithms and compilation techniques for the related language KL1. The scheme developed by Taylor *et al.* is intended for use on message-passing multiprocessors; simpler mechanisms can be employed on shared-memory multiprocessors [Sato *et al.*, 1987b; Crammond, 1988].

The SPM provided a basis for early experimentation in both kernel and OS design, but proved to be too complex to serve as a basis for a minimal OS kernel. The mechanisms required to maintain a process tree are the primary source of complexity. As the flat model does not require these mechanisms, this was adopted as an alternative and a FP abstract machine was developed, based on Taylor's FCP machine [Taylor 1989]. The resulting FP machine (FPM) was then extended to incorporate task management and processor scheduling facilities [Foster and Taylor, 1988].

For ease of exposition, this chapter first describes the FPM in a simplified form, without extensions required for systems programming. Support for a global address space, uniprocessor task management, and multiprocessor task management are then introduced as incremental extensions to the basic design. Distributed unification algorithms for FP are also described. A novel feature of these algorithms is their support for distributed termination and quiescence detection.

5.2 PROCESS MANAGEMENT AND INTERPROCESS COMMUNICATION

This section provides an overview of the FP machine (FPM), an abstract uniprocessor for the FP language which implements the kernel's process management and interprocess communication facilities.

The FPM is described in detail elsewhere [Foster and Taylor, 1988]. The purpose of this overview is to provide essential background material for subsequent sections which describe extensions to the FPM to support interprocessor communication, task management, and processor scheduling.

5.2.1 Operational model

The FPM implements the FP operational model described in Chapter 3 and Appendix II. Recall that in this model the state of a computation is represented as a process pool. Evaluation proceeds by repeatedly selecting processes from this pool and attempting to reduce them. The FPM represents the state of a computation in terms of this model and executes instructions that encode basic operations on this computation state. Programs to be executed by the FPM are encoded as sequences of FPM instructions.

The FPM applies the two optimizations described previously in the context of the SPM, namely a *scheduling structure* and *tail recursion*. The scheduling structure consists of a single *active queue* containing reducible processes plus multiple *suspension lists* which link together processes that require particular data. Suspension lists enable suspended processes to be located and moved to the active queue when the variable that they are suspended on is instantiated.

The tail recursion optimization is a generalization of that commonly used in Prolog implementations. When a clause with body processes is used to reduce a process, reduction can continue with one of those processes. This saves the overhead of adding that process to the process pool and subsequently reselecting it. Tail recursion optimization is only applied a finite number of times before the current process is moved to the end of the active queue and a new process selected for reduction. The number of tail recursive calls permitted before such a *process switch* occurs is a *process timeslice*. This ensures that any process capable of being reduced will eventually be reduced.

When trying to reduce a process, the FPM tries each clause in the associated procedure. Each such *clause try* may suspend, succeed, or fail. If any clause try succeeds, that clause is used to reduce the process. If a clause try suspends because data are not available, the variable(s) for which it requires values are recorded. If no clause try succeeds, but at least one clause try suspends, the process is linked into the suspension lists of all recorded variables. If all clause tries fail, the process try and hence the FP computation fails.

5.2.2 Machine architecture

The principal data area in the FPM is a *heap*. This holds tagged words representing both FP data structures (terms) and process records representing processes. Valid data types are variables, constants (numbers, strings, nil, and object code modules), structured terms (tuples and lists), variables and references to other data structures. The format of all data types except the module is straightforward; the representation of the latter is described in appendix III. A process record contains pointers to the code that the process is executing, its sibling in the scheduling structure and a fixed number of arguments. The only other data structure used by the FPM is the *suspension table* used during a reduction attempt to record variables to suspend upon if no clause try succeeds.

The current state of the abstract machine is recorded in various registers. These form three distinct groups according to the time at which their values are relevant. General registers are used for storing global aspects of the machine state. Process registers are only used during a reduction attempt. Clause registers are used at each clause try. Registers relevant to the present discussion are:

General registers

    QF   Queue Front, points to the first process in the active queue.

    QB   Queue Back, points to the last process in the active queue.

Process registers

    CP   Current Process, points to the process currently being reduced.

    TS   Time Slice, the remaining timeslice for the current process.

    PC   Program Counter, the instruction pointer. Contains the address of the next instruction to be executed.

Figure 5.1 represents the data structures of the FPM. Here the active queue is depicted as containing three process records, labelled P1, P2 and P3. A process P0 is currently being reduced. This has a remaining timeslice of 16.

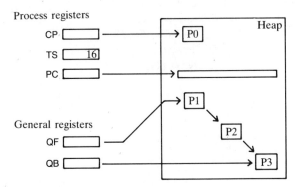

Figure 5.1 FPM architecture.

5.2.3 Instruction set

The FPM's instruction set comprises *unification* instructions used to encode FP's matching and unification operations, and *control* instructions used to encode the language's computational model. The control instructions are based on those developed by Houri and Shapiro [1987] for FCP and encode actions such as the creation, termination and suspension of processes. The unification instructions are similar to those used in Taylor's [1989] FCP machine and in the SPM [Gregory *et al.*, 1989], and encode test and unification operations on process arguments. A complete specification of these instructions can be found in [Foster and Taylor, 1988]. The encoding of the following clause, taken from the lookup procedure in Program 3.1, is presented here to illustrate their use.

```
lookup (Key, [{Key1, Value1} | Db], Value) ←
    Key == Key1 :
    Value = Value1.
```

The following sequence of instructions encodes this clause. The *load* instruction encodes the start of the procedure. It loads process arguments into a set of machine registers called X registers. The *try_me_else* instruction encodes the beginning of a clause try. This takes a label *L1* as an argument, which indicates where execution should continue if the clause try fails. A series of *test* instructions follows. These encode the testing component of the clause try. If any test fails or suspends, execution proceeds at label *L1*. The *unify* instruction encodes the unification operation. Finally, as the clause does not spawn body processes, a *halt* instruction is used to terminate the clause. If all clauses fail or suspend, execution eventually reaches a *suspend* instruction. This suspends the process on any variables included in the suspension table and fails the process if this table is empty.

```
lookup/3:
        load(3)              % Load arguments into registers X0–X2.
        try_me_else(L1)      % Start first clause.
        test_list(1,3,4)     % Is second arg a list? Head in X3, tail in X4.
        test_tuple(2,3,5)    % Is head of list a tuple {_,_}? Args in X5, X6.
        equal(0,5)           % Key == Key1?
        unify(2,6)           % Value = Value1.
        halt                 % Terminate process.
L1:                          % Next clause.
        . . .
Ln:     suspend              % Suspend or fail process.
```

5.3 GLOBAL ADDRESS SPACE

An important feature of the parallel logic programming model is its uniformity. Processes communicate in exactly the same way if they are located on the same or different processors: by reading and writing shared logical variables. Programs are effectively provided with a global address space. A multiprocessor kernel must provide run-time support for this abstraction.

5.3.1 Principles

Taylor *et al.* [1987b] describe the following implementation of a global address space. A logical variable shared by processes located on different processors is represented by a single occurrence and one or more remote references to that occurrence. A *remote reference* specifies a processor and a location within a processor. Each processor is assumed to have a unique identifier. For example, in Figure 5.2 a variable X is located on processor n2 and is represented on processors n1 and n3 by remote references.

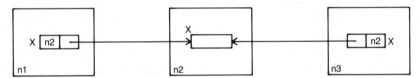

Figure 5.2 Remote references.

A language implementation incorporates *distributed unification* algorithms which generate communications when processes attempt to read or write values represented by remote references (*remote values*). These algorithms permit processsses to access remote values as if these values were located locally. In a compiler-based language implementation, the communication required for distributed unification can be incorporated in the compilation process. This is achieved by incorporating interprocessor communication mechanisms in an abstract machine and extending the abstract instruction set to invoke these mechanisms when remote references are encountered. For example, recall the encoding of the lookup clause presented in the previous section. Both test (*test_list, equal,* etc.) and unification (*unify*, etc.) instructions can encounter remote references. A test instruction that encounters a remote reference acts as if the remote reference denoted a variable: it places an entry in the suspension table and continues to the next clause. If execution reaches the *suspend* instruction, messages are generated to request the values of any remote references recorded in the suspension table. The process is suspended on these remote references; it will thus be woken when a requested remote value is returned. A unification instruction that encounters a remote reference generates a message to request the remote processor to continue the unification operation.

Assume that run-time support for FP is provided on each processor in a multiprocessor. This support can take the form of an implementation of the FPM. The additional kernel mechanisms required to support a global address space consist of a mechanism for receiving and processing incoming messages (potentially modifying FPM data structures) and a mechanism for transmitting outgoing messages. Figure 5.3 illustrates this extended architecture.

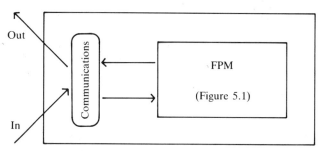

Figure 5.3 Kernel support for distributed unification.

5.3.2 Data manipulation in FP

The distributed unification algorithms required in an implementation of a particular language are determined by the data manipulation operations incorporated in that language. FP's operational model distinguishes two fundamental operations on data. *Test* operations are performed when seeking to reduce a process; *unification* operations are performed by unification processes. It is useful to further distinguish between strict and nonstrict tests. Most FP tests are *strict*: they suspend until all input arguments are instantiated and then succeed or fail. For example, data or integer. A few, such as == and =\=, can in certain cases proceed when their input arguments are variables. These are said to be *nonstrict* in these cases. For example, a call X==Y succeeds if its two arguments are syntactically identical; this includes the case when they are identical variables. A call X==Y can thus succeed when its arguments are both variable, if they are the *same* variable.

The distinction between strict and nonstrict tests is important because different actions must be performed when these tests require remote values. As a strict test cannot proceed until a remote term is instantiated, it is not necessary to return the value of a remote term required by a strict test until it is nonvariable. A nonstrict test, on the other hand, must be informed of the location of a remote variable. This allows a call X==Y to succeed if X and Y are remote references to the same variable.

A *unification* operation applied to a remote reference can be translated into a message requesting the processor on which the remote term is located to perform the unification operation.

5.3.3 Distributed unification algorithms

The extensions to an FP implementation required to support a global address space are encoded in three distributed unification algorithms. These algorithms are defined in terms of:

> When messages are generated.
> What messages are generated.
> How messages are processed.

The *read* and *ns_read* algorithms are used to retrieve remote terms required by strict and nonstrict test operations. These algorithms are invoked when a process suspends and is found to require remote values. The *unify* algorithm is used to perform unification operations involving remote terms. It is invoked when unification operations encounter remote references. Messages generated as a result of test and unification operations or while processing messages are handled by communication mechanisms provided by the kernel. These mechanisms may generate further messages and/or modify local data structures. Processors are assumed to alternately perform reduction attempts and process messages; this ensures that data structures are not accessed while in inconsistent states.

Messages are represented here as structured terms: read(T,F), unify(X,T,Y), etc. The functor (read, unify) represents the message type; the first subterm (T,X) is always a remote reference representing the message's *destination*. Recall that a remote reference is a {processor, location} pair. When a message is generated, it is sent to its destination processor. A processor receiving a message examines the destination location. If this contains a remote reference, the message is forwarded, thus dereferencing chains of remote references. Otherwise, the message can be processed. Dereferencing of remote reference chains is assumed in the following descriptions and is not mentioned explicitly.

A chain of remote references may lead a message back to its source processor, making an apparently remote operation a local operation [Taylor, 1989]. For clarity of presentation, the descriptions that follow ignore such special cases. Only minor modifications to the algorithms are required to deal with them.

THE *READ* ALGORITHM

If a *strict* test requires the value of a remote term, a read message is generated to the processor indicated in the remote reference. A processor receiving a read message returns the value of a *nonvariable* term immediately using a value message. The value of a *variable* is not returned until the variable is bound. A *broadcast note* is attached to the variable to record the pending request. It is thus necessary to check for broadcast notes when binding variables and to respond to the pending requests that they represent with value messages. Note that a read message is only generated for the first process to suspend on a particular remote reference.

The *value* of a term is defined to be the scalar value of a constant, one or more levels of a structure (including constant subterms and remote references to other subterms) and a remote reference to a variable. A value message copies the value of a term from one processor to another. A processor receiving a value message replaces the remote reference with the value and awakens any processes suspended waiting for it. Subsequent accesses to a nonvariable value do not require communication. This copying of nonvariable terms is possible because of the single-assignment property of the logical variable. The read and value messages have the form:

    read(To, From)
    value(From, Value)

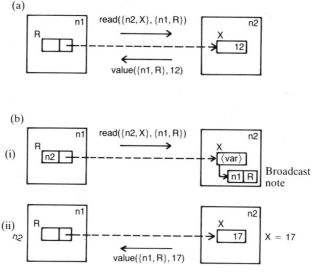

Figure 5.4 The *read* distributed unification algorithm. (a) Value is available. (b) Value is not available.

where To is a remote reference to the remote term (that is, a representation of its processor and location), From is a remote reference to the original remote reference and Value is the value of the remote term.

Figure 5.4 shows two examples of remote reading. In each case, the value of a term represented by a remote reference (represented here as {n2, X}: that is, location X on processor n2) is required by a strict test (for example, integer(X)). The value of X is requested using a read message. In the first example, the remote term is available (it is the integer 12) and is returned immediately using a value message. In the second case, the remote term is not available: location X is a variable. A broadcast note is therefore associated with the variable (a). When this variable is instantiated (X = 17), its value is returned using a value message (b).

THE *NS_READ* ALGORITHM

The *ns_read* algorithm is applied when a nonstrict test requires the value of a remote term. If differs from the *read* algorithm in a single aspect: if the remote term that it requests is a variable, a broadcast note is attached to the variable and a remote reference to the variable is returned in an ns_value message. The processor that initiated the request can replace the initial remote reference (which may have been the head of a reference chain) with this direct remote reference. Nonstrict tests that require the remote term may then be repeated. If these tests still suspend, the value of the remote term need not be requested again: the broadcast note attached to the remote variable means that its value will be returned as soon as the variable is bound. An ns_read message is generated for the first process to suspend on a particular remote reference because of a nonstrict test.

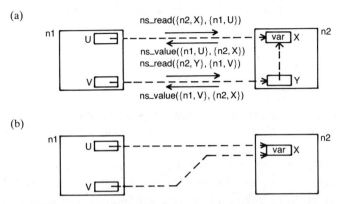

Figure 5.5 The *ns_read* distributed unification algorithm. (a) U==V suspends.
(b) U==V succeeds.

Figure 5.5 illustrates the use of ns_read and ns_value messages. In (a), a nonstrict test
U==V encounters two remote references. Note that although these indicate different
locations on processor n2 they in fact refer to the same variable, X. The test U==V initially suspends and ns_read messages are generated. Reference chains are dereferenced
and 'direct' remote references returned to processor n1. These replace the original remote references. In (b), the test U==V is repeated and, as U and V are now identical
remote references, succeeds.

THE *UNIFY* ALGORITHM

If a unification operation encounters a remote reference, a unify message is generated
to request processors on which remote term(s) are located to perform the unification.
Failure of a remote unification operation is signalled to the processor on which it was
initiated by a failure message. This permits an exception message to be signalled on the
status stream of the task that performed the unification operation.

Consider a unification operation X=Y. If one of the terms X or Y is represented by a
remote reference (say X), a unify message is generated to the processor on which the
remote term is located. The value of the other term (Y) is included in this messsage. If
both terms to be unified are remote, a unify1 message containing remote references to
both terms is dispatched to the processor on which the first is located; a processor receiving such a message forwards a unify message containing the value of that term to the
processor on which the second term is located. In both cases, a unify message eventually
arrives at a processor on which one of the terms to be unified is located, carrying the
value of the other term. The unification operation can then proceed. A unify message
has the form:

    unify(X, T, Y)

where X is a remote reference to one term to be unified, T denotes the task which initiated the unification operation and Y is the value of the other term. A unify1 message

has the same form: unify1(X, T, Y) but both X and Y are remote references. A failure message has the form:

failure(T, X, Y)

where T specifies the task which initiated the unification operation that resulted in failure and X and Y are the terms that could not be unified.

Figure 5.6 illustrates the messages that may be generated by the *unify* algorithm if one or both arguments in a unification operation are remote terms. In (a), only one of the terms to be unified, X, is represented by a remote reference. A unify message is generated to processor n2. This message contains remote references to X and to the task in which the unification operation occurs (T), plus the value of the other term, Y (<yval>).

In (b), both terms to be unified are represented by remote references. A unify1 message is generated to n3, the processor on which one of these terms, Y, is located. This message carries remote references to X and Y. Processor n3 receives the unify1 message, determines the value of Y (<yval>) and forwards a unify message to processor n2. As in (a), this contains remote references to X and to the task T, plus the value of the other term, Y (<yval>).

In both cases, the processor n2 on which the term X is located receives a unify message containing the value of Y. It then performs the actual unification operation, potentially generating further unify or failure messages. The algorithm used to process a unify message is summarized here. The annotations A, B and C refer to Figure 5.6.

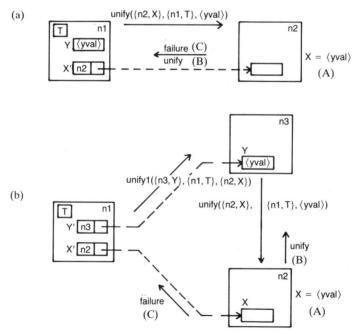

Figure 5.6 The *unify* distributed unification algorithm. (a) One local, one remote. (b) Both remote.

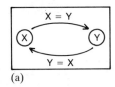 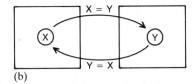

Figure 5.7 Circular references. (a) Uniprocessor. (b) Multiprocessor.

- If X and Y are the same constant, nothing is done.
- A local variable X is bound to a reference to a remote constant or structure Y (A).
- If Y is a variable and X is not, a unify message is generated to request the processor containing Y to unify Y with X (B).
- If both X and Y are variable, an order check (defined below) is performed; this may generate a further unify message (B).
- If X and Y are tuples of the same arity, corresponding subterms are recursively unified; this may generate further unify and unify1 messages (not shown).
- In all other cases, a failure message is generated (C).

CIRCULAR REFERENCES

In logic programming systems, circular references can be created if a variable X can be bound to a variable Y at the same time as Y is bound to X. This situation is illustrated in Figure 5.7. This problem can be avoided on shared-memory machines by using pointer comparison to ensure that variable to variable bindings are only created in a certain direction (from low address to high address, for example). A similar technique can be used on nonshared-memory machines. An ordering is defined on processor identifiers. An *order check* compares processor identifiers when variables located on different processors are unified. Bindings are only permitted from a processor of lower identifier to a processor of higher identifier.

The order check is applied when a local variable X is unified with a variable represented by a remote reference Y. If the ordering constraint is violated (that is, $processor(X) > processor(Y)$), the unify message is forwarded to the other processor. This causes the unification operation to be repeated in the opposite direction. Otherwise, X is bound to a remote reference to Y (unless both variables are located on the same processor). In both cases, the binding is created in the correct direction, from low to high processor.

5.3.4 Application of distributed unification

A simple example illustrates the use of distributed unification algorithms and motivates some observations on their complexity. Consider the program

```
producer(Xs, synch) ← Xs = [X |Xs1], producer(Xs1, X).

consumer([X |Xs]) ← X = synch, consumer(Xs).
```

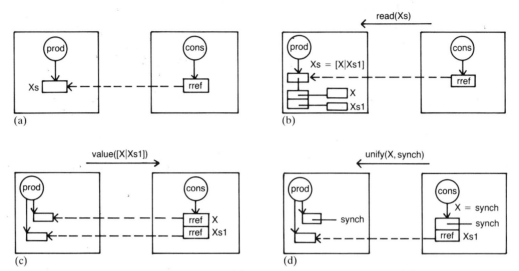

Figure 5.8 Distributed unification. (a) producer(Xs,_), consumer(Xs). (b) prod binds Xs; cons reads Xs. (c) cons obtains X and Xs1. (d) cons binds X.

and the initial processes

    producer(Xs, synch), consumer(Xs).

The program implements synchronous communication between two processes producer and consumer. The producer process repeatedly communicates a variable to consumer by instantiating the shared variable Xs to a list structure containing the variable. It then suspends until the variable that it has sent is bound. The consumer process acknowledges each such 'communication' by instantiating the variable to synch. This acknowledgement permits producer to generate a further communication.

Assume that the producer and consumer processes are located on different processors and that the kernel supports the *unify* and *read* distributed unification algorithms. Figure 5.8 illustrates the messages generated when these processes are executed. In (a), the initial situation is represented. It is assumed that the variable Xs is located on the same processor as the producer process; the consumer process thus possesses a remote reference to this variable. In (b), producer generates a value for Xs (say [X | Xs1]) on its own processor; when consumer attempts to read the shared variable Xs, a read message is generated to retrieve that value. In (c), a value message returns the list structure generated by producer to consumer; this contains remote references to X and Xs1. In (d), consumer unifies X with the constant synch. As X is a remote reference to a variable located on producer's processor, a unify message is generated.

Distributed unification thus generates three messages to send and acknowledge a communication. Two messages are required to 'read' the original value and one message is required to 'write' the value synch to the variable X. In contrast, if this algorithm were to be implemented in a language with explicit *send* and *receive* primitives, two messages would be required for each communication: one to send it and one to acknowledge it.

Two points can thus be made about the distributed unification algorithms presented here.

- They are *in general* optimal in their communication complexity. That is, $O(N)$ messages are required to communicate $O(N)$ values between processors. ('In general' because when unifying two variables, order checks may cause additional communications. This is, however, a special case as variables rather than values are involved.)
- They are lazy: a value must be requested by a reader before it is transmitted. This is why three messages are required to communicate two values. There is scope for optimizations that eagerly propagate values when readers are known to require them.

5.4 UNIPROCESSOR TASK MANAGEMENT AND SCHEDULING

Recall that the kernel's task management and processor scheduling facilities have been defined in terms of a set of primitive operations. Kernel mechanisms that support these facilities on a uniprocessor are presented here as extensions to the architecture and instruction set of the abstract machine introduced in Section 5.2.

5.4.1 Extensions to operational model

The introduction of the notion of task into a process-oriented language implies a need for an extended operational model. As the processes comprising a task must be managed as a unit, each task can usefully be viewed as a separate process pool. The state of a computation is hence represented as a pool of tasks, each of which is a pool of processes. Figure 5.9 contrasts the original and extended operational models.

Computation in the extended model proceeds by repeatedly selecting both a task and a process within that task, and attempting to reduce the process. A reduction attempt may succeed, suspend or fail as before. Failure now causes an exception message (Section 4.2.3) to be generated on the corresponding task's status stream and a continuation variable to be placed in the task's process pool. An empty process pool corresponds to successful termination of a task. A nonempty process pool which contains no reducible processes corresponds to task quiescence.

An abstract machine named the extended FPM (eFPM) is used to implement this

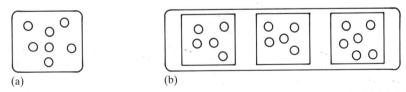

(a)   (b)

Figure 5.9 Simple and extended operational models. (a) Process pool. (b) Multiple process pools.

extended operational model. The eFPM applies optimizations similar to the FPM's tail recursion and scheduling structure. These are the notions of *current task*, which avoids the overhead of selecting a task at each reduction, and *scheduler*, which avoids the overhead of repeatedly selecting quiescent or suspended tasks for reduction.

A separate active queue is maintained for each task. One task is identified as the current task. The eFPM repeatedly reduces processes from the active queue of this task until a task timeslice (defined subsequently) ends, the task blocks or a higher-priority task requires resources. A *task switch* then occurs. This causes the scheduler to be run. The scheduler is a kernel routine that maintains a scheduling structure (a *task queue*) representing tasks that require processor resources. Each time it is invoked, it selects and schedules as the current task the highest priority task in this queue. When a time-slice ends, the current task is inserted in the task queue *after* tasks with the same priority: tasks with the same priority are hence scheduled round-robin. Tasks are only inserted in the task queue by the kernel if they require processor resources; quiescent and suspended tasks are hence never selected for execution.

5.4.2 Extensions to architecture

Recall that in the FPM, the current state of the abstract machine is recorded in three sets of registers: general registers, process registers, and clause registers. The general registers include the queue head and queue tail registers, which point to the head and tail of the active queue.

In the eFPM, a separate active queue is maintained for each task. The head and tail of a task's active queue, and other information about the task, are maintained in a data structure much like a process record called a *task record*. The fields of the task record include the following:

> NX   Next, the next task record in the task queue.
> SV   Status Variable, points to the task's status variable.
> QF   Queue Front, points to the first process record in the task's active queue.
> QB   Queue Back, points to the last process record in the task's active queue.
> PK   Process Count, the number of processes in the task
> MK   Message Count, the number of outstanding messages (see section 5.5).
> ST   State, indicates whether the task is active, suspended, aborted, etc.
> PR   Priority, the priority associated with the task.
> TY   Type, the type of the task.

Figure 5.10 illustrates the run-time structures used to represent tasks. Three different structures are represented: task records, process records, and a status variable. Two task records are linked in the task queue; the first is expanded to show its internal structure. This contains a pointer to the next entry in the task queue, a pointer to the task's status variable and pointers to the head and tail of the task's active queue. The task has a process count of four: three processes are in the active queue and one is suspended. The

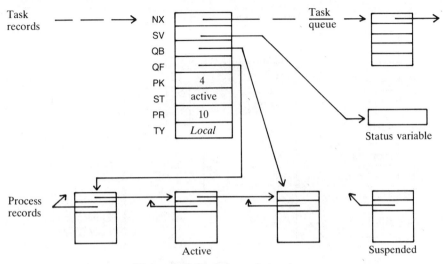

Figure 5.10 Task record structure.

task is *active*, has a priority of 10 and has been assigned type *Local*. The upward pointers in the process records reference the task record. These pointers are contained in an additional task field (TA) in the process record.

New machine registers, termed *task registers*, are used to buffer some of the data contained in the task record when a task is current. These include the following:

CT	Current Task, points to the current task.
QF	Queue Front, buffers the current task's QF field.
QB	Queue Back, buffers the current task's QB field.
PK	Process Count, buffers the current task's PK field.
MK	Message Count, buffers the current task's MK field.
TY	Type, buffers the current task's TY field.
SL	Task Slice, the remaining task timeslice for the current task.

The scheduling structure used by the eFPM is a queue of task records ordered according to priority. Two general registers provide access to this queue:

TF	Task queue Front, points to the first task record in the task queue.
TB	Task queue Back, points to the last task record in the task queue.

The only other new data structure is an interrupt vector that specifies kernel routines that handle run-time errors, timer interrupts, etc. Figure 5.11 represents the data structures of the eFPM. Four tasks are represented in this figure. One of these, labelled T3, is the current task; its fields are buffered in the task registers. Two tasks (T1 and T4) are recorded in the task queue. T2 is quiescent – its active queue is empty – and is hence not recorded in the task queue.

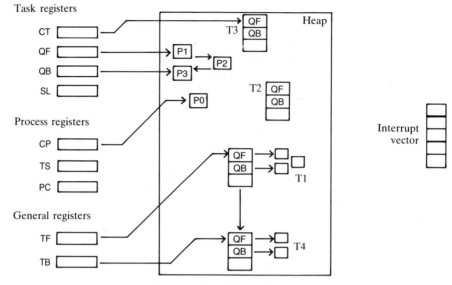

Figure 5.11 eFPM architecture.

5.4.3 Implementation of task management primitives

The implementation of the task management primitives is defined in terms of their effect on eFPM data structures.

- 'TASK'(S, TR, T, P): allocates a task record on the heap and returns it as TR. The new task's process count (PK) is set to one, its message count (MK) to zero and its state (ST) to active. Its priority is the same as its parent. S is recorded as its status variable (SV) and T as its type (TY). A new process is created to execute P; this is added to the active queue of the new task. The new task is inserted in the task queue.
- 'SUSPEND'(TR, Done): sets the state field of the task record TR to suspended and binds the variable Done to the constant ok.
- 'CONTINUE'(TR, Done): if the state field of the task record TR is suspended, it is set to active and the task record is inserted in the task queue. The variable Done is bound to the constant ok. A task switch occurs if the resumed task's priority is greater than that of the current task.
- 'STOP'(TR, Done): sets the state field of the task record TR to aborted. The variable Done is bound to the constant ok.
- 'PRIORITY'(TR, P, Done): sets the priority field of the task record TR to P and reschedules the task in the task queue. The variable Done is bound to the constant ok. A task switch occurs if the new priority is greater than that of the current process.

5.4.4 Extensions to instruction set

The eFPM instruction set is extended to perform the operations on eFPM data structures necessary for task management. Task management functions are hence incorporated in the compilation process.

The abstract machine instructions that encode the creation and termination of processes increment and decrement the current task's process count (the task record field PK, buffered in the register PK when a task is current). The instruction that encodes process termination also checks for (and reports) termination and quiescence. If a task's process count is zero, the current task (CT) register is used to access its task record and:

- The status variable is accessed using the SV field and is instantiated to succeeded to report successful termination.
- The state field is set to terminated.
- A task switch occurs.

If a task's active queue is empty and its message count is zero, but its process count is not zero:

- A quiescent(N) exception is signalled on its status stream, where N is the process count. (This involves binding the status variable to a list [quiescent(N) | Var] and setting the task record's SV field to reference the new variable Var.)
- The state field is set to quiescent.
- A task switch occurs.

A task switch involves saving the contents of the task registers in the current task's task record and then executing the scheduler. Failure of a process reduction is also signalled on the current task's status stream by an exception message.

In the FPM, unification operations check for suspended processes when they instantiate a variable. They move any such processes from the variable's suspension list to the active queue. In the eFPM, an awakened process's task record is consulted to determine the active queue to which the process is to be appended. Furthermore, if the awakened process's task was quiescent, its task record's state field is set to active and the task record is inserted in the task queue. An active exception is signalled on its status stream. The process record's task (TA) field gives access to its task's task record and hence to the task's active queue, state, and status variable. An active exception is also signalled if a quiescent task's message count becomes nonzero (see Section 5.5). Whenever a new task is inserted in the task queue its priority is compared with that of the current task. If it is greater, an immediate task switch occurs.

Interrupts are handled by kernel procedures referenced by the interrupt vector. Interrupts indicating process error conditions are signalled on the current task's status stream as exception messages. Timer interrupts cause a task switch if the current task's task timeslice is exhausted.

5.5 MULTIPROCESSOR TASK MANAGEMENT

The kernel facilities described in the previous chapter report two changes in the state of a task:

1. *Termination:* the process pool representing the task is empty.
2. *Quiescence:* the process pool is not empty, but all processes are suspended due to dataflow constraints.

As noted in the previous section, a uniprocessor kernel can maintain a process count for a task in order to detect its termination. A task's process count is incremented when a new process is created and decremented when a process terminates. If a task's process count reaches zero, the task has terminated. Similarly, the active queue can be used to detect quiescence. An empty active queue (and a nonzero process count) signify quiescence.

Now consider a task executing on a single processor in a multiprocessor. If this task's processes share data with remote processes, the mechanisms just described are no longer adequate for detecting termination and quiescence. Unification operations that encounter remote terms generate messages to request remote unification operations. As these operations may result in exceptions, a task cannot be said to have terminated until both its process count is zero and it is known that all remote unifications that it has initiated have completed without error. Read operations on remote terms cause similar problems. As processes suspend until a reply to a request for a remote value is received, a task cannot be said to be quiescent until both its active queue is empty and it is known that all remote read requests have either completed or are suspended waiting for data.

Alternative distributed unification algorithms are defined to avoid these problems. These are used when termination and/or quiescence detection is required in tasks that are known to access remote data. The algorithms are *symmetric*: they acknowledge messages to indicate that (say) unifications have terminated or remote reads have suspended. This permits the use of message counting to detect termination and quiescence. The eFPM supports this message counting by means of the message count field (MK) in task records.

Three additional algorithms are defined: *s_unify*, *s_read* and *d_read*. The algorithm *s_unify* differs from *unify* in that it acknowledges successful unifications. The algorithm *s_read* differs from *read* in that it acknowledges read messages when a value is not immediately available. The *d_read* algorithm acknowledges both read and value messages.

The various distributed unification algorithms vary in their run-time costs and the task management functions that they support. Different tasks are permitted to use different combinations of these algorithms; which combination is to be used in a particular task is specified when the task is created. The four combinations supported by the TASK primitive are listed in Table 5.1.

Type *Local* permits efficient communication in tasks for which neither termination nor quiescence detection is required. For example, system services, which are not

Table 5.1 Task types

Type	Algorithms	Functions supported
Local	unify, read	Neither termination nor quiescence detection
GlobalT	s_unify, read	Termination detection
LocalQ	s_unify, s_read	Quiescence detection in uniprocessor tasks
GlobalQ	s_unify, d_read	Quiescence detection in multiprocessor tasks

expected to terminate but which are represented as separate tasks for scheduling purposes or to localize failure. Type *GlobalT* permits termination detection at the cost of some additional communication. This can be used for application programs in which it is not necessary to detect quiescence. Finally, types *LocalQ* and *GlobalQ* can be used when quiescence detection is required in uniprocessor or multiprocessor tasks.

5.5.1 The *s_unify* algorithm

The symmetric *s_unify* algorithm acknowledges successful remote unifications. This acknowledgement permits termination detection in uniprocessor tasks. The *s_unify* algorithm differs from the *unify* algorithm (Section 5.3.2) in three respects:

1. s_unify and s_unify1 messages are used in place of unify and unify1 messages.
2. Successful remote unifications are acknowledged. A processor receiving an s_unify message processes it as it would a unify message, but acknowledges successful completion of the remote unification operation using an ack message.
3. Remote unification operations involving two structures are not performed. Instead, a structure message is generated to return both structures to the processor which initiated the unification. New unification operations can then be initiated, one per structure element. The structure message avoids a need for the complex kernel mechanisms that would be required to detect termination of the recursive unification of two remote structures.

A processor increments its process and message counts when it generates an s_unify message and decrements them when it receives a failure or ack message. A process count of zero then signifies that both all a task's processes and all remote unifications that it has initiated have terminated. This is termination. (The message count is modified to permit quiescence detection: see below.)

Figure 5.12 illustrates the messages generated by the *unify* and *s_unify* algorithms. The *unify* algorithm generates a unify message, which *may* receive a failure response. The *s_unify* algorithm generates an s_unify message, which *always* receives a failure, structure, or ack response. In this figure, PC++, MC−−, etc., indicate the increment and decrement of the process and message counts of the task that initiated the unification operation.

s_unify messages have the same form as unify messages

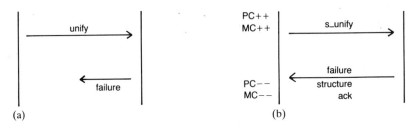

Figure 5.12 Distributed unification algorithms. (a) *unify.* (b) *s_unify.*

> s_unify(X, T, Y)
> s_unify1(X, T, Y)

The ack and structure messages have the form

> ack(T)
> structure(T, X, Y)

where T specifies the location of the task which initiated the remote unification operation and X and Y are the two structures that are to be unified.

5.5.2 The *s_read* algorithm

For brevity, this description of symmetric *read* algorithms only deals with the read/value protocol used to retrieve remote values required by strict tests. The ns_read/ns_value protocol that supports nonstrict tests uses similar algorithms.

The symmetric *s_read* algorithm acknowledges remote read requests. This acknowledgement permits quiescence detection in uniprocessor tasks. The *s_read* algorithm differs from the *read* algorithm (Section 5.3.2) in three respects:

1. s_read messages are generated in place of read messages.
2. A processor receiving an s_read message acknowledges it with an ack message if the value requested is not immediately available.
3. If the value is available, it is returned in an s_value rather than a value message. (If it is not immediately available, the value is returned when it becomes available in a value message, as in the *read* algorithm.)

A processor increments a task's message count when it transmits an s_read message; it decrements it when it receives an s_value or an ack message. The s_value message effectively combines the acknowledgement to the read (ack) with the message that returns the value (value). This optimization reduces communication when a value is immediately available.

When the *s_read* and *s_unify* algorithms are used together, a message count of zero signifies that all remote unifications that a task has initiated have terminated and that all remote reads it has initiated have either completed or suspended. If the active queue is also empty, indicating that the task has no active processes, the task is quiescent.

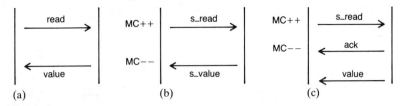

Figure 5.13 Distributed unification algorithms. (a) *read*. (b) *s_read* (data available). (c) *s_read* (data not available).

Figure 5.13 illustrates the messages generated by (a) the *read* algorithm, (b) the *s_read* algorithm when a remote value is available and (c) the *s_read* algorithm when a remote value is not available. In (b) and (c), MC++ and MC−− denote the increment and decrement of the message count of the task that initiated the s_read operation.

The s_read and s_value messages differ from the read and value messages in incorporating the location of the task that initiated the read, T. They have the form:

    s_read(From, T, To)
    s_value(From, T, To)

5.5.3 The *d_read* algorithm

The second symmetric *read* algorithm, *d_read*, acknowledges both read and value messages. These acknowledgements permit quiescence detection in multiprocessor tasks constructed using two or more uniprocessor tasks (Section 4.5). The *d_read* algorithm differs from the *s_read* algorithm just described in three respects:

1. d_read messages are generated in place of read messages.
2. Values that are not immediately available are returned by a d_value rather than a value message when they become available. (The broadcast note generated for a d_read request must indicate that a d_value message is to be generated).
3. A d_value message is acknowledged with an ack message.

A d_value message includes a remote reference to the task that performed the unification operation that bound the remote variable. (Note that this is *not* the same as the task that generated the d_read message; it is located on a different processor.) The processor that receives the d_value message sends its acknowledgement to this task.

A processor increments a task's message count when it transmits a d_read or a d_value message; as before, it decrements it when it receives an s_value or an ack message. The *d_read* algorithm can thus modify the message counts both of tasks that require values (those that generate d_read messages) and of tasks that generate values (those that instantiate variables required by d_read requests). When the *d_read* algorithm is used in conjunction with the *s_unify* algorithm (type *GlobalQ*), a message count of zero signifies that all basic messages (read, value and unify) that a task has generated have been received.

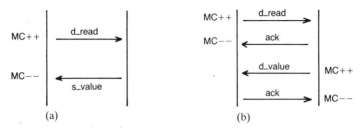

Figure 5.14 The *d_read* distributed unification algorithm. (a) Data available. (b) Data not available.

Figure 5.14 illustrates the messages and message count changes when the *d_read* algorithm is used and (a) a value is available; (b) a value is not available.

The d_read and d_value messages have the form:

d_read(To, T, From)

d_value(From, T, R, Value)

To and From specify the processor and location of the value to be read and the original remote reference, respectively. Value is the value of the remote term, T specifies the location of the task that initiated the read operation, and R is a remote reference to the task that generated the d_value message by supplying the value To. R is used when acknowledging the d_value message. The acknowledgement is the message: ack(R).

5.5.4 Discussion

Distributed unification algorithms permit processes located on different processors to communicate by reading and writing shared logical variables. Extended algorithms have been defined that support termination and quiescence detection in multiprocessor tasks. These generate additional acknowledgement messages and hence are more costly to use than the standard algorithms. However, they only generate one or two additional messages per remote operation and hence do not alter the communication complexity of programs that use them.

The kernel mechanisms required to support the extended algorithms are simple. In particular, the kernel only need maintain local information for each uniprocessor task. Remote information would be required in the *s_unify* algorithm, to detect termination of remote structure-to-structure unifications. (The information to be maintained here would be the number of outstanding substructure unification operations.) This complexity is avoided by the structure message, which returns remote structures to the processor that initiated the remote unification operation.

The structure message is, strictly speaking, an unnecessary communication. It may thus appear to be a source of inefficiency. However, unification of two structures, though possible, rarely occurs in practice. To determine the approximate frequency of such operations, ten parallel logic programs were executed on an instrumented uniprocessor implementation. These included both large system programs (operating system, programming environment) and applications. Less than one percent of all unification operations were found to involve two structures. As remote structure-to-structure unifications are a subset of all structure-to-structure unifications on a multiprocessor, it can be expected that such operations will occur very rarely. The structure message thus appears to be a useful and inexpensive simplification.

5.6 MEMORY MANAGEMENT

A computational model that supports dynamic process, data and communication structures requires either sophisticated compilers capable of determining memory requirements at compile-time or dynamic memory management mechanisms. The first approach is beyond the state of the art in the general case and as a subject is beyond the scope of this book. Dynamic memory management has been assumed in this chapter.

Dynamic memory management requires that the kernel provide two mechanisms: one to allocate memory when messages are sent or processes are created and the other to reclaim this memory when it is no longer required. The latter function is referred to as *garbage collection* [Cohen, 1981]. Garbage collection can either execute concurrently with normal execution or be performed at intervals. The former approach is to be preferred if an application must satisfy real-time requirements but is more costly in the absence of hardware support. Both approaches become more complicated in a multiprocessor because interprocessor references make it more difficult to determine when memory is no longer required. The reader is referred to Foster, [1988c] for a discussion of different approaches and a description of a novel garbage collector for multiprocessors. This collector allows individual processors to reclaim storage independently. It applies optimizations made possible by the single-assignment property of the logical variable to reduce communication and memory requirements. It represents a partial solution to the problem of dynamic memory management in a multiprocessor.

5.7 SUMMARY

This chapter has presented implementation techniques for the kernel facilities described in Chapter 4. A simple abstract machine has been used as a framework for the presentation. This FP machine (FPM) provides process management and data manipulation functions. Implementation techniques for the kernel's task management, interprocessor communication, and termination and quiescence detection facilities have been defined as extensions to the FPM.

A novel and important feature of the approach is that task management functions are incorporated in the compilation process. This is achieved by extending an abstract machine with data structures that support these functions and incorporating operations on these data structures in the abstract instructions used to encode programs. This permits frequently used functions (for example, termination detection) to be compiled to simple operations on machine registers.

The extended machine can be implemented in software, hardware, or microcode to provide an OS kernel. Abstract machine programs can also be further compiled to the machine code of a particular physical machine. Emulators for the kernel have been constructed and used for performance studies. These studies are reported in the following chapter.

6

PERFORMANCE STUDIES

Previous chapters have described kernel facilities that support systems programming in parallel logic languages. This chapter presents performance studies that permit evaluation of the efficiency of these facilities. These studies have two aims:

1. To determine whether the abstract machine used as a basis for kernel implementation, the FPM, provides an adequate basis for performance studies.
2. To quantify overhead associated with the mechanisms introduced to support:

   - uniprocessor task management;
   - interprocessor communication;
   - multiprocessor task management.

Efficiency is a central issue in OS design. Early operating systems were hence implemented entirely in machine language. Advances in compilation techniques and processor design have since permitted moves to higher-level languages. However, the performance problems of computational models that require dynamic storage management have yet to be properly addressed. For example, Ross Overbeek [personal communication, 1988] found that a Prolog theorem prover ran ten times slower than an equivalent C program, even when carefully optimized. Fortunately, the state of the art in compilation of such languages is advancing rapidly. Techniques such as decision tree compilation [Augustsson, 1985; van Roy *et al.*, 1987], native code compilation [Kliger, 1987], and compile-time storage reclamation [Bruynooghe, 1986] can be expected to reduce the performance gap. Improvements in processor design can also contribute: process-oriented and symbolic languages run faster on processors that provide appropriate run-time support [May and Shepherd, 1984; Tick and Warren, 1984; Chu and McCabe, 1988].

Both performance requirements and achievable performance are rapidly changing. Hence the studies reported in this chapter do not focus on the efficiency of basic data manipulation and process management mechanisms; instead, they evaluate the extensions to these basic mechanisms introduced to support task management and interprocessor communication. They also evaluate the efficiency of similar mechanisms proposed by other researchers. In addition, a preliminary study compares the FP machine that implements basic mechanisms with other similar machines. This study is intended to verify that the FPM constitutes an efficient approach to parallel logic language implementation, and hence provides a valid basis for the main studies.

6.1 UNIPROCESSOR STUDY

The purpose of this study was to compare the basic FP machine described in Section 5.2 with similar abstract machines developed by other researchers. Four implementations were benchmarked: the FP machine (*FP*); a similar abstract machine for the FCP language (*FCP*) [Taylor, 1989]; the Sequential Parlog Machine (*SPM*) [Foster *et al.*, 1986] and Houri and Shapiro's FCP machine (*Emu*) [Houri and Shapiro, 1987]). The implementations are all C-coded emulators.

6.1.1 Method and results

Five benchmark programs were executed on each implementation. These were a program proposed by Takeuchi (*Takeuchi*), quicksort of a one-thousand-element list (*QSort*), all solutions to the eight queens problem (*Queens*), naive $O(n^2)$ reverse of a five-hundred-element list (*Reverse*), and an assembler assembling itself (*Assembler*). Table 6.1 characterizes the programs by presenting the number of process reductions performed and process suspensions that occur during the program executions.

Reverse is a tight computational loop that performs many process reductions but little reading and writing of variables and few process suspensions. Queens is a search program that performs more complex variable manipulations but no suspension. *Qsort* and *Takeuchi* generate many suspensions. The assembler is a typical application program that uses common parallel logic programming techniques such as incomplete messages [Shapiro, 1986] and difference lists [Clark and Tärnlund, 1977].

Table 6.2 presents the performance results, in reductions per second, for the programs executed on a CCI (Power 6) processor by each implementation. These are accurate to within 0.5 percent.

Table 6.1 Uniprocessor benchmark programs

Name	Reductions ('000s)	Suspensions ('000s)	Suspensions /Reduction
Assembler	35.9	10.1	0.28
Takeuchi	63.6	12.1	0.19
QSort	16.9	9.4	0.56
Queens	62.1	0.0	0.00
Reverse	126.2	0.5	0.00

Table 6.2 Uniprocessor performance in RPS

	FP	FCP	Emu	SPM
Assembler	5,703	5,012	4,215	–
Takeuchi	8,274	7,488	3,394	1,537
QSort	7,388	6,428	4,042	2,074
Queens	6,640	6,262	2,755	2,318
Reverse	17,045	16,157	14,914	4,774

6.1.2 Discussion

The *FP* and *FCP* emulators implement similar abstract machines and were constructed using the same techniques. Great care was taken to ensure that performance differences reflected differing language semantics. The results show that FP executes between 5 and 15 percent faster on the benchmark programs. These differences are attributed to FCP's more complex unification mechanisms [Foster and Taylor, 1988].

The other implementations, *Emu* and *SPM*, implement different abstract machines and do not necessarily employ the same implementation techniques or optimizations. In addition, *SPM* supports a computational model based on a process tree rather than a process pool. Performance differences hence only give an indication of the effectiveness of the implementations. *FP* executes significantly faster than both *Emu* and *SPM*. *SPM* is particularly slow; this suggests that run-time overhead associated with its more complex process structures is high.

6.2 UNIPROCESSOR TASK MANAGEMENT STUDY

It was proposed in Chapter 5 that task management facilities be supported directly in the kernel. Implementation techniques that provided this support were defined in terms of extensions to the FP abstract machine. Hirsch *et al.* [1987] have proposed an alternative approach to implementation based on program transformation. (This was illustrated in Section 4.2.5.) This section describes performance studies designed to quantify the costs associated with the two approaches.

6.2.1 Method

Any task management mechanism necessarily introduces some overhead. This overhead may take the form of increased code size, CPU time and run-time memory requirements. Task management overheads may thus affect two classes of program:

1. Programs that form part of a controlled task (*controlled* programs).
2. Programs that do not form part of a controlled task (*uncontrolled* programs).

Table 6.3 Implementation costs of task management functions

	Overhead$_{\text{uncontrolled}}$	Overhead$_{\text{controlled}}$
Kernel support	C_1	C_1
Transformation	0	C_2

For example, consider a simple OS consisting of a shell that initiates, monitors, and controls application programs. The shell may not need to be monitored or controlled itself. Task management functions do, however, need to be applied to application programs. If control is provided by kernel mechanisms, both controlled and uncontrolled programs incur the same overhead, as both are executed using the same kernel. If control is provided by transformation, only controlled programs incur overhead. Table 6.3 illustrates this.

The values C_1 and C_2 are most easily determined by experimental studies. Some figures for C_2 have been previously obtained by Hirsch *et al.* [1987]; these are summarized below. It is more useful however to obtain figures for C_1 and C_2 using the same implementation, to minimize discrepancies due to implementation differences.

Levels of control. For the purposes of evaluation, it is useful to isolate the functions represented by the task management primitives presented in Section 4.2. This yields a number of control levels, each generally requiring mechanisms provided by lower levels for its implementation. The levels are named 0 to 3 and are characterized in Table 6.4.

Level 0 provides no additional functionality: it implements the basic computational model. Level 1 introduces the task. Every process is part of a task and process failure in a task is reported. This provides support for the status message exception/3. Level 2 in addition permits a task to be suspended, resumed, and aborted; it supports the SUSPEND, CONTINUE and STOP primitives. Level 3 provides for reporting of successful termination of a task: the status message succeeded. Level 3 is effectively the level of control provided by the TASK primitive (Section 4.2).

Implementations. Kernel support for task management has previously been incorporated in the Sequential Parlog Machine (SPM). Recall that the SPM represents the state of a computation as a process tree. It incorporates mechanisms for detecting termination of subtrees and aborting subtrees. A task can be implemented as a new type of

Table 6.4 Levels of control

i	Description
0	No controls
1	Report process failure and exceptions
2	Suspend, resume and abort task
3	Report task termination

tree node: existing tree management mechanisms require little modification to deal with tasks [Gregory *et al.*, 1989]. It is thus not surprising that task management overhead is found to be negligible in the SPM. However, the results reported in the previous section suggest that run-time support for a process tree is expensive. As this cost is partly due to mechanisms which can be used for task management, the SPM cannot be used for comparative studies of task management mechanisms.

The FP machine described in Section 5.2 provides a suitable basis for comparative studies. This abstract machine provides no inherent support for task management. Furthermore, the results reported in the previous section indicate that it is particularly efficient. This is important, as small task management overheads may not be apparent in inefficient implementations.

For the purposes of this study, an implementation of the FP machine (henceforth referred to as FP_0) was progressively extended to implement the control levels 1 to 3 described above, yielding new machines FP_1, FP_2 and FP_3. This permitted precise measurement of the costs associated with each control level. The extensions to FP_0 required to implement machines FP_1, FP_2 and FP_3 are described in detail in Foster [1987b]. FP_3 is essentially the eFPM described in Section 5.4.

To permit benchmarking of the transformation approach, three transformations described by Hirsch *et al.* [1987] were also implemented. These transformations implement control levels 1, 2 and 3 and are termed here T_1, T_2 and T_3.

Benchmark programs. Four benchmark programs were selected. To facilitate comparison with the results reported by Hirsch *et al.*, similar programs were used. *Reverse* performs naive reverse of a list of thirty two elements, thirty-two times. *Primes* generates all primes less than 1,000 using the parallel sieve of Eratosthenes. *QSort* applies the quicksort sorting algorithm to a one-thousand-element list. The last program, *Compiler*, is the program that translates parsed FP programs into sequences of FP machine instructions. This program is run with the FP assembler as data.

Summary. Four levels of control (0 to 3), four machines (FP_0 to FP_3) and three transformations (T_1 to T_3) were defined. Four benchmark programs were selected. Experiments were then performed to determine the overhead incurred when the benchmark programs were executed on each of the machines $FP_0, \ldots, FP_3$ and, when transformed using transformations T_1, T_2 and T_3, on FP_0. CPU time, code size, and run-time memory requirements were measured.

6.2.2 Results

Hirsch *et al.* [1987] measured code size and execution time when three benchmark programs, transformed using transformations T_1, T_2 and T_3, were executed on an FCP emulator. Their results are summarized in Figures 6.1 and 6.2. The benchmark programs *Reverse* and *Primes* are as described above. For the *Compiler* benchmark, an FCP compiler was used to compile the primes program.

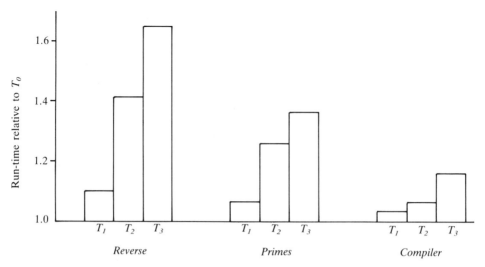

Figure 6.1 Transformation run-time relative to T_0 [Hirsch *et al.*, 1987].

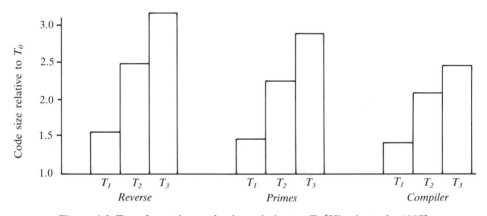

Figure 6.2 Transformation code size relative to T_0 [Hirsch *et al.*, 1987].

Figure 6.3 and 6.4 summarize the results of the experiments described in Section 6.2.1. Figure 6.3 shows execution time (relative to an untransformed program running on machine FP_0) when various levels of control were provided by both kernel support and by transformation. Figure 6.4 shows code sizes when transformations T_1, T_2 and T_3 were applied. Additional run-time memory requirements were also measured for both kernel support and transformation, but were not found to be significant.

6.2.3 Discussion

The results presented in Figure 6.3 indicate that kernel support only introduces small overheads on uniprocessors. In the most complex benchmark, *Compiler*, the perform-

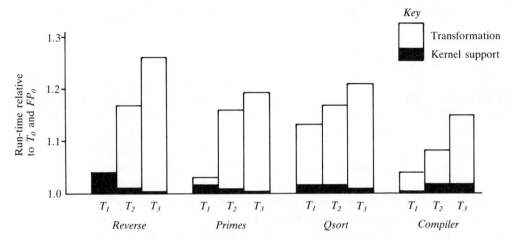

Figure 6.3 Run-time relative to T_0 and FP_0.

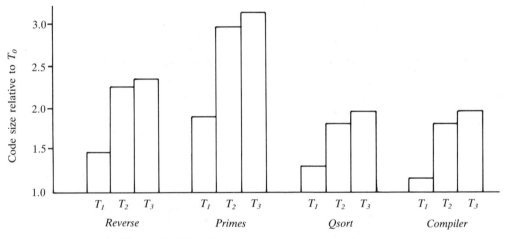

Figure 6.4 Transformation code size relative to T_0.

ance difference between FP_3 and FP_0 is 2 percent. Code size is of course the same on all machines. Study of the extensions to the FPM introduced to support task management (Section 5.4) indicates why kernel support is so inexpensive. Overheads are only incurred at certain points in a computation, such as process creation, process termination and process switching. Overheads are generally small, consisting of simple operations on registers. Most significantly, the notion of *current task* is introduced. Tasks are reduced in turn using (for these benchmarks) a round-robin strategy. The contents of a current task's task record is buffered in global registers. This ensures that overheads associated with task selection are incurred only in the rare event of a switch to another task. (For the benchmarks, a task switch was performed once every five hundred reductions; in an FP processor, it could be triggered by a timer interrupt.) Otherwise, reduction proceeds almost as efficiently as in a machine that does not support tasks.

It will be observed that performance overheads do not increase uniformly across the FP_i with increasing i. For example, *Primes* suffers a 2 percent performance degradation on FP_1 but virtually none on FP_3. This is due to reasons unconnected with the functionality of the FP_i. Because performance differences are so small, machine-dependent factors related to the swapping behavior of the different implementations become significant. These factors hinder precise comparisons of the various control levels. They do not, however, invalidate the conclusion that kernel support only incurs low overhead.

The transformation overheads observed in this study are generally lower than those reported by Hirsch *et al.* [1987]. These lower overheads are attributed to differences in the language implementations used to perform the benchmarks. For example, the FP machine (FP_0) used to benchmark the transformations provides a particularly efficient implementation of test primitives introduced by transformation. Nevertheless, time and space overhead due to transformation is still substantial.

In summary, referring to the most substantial benchmark, *Compiler*, and the most comprehensive level of control, level 3:

- The CPU cost of kernel support is 2 percent: this cost is incurred whether or not the program is to be controlled.
- The CPU cost of transformation is 15 percent: this cost is incurred only if the program is to be controlled.
- Kernel support does not affect code size.
- Transformation increases code size 98 percent.
- Run-time memory requirements are not a significant source of overhead.

A potential disadvantage of kernel support is that overhead is incurred by all programs whether controlled or not. The overhead associated with kernel support is, however, so small that this is not considered important. The higher overheads associated with transformation can be reduced using better compilation techniques. Kernel support overheads represent at the very least an upper bound on the improvements that can be expected, as any optimization introduced by compilation can be incorporated in a kernel mechanism.

6.3 INTERPROCESSOR COMMUNICATION STUDY

A novel feature of the parallel logic programming model is its use of a rather abstract mechanism – shared logical variables – to provide interprocess communication. On a multiprocessor this requires distributed unification algorithms which translate read and write operations on remote terms into messages to other processors. Interprocessor communication is expensive on many architectures. The use of an abstract communication mechanism may thus cause unacceptably high communication overhead. The performance study reported in this section was designed to quantify the cost of distributed unification. It sought to determine whether communication costs attributable to the use of logical variables become excessive in typical applications. As communication costs depend on both communication rates and message transmission costs, the study investigated the effect of these factors.

6.3.1 Method

A different language implementation was used for this study. A multiprocessor implementation of a parallel logic language closely related to FP, Strand [Foster and Taylor, 1989], was extended to incorporate the distributed unification algorithms described in Chapter 5. This implementation was initially developed on a network of workstations connected by a local area network and was ported for the purposes of this study to a shared memory multiprocessor, an Encore Multimax. On the Encore, message passing was implemented as message copying in shared memory.

The Encore implementation was instrumented and modified to permit the cost of sending a message to be increased by constant factors. This permitted measurement of the effect of varying message transmission costs in an otherwise uniform environment. Table 6.5 presents approximate message transmission times for three classes of machine: shared-memory multiprocessors, message-passing multiprocessors (e.g., hypercubes), and local area networks (LANs). These times are expressed in terms of the mean time to send or receive an empty message (P) and the time per four-byte word in a message (Q). The time T to send or receive an N-word message on a machine of type x is given by equation E:

$$T = P_x + NQ_x \tag{E}$$

It must be emphasized that these figures are intended only as approximations to true costs. Precise values depend on hardware characteristics, kernel design, and the mechanisms used to implement communication. For example, significantly faster communication can be achieved on shared memory machines by copying pointers rather than messages. The present generation of hypercubes promise significantly lower communication costs (by up to three orders of magnitude). Note also that the effect of communication latency is ignored in this study as it is not believed to be a significant factor on the architectures considered.

Four benchmark programs were executed on the parallel implementation while the

Table 6.5 Constants P_x and Q_x in equation E (msec)

x	P_x	Q_x
Shared-memory	0.7	0.015
Message-passing	1.7	0.006
LAN	3.7	0.060

Table 6.6 Multiprocessor benchmark programs

Benchmark	Reductions/ communication	Mean message size (words)	Runtime (sec)
Circle	6.5	39	15.8
TP1	30	12	5.4
TP2	110	14	178
DNA	980	25	560

value of P was varied between 0.7 and 3.7. Q was maintained at a constant ⅟₅₀th of P (this only approximates the values of Q in Table 6.5 but is sufficiently close for the present study as messages were found to be generally small). The benchmark programs were selected to present a range of communication patterns. Table 6.6 characterizes them in terms of communication rates, mean message size, and run-time. Communication rates are expressed as the mean number of reductions between communications.

The *Circle* benchmark executes a program that communicates a stream of small messages around a ring of processors. It is a very fine grained application that achieves extremely high and regular communication rates.

Benchmarks *TP1* and *TP2* execute a propositional theorem prover, run on a small and medium sized problem respectively. This theorem prover is structured as a single manager and one or more workers; in a parallel machine, the manager and workers can be placed on different processors. The manager manages a database containing information about a problem. It allocates pieces of information to the workers, which attempt to infer new information from this and previously provided information. New information is passed back to the manager, which assimilates it into its database. As Table 6.6 shows, the small theorem proving problem (*TP1*) is quite fine grained. The larger problem (*TP2*) achieves somewhat lower communication rates. This is because the workers must do more to process each piece of information that they are given.

DNA implements part of an algorithm for sequencing genetic material and is also structured as a manager and a number of workers. The manager is responsible for allocating work to workers and performs relatively little computation. The workers, in contrast, perform substantial amounts of computation for each unit of work. This benchmark was run on nineteen processors. The communication rate given in Table 6.6 counts communications for the manager (which performs eighteen times more communication than a worker) but counts reductions performed by a worker. Even with eighteen workers, the manager's communication rate is still low.

6.3.2 Results

Figure 6.5 presents the benchmark results. The y-axis in this graph shows the percentage of time that each benchmark spent communicating rather than processing. (No significant overlapping of communication and computation is possible in the implementation

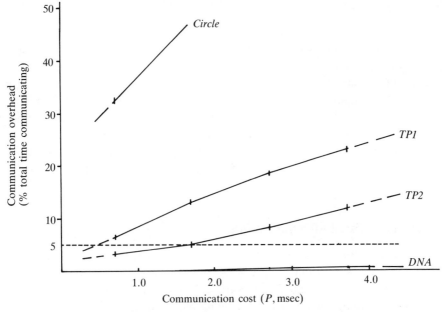

Figure 6.5 Communication overhead vs communication cost.

used for this study.) The x-axis gives the communication cost as the term P in equation E given above.

6.3.3 Discussion

For simplicity, assume that all communication cost measured represents overhead from distributed unification. (This is obviously a pessimistic assumption as even an optimal implementation of communication using more primitive mechanisms incurs some overhead: however, it gives an upper bound on the cost of distributed unification.) Those applications with high communication rates (*Circle* and *TP1*) incur substantial communication overhead, particularly when communication costs are high. In contrast, both the less fine grained applications (*TP2* and *DNA*) incur less than 5 percent overhead at communication costs corresponding to those found in tightly-coupled multiprocessors ($P \leq 1.7$ msec). *DNA* performs well even when communication costs are substantially higher.

These results suggest one definite and one tentative conclusion. The logical variable can definitely be used as a communication mechanism in tightly coupled systems: overhead of more than 5 percent is incurred only in extremely communication-intensive applications. However, it appears possible that logical variables are not an appropriate communication mechanism when communication is more costly, as in local area networks. The logical variable can still be used effectively in such systems but communication rates appear to be more critical.

6.4 MULTIPROCESSOR TASK MANAGEMENT STUDY

Recall that the kernel facilities described in Chapter 4 do not provide direct support for multiprocessor task management. Instead, multiprocessor tasks are constructed from uniprocessor tasks managed by networks of communicating processes. Symmetric distributed unification algorithms support termination and quiescence detection. This section describes performance studies designed to quantify overheads associated with multiprocessor task management. Both the acknowledgement messages generated by symmetric distributed unification algorithms and the process networks used for task management represent potential sources of inefficiency. These two problems are studied separately.

6.4.1 Symmetric distributed unification

In order to quantify the overhead associated with symmetric distributed unification, the parallel implementation used in the previous study was further extended to support the symmetric algorithms. The same benchmark programs were then executed on the extended implementation, again at varying communication costs.

Figure 6.6 presents execution times for the benchmarks *TP1*, *TP2* and *DNA* when executed using the four extended algorithms: *Local*, *GlobalT*, *LocalQ* and *GlobalQ*. The communication cost *P* is varied between 0.7 and 3.7 as before. Times are relative to the time taken to execute the benchmark using algorithm *Local*, with *P* = 0.7.

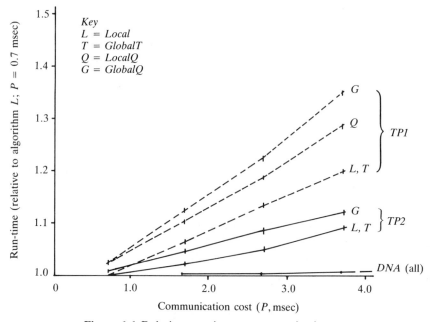

Figure 6.6 Relative run-time vs communication cost.

As may be expected, *DNA* shows no appreciable performance degradation when different algorithms are used. *TP2* performance degrades an additional 1 percent when the most complex algorithm, *GlobalQ*, is used at tightly-coupled communication speed and 3 percent at LAN speeds. The most fine grained application, *TP1*, experiences 2 and 15 percent degradation respectively. (For *Circle*, not depicted in the figure, the numbers are 8 and 21 percent). Algorithm *GlobalT* does not incur significant overhead on any benchmark.

Figures 6.7 and 6.8 present message and data counts for applications *TP1* and *TP2* when executed using the different distributed unification algorithms. These data explain why overhead is not generally high. Consider firstly the most costly algorithm, *GlobalQ*, Substantially more messages are generated by this algorithm than by the *Local* algorithm: 65 percent more in both cases. However, these additional messages are small acknowledgement messages and do not impact significantly on the total amount of data sent: this increases by only 18 and 15 percent for *TP1* and *TP2* respectively.

Consider secondly the simplest symmetric algorithm, *GlobalT*. Recall that this only acknowledges unification operations. The low overheads associated with this algorithm in the benchmarks are attributed to the small number of remote unification operations performed. *Unify* messages made up only 0.1, 7, 4, and 28 percent of all messages sent by benchmarks *Circle, TP1, TP2,* and *DNA* respectively. That is, most communications are concerned with reading rather than writing. Taylor [1989] confirms this observation in studies of programs in the related language FCP. This suggests that it is typical of parallel logic programs in general.

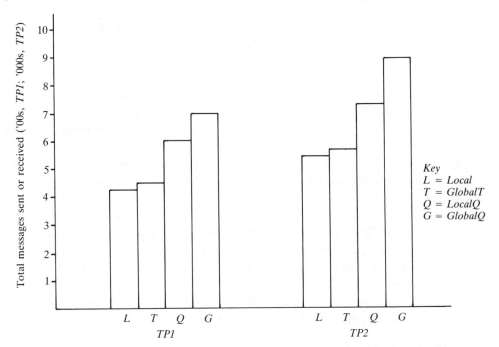

Figure 6.7 Message counts for *TP1* and *TP2* vs distributed unification algorithm.

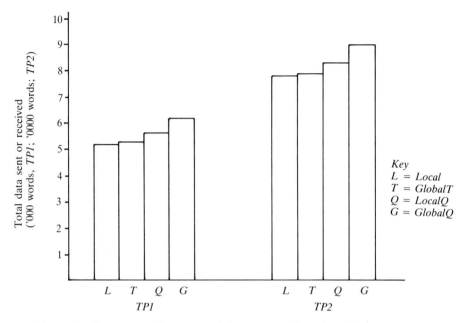

Figure 6.8 Data counts for *TP1* and *TP2* vs. distributed unification algorithm.

6.4.2 Process networks

The use of supervisory networks to implement multiprocessor task management functions can lead to additional costs in three areas: task creation, task monitoring, and task control. None of these costs can easily be measured. However, it is possible to estimate them and hence to determine whether the process network introduces extra complexity.

Assume that the network defined by Programs 4.3 and 4.4 and illustrated in Figure 4.4 is used to control a multiprocessor task executing on N processors. This network consists of a supervisor process on each processor plus a central coordinator. These processes are linked in a circuit using shared variables. Consider firstly the problem of aborting this task. This is achieved by passing a stop request around the circuit. The kernel on each processor must generate or receive two messages: one containing the stop request, and one to pass on the stop request to the next processor. One or two additional messages may be generated if symmetric algorithms are used. In addition, each supervisor executes the STOP task management primitive and also performs two reductions. Each processor hence performs a small, constant amount of work. The elapsed time taken to abort the task is the time required to perform $2N$ reductions, N STOP calls and $2N$ communications.

Now consider the problem of creating the process network required to control the multiprocessor task. A central manager must send a request to a mapping server on each of the processors on which the task is to execute. Each request specifies an initial process and the module that process is to execute. The central manager must hence perform

$O(N)$ reductions and communications; other processors perform a constant amount of work.

Finally, consider the problem of signalling exceptions detected in the multiprocessor task. Program 4.4 specifies that supervisors forward exception messages to the central manager using the circuit that links the supervisors. This requires a small, constant number of reductions and communications at each processor; altogether $O(N)$ reductions and communications are required and the elapsed time required to signal an exception is also $O(N)$.

These examples indicate that only a small number of operations are required to create a task, detect exceptions and abort execution. No additional algorithmic complexity is introduced by the use of a process network. The elapsed time required for some functions can be high: in a massively parallel machine, an elapsed time of $O(N)$ to signal an exception or to abort a task may be unacceptable. However, these times are determined by the process structure specified by Program 4.3, not by the kernel. More efficient structures can easily be specified: for example, each supervisor can be given a stream to the coordinator to permit direct reporting of exceptions or may be modified to process exceptions locally.

6.5 SUMMARY

This chapter has presented performance studies of four kernel components: basic uniprocessor execution, uniprocessor task management, interprocessor communication, and multiprocessor task management. These studies indicate that the implementation techniques developed in Chapter 5 provide efficient support for kernel facilities.

A comparative study of abstract machine implementations showed that the FP abstract machine is significantly faster than parallel logic language implementations developed by other researchers. The SPM, which supports a process tree computational model, is particularly slow. Carefully controlled studies of the FP machine and an equivalent FCP machine show that FP executes 15 percent faster on a large application, an assembler. These differences are due to FCP's more complex data manipulation primitives.

Kernel support for task management functions incurs substantially less overhead than an alternative approach based on program transformation. A substantial application, a compiler, incurred run-time overhead of 15 percent with transformation but only 2 percent with kernel support. In addition, transformation increased code size by 98 percent. These results suggest that transformation is currently only useful for task management functions that are applied rarely: for example, suspending a computation.

The use of logical variables as a communication mechanism is a potential source of overhead. When total communication costs were measured as a function of both message transmission costs and communication rates, only very fine grained problems incurred communication overhead in excess of 5 percent, and then only when communication costs were substantially higher than would be expected in tightly-coupled machines. This suggests that logical variables are a practical communication mechanism on tightly-coupled architectures. However, it is not clear that they are appropriate for distributed systems.

The kernel facilities proposed in Chapter 4 require the use of process networks to manage multiprocessor tasks and extended distributed unification algorithms to detect termination and quiescence. The extended algorithms were found to only cause significant overhead when both communication rates and communication costs were high. When communication costs corresponded to those on tightly-coupled architectures, the overhead associated with the most complex extended algorithm was 3 percent or less for all but the most fine grained application. Analysis of the process networks created to manage multiprocessor tasks suggests that run-time costs attributable to these networks are low.

7

THE NUCLEUS

Recall that the nucleus uses kernel facilities to provide services.

USER
Various services
NUCLEUS
Essential services
KERNEL
Basic facilities
HARDWARE
e.g. Parallel machine

This chapter demonstrates that the kernel facilities described in Chapter 4 are sufficient to: (1) provide essential services required in any OS; (2) provide other programs with access to these services; and (3) protect these services against malicious or erroneous access.

The material in this chapter has been tested in a working OS. The nucleus of this system provides basic services such as disk and terminal I/O. It has been used to support substantial applications such as a sophisticated programming environment. Fragments of this implementation are presented in this chapter to illustrate the techniques used to construct an OS using lightweight processes, tasks and logical variables.

7.1 PROVIDING SERVICES

An OS kernel provides basic management facilities for resources such as terminals and disks. The use of these resources must be controlled and sometimes synchronized to prevent indiscriminate use by user-level programs. An OS nucleus hence uses kernel facilities to define services to which user-level programs make requests for resources. A service encapsulates a resource, protecting it and synchronizing access when required. This section is concerned with the techniques used to implement services in a lightweight process model. It also considers the related issue of how more complex services can be constructed as either nucleus or user-level programs using facilities provided by basic services.

Services are commonly represented as monitors in shared resource models and as processes in message passing models. The process is the more appropriate represent-ation here. A service is implemented as a lightweight process which consumes a stream of messages representing requests for service. It may also maintain an internal state. It processes a request by performing some combination of the following five actions:

1. Creating further processes to perform computation.
2. Invoking kernel mechanisms to control hardware.
3. Generating requests to other services.
4. Returning values to the requesting process.
5. Either terminating or recursing with altered internal state.

The order in which requests arrive on a service's input steam defines a total temporal ordering on the arrival of requests. Dataflow constraints within the service define a total or partial temporal ordering on the processing of requests.

It is useful to characterize services in terms of the actions they perform when pro-cessing requests. *Physical* services interact with the kernel by invoking kernel mecha-nisms or consuming data generated by the kernel; *logical* services do not. *Basic* services do not communicate with other services. A *filter* is a service which is composed with other services to augment their functionality. It accepts a stream of requests and passes on a modified stream. A *mailbox* consumes a stream of requests and stream(s) of data and matches requests with data items. Figure 7.1 illustrates a number of services.

Some examples illustrate the techniques used to implement services. First, consider what is perhaps the simplest service possible: a *memory cell* that maintains a single value and responds to requests to read and replace this value. This can be implemented as a basic logical service, as illustrated in the following program. The procedure cell/2 takes as arguments a stream of requests and a value representing its contents. It responds to read and write requests by returning (C1) or updating (C2) its contents. The processing of read and write requests is not explicitly sequenced; nevertheless, avail-

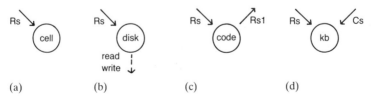

Figure 7.1 Types of service. (a) A basic logical service: memory cell. (b) A basic physical service: disk service. (c) A filter: code service. (d) A mailbox: keyboard service.

ability of data ensures that each read accesses the value deposited by the most recent write. Note that the argument to a read request is assumed to be a variable: this serves as a return address and is used to return the cell value to the requesting process:

cell([read(V1) |Rs], V) ← V1 = V, cell(Rs, V).   % Return contents   (C1)
                                                     (V1 is variable)
cell([write(V1) |Rs], V) ← cell(Rs, V1).   % Update contents   (C2)
                                                     (V1 is new value)

As a second example, consider the problem of providing access to a disk. This can be achieved using a basic physical service that uses read and write primitives to control hardware. These primitives invoke kernel mechanisms to read and write a disk block at a specified address. The service should synchronize read and write operations so that they are performed in the order in which the corresponding requests are received. This ensures that each read at a particular address accesses the value deposited by the most recent write.

The mutually recursive procedures disk/2 and disk/3 in Program 7.1 implement a disk service with these characteristics. They process a stream of read and write requests using primitives read/4 and write/4 (C2, C3). Calls to these primitives suspend until a requested I/O operation has completed and then bind a status variable. This variable is used to sequence I/O operations: the data guard test in C1 ensures that the disk service does not proceed to another operation until the previous operation has completed. (FP's data primitive suspends until its argument is instantiated, and then succeeds.)

---

disk(Device, Requests, Status) ← data(Status) : disk(Device, Requests).   %   (C1)

disk(Device,[read(Addr, Block) |Requests]) ←   % Read request (Block is var).   (C2)
    read(Device, Addr, Block, Status),   %   Read block from disk.
    disk(Device, Requests, Status).   %   Synchronize and proceed.
disk(Device, [write(Addr, Block) |Requests]) ←   % Write request (Block is data).   (C3)
    write(Device, Addr, Block, Status),   %   Write block to disk.
    disk(Device, Requests, Status).   %   Synchronize and proceed.

Program 7.1 Disk service.

7.1.1 Filters: a code service

A somewhat more complex example illustrates how new services can be constructed by composing processes called filters with existing services. The problem here is to provide a code service that permits other processes to read and write named object code modules. This functionality could be provided by specializing the disk service. However, this would require that the code service execute on the processor to which the disk is attached. It also prevents replacement of disk or code services. A more modular approach is to define a *filter* process that accepts requests to read and write modules and generates requests to read and write the disk blocks occupied by these modules. The filter takes as arguments an incoming stream of module requests (Rs) and an outgoing stream of block requests (Ds). It is composed with a disk service as follows to implement a code service:

> ..., code(Rs, Ds), disk(Device, Ds), ...

A complex abstraction (code modules) is hence constructed from a simple abstraction (blocks) by process composition. The following program implements the filter.

```
code(Rs, Ds) ←                              % Initialize code service.      (C1)
    read_table(As, Ds, Ds1),                %    Load file table.
    code(Rs, As, Ds1).                      %    Process requests.

code([read(Name, Module) |Rs], As, Ds) ←    % Retrieve module request.      (C2)
    load(As, Name, Module, Ds, Ds1),        %    Load from disk.
    code(Rs, As, Ds1).                      %    Recurse.
code([write(Name, Module) |Rs], As, Ds) ←   % Update/add module request.   (C3)
    save(As, As1, Name, Module, Ds, Ds1),   %    Save on disk.
    code(Rs, As1, Ds1).                     %    Recurse.
```

The procedure code/2 first loads a *file table*: a list of {module-name, disk-address} pairs specifying where named modules are to be found on disk (C1). It then calls the procedure code/3 which recursively processes a stream of requests to read and write named modules. code/3 processes a request read(Name, Module) by determining the disk address of the module named Name and generating requests to a disk service to load the module (C2). It processes a request write(Name, Module), which provides a new definition for a named module, by generating requests to the disk service to save the new module on disk (C3). These actions are performed by the procedures load/5 and save/6, which are not defined here.

This code service is simple but inefficient: it reloads modules from disk each time they are requested. To avoid this repeated loading, the previous program can be refined to maintain a cache. Program 7.2 maintains a fixed-size cache using a least recently used (LRU) algorithm. The cache is represented as a list of named modules. It is initially primed with the first N modules found in the file table (C1) and subsequently updated following each read and write request (C2, C3).

The new code/4 procedure only loads a module from disk if it is not present in the cache. The procedure lookup/5 is used to scan the cache when processing a read request. This procedure returns a result found (C7), indicating that a cached module can be used (C4), or notfound (C6), in which case the module is loaded from disk (C5). A module is deleted from the cache following the processing of a request (C3, C5, C7) and the new module is added to the front (C3, C4, C5): this implements the LRU algorithm. As this code service always recurses with a new cache, and each request is processed with respect to the cache, requests are processed in sequence. Yet processing is nonblocking: if a

```
code(N, Rs, Ds)←
    read_table(As, Ds, Ds1),                               % Load file table.            (C1)
    prime_cache(N, As, Cache, Ds1, Ds2),                   % Prime cache: N modules.
    code(Rs, As, Cache, Ds2).                              % Process requests.

code([{read(Name, Module) |Rs], As, Cache, Ds) ←          % Request for module.          (C2)
    lookup(Name, Cache, NewCache, Module1, Result),        % Look in cache.
    find(Rs, As, NewCache, Ds, Name, Module, Module1, Result).
code([{write(Name, Module) |Rs], As, Cache, Ds) ←         % New module.                  (C3)
    save(As, As1, Name, Module, Ds, Ds1),                  % Save on disk.
    purge_oldest(Cache, NewCache),                         % Purge oldest entry.
    code(Rs, As1, [{Name, Module} |NewCache], Ds1).        % Add to cache.

find(Rs, As, Cache, Ds, Name, Module, Module1, found) ←   % Found in cache.              (C4)
    Module = Module1,                                      % Return to requestor.
    code(Rs, As, [{Name, Module} |Cache], Ds).             % Add to front of cache.
find(Rs, As, Cache, Ds, Name, Module, _, notfound) ←      % Not found in cache.          (C5)
    load(As, Name, Module, Ds, Ds1),                       % Load from disk.
    purge_oldest(Cache, NewCache),                         % Purge oldest entry.
    code(Rs, As, [{Name, Module} |NewCache], Ds1).         % Add to front of cache.

lookup(_, [], Cache,_, Res) ← Cache = [], Res = notfound.  % Not found!                   (C6)
lookup(Name, [{Name1, Mod1} |Cache], NewCache, Mod, Res) ← % Located: delete.             (C7)
    Name == Name1 :
    NewCache = Cache, Mod = Mod1, Res = found.
lookup(Name, [{Name1, Mod1} |Cache], NewCache, Mod, Res) ← % Continue search.             (C8)
    Name =\= Name1 :
    NewCache = [{Name1, Mod1} |NewCache1],
    lookup(Name, Cache, NewCache1, Mod, Res).

purge_oldest([ B ], Cache) ← Cache = [].                   % End: delete oldest module.   (C9)
purge_oldest([B, C |Cache], NewCache) ←                    % Recurse to end.              (C10)
    NewCache = [B |NewCache1], purge_oldest([C |Cache], NewCache1).
```

Program 7.2 Code service.

module must be requested from the disk service, code can proceed to process further requests while a load process loads the module (C5). Subsequent requests for the same module do not require further disk accesses, unless it has been purged from the cache in the meantime.

7.1.2 Mailboxes: a keyboard service

A further example illustrates the use of mailboxes. Assume that the kernel generates a stream containing both ascii values representing characters typed at a keyboard and 'break' values representing interrupts. The problem is to construct a keyboard service that does the following:

1. Responds to requests for characters typed at the keyboard.
2. Echoes characters typed on a screen.
3. Discards pending characters and echoes break when it detects an interrupt.

A simple keyboard service that satisfies requirement (1) can be implemented as follows:

    kb1([C |Cs], [R |Rs]) ← R = C, kb1(Cs, Rs).

This program takes as arguments a stream of keyboard input (Cs) and a stream of requests for input (Rs). A request for input consists simply of a variable to be instantiated to an input character. A request variable represents a return address, in the same way as the Block component of the read request processed by the code service. The program waits until both a character and a request are available and then 'receives' the character, returning it to the requesting process using the supplied return address.

This program does not receive characters typed until they are requested. In order to satisfy requirements (2) and (3), it is necessary to receive characters before they are requested. In most message passing models, this can only be achieved by explicitly receiving and buffering characters. The logical variable permits a more elegant formulation. Two references to the input character stream are maintained. One is used to *eagerly* receive and echo characters as they are typed; they other is used in a *lazy* fashion, to select characters as requests are received. The difference between the two references to the stream represents buffered characters: characters received but not yet requested. The input stream is hence treated as both a data structure and a communication stream.

Program 7.3 uses this technique to implement a keyboard service that fulfills all three requirements. This service might execute in conjunction with a *screen service*, that accepts and displays a stream Ts containing characters and control sequences (such as nl: newline) on a screen, and a *user*, which generates a stream of requests Rs for characters. The following set of processes represents this scenario. The stream Cs is generated by the kernel.

    kb(Cs, Rs, Ts), screen(Ts), user(Rs)

The procedure kb/3 in Program 7.3 immediately calls kb/4 to create two identical

kb(Cs, Rs, Ts) ← kb(Cs, Cs, Rs, Ts).	% Initialize buffer.	(C1)
kb([break |Cs], Cs1, Rs, Ts) ←	% Interrupt received.	(C2)
Ts = [nl,b,r,e,a,k,nl |Ts1],	% Echo break.	
kb(Cs, Cs, Rs, Ts1).	% Discard characters.	
kb([C |Cs], Cs1, Rs, Ts) ←	% Character received.	(C3)
C =\= break :	%	
Ts = [C |Ts1],	% Echo character.	
kb(Cs, Cs1, Rs, Ts1).	% Recurse.	
kb(Cs, [C |Cs1], [R |Rs], Ts) ←	% Request received.	(C4)
R = C,	% Service request.	
kb(Cs, Cs1, Rs, Ts).	% Recurse.	

Program 7.3 Keyboard service.

references to the input stream Cs (C1). These are to serve as the input stream and buffer respectively. The procedure kb/4 then both matches user requests for input with characters typed (C4) and scans ahead on the input stream, processing interrupts (C2) and echoing characters typed by passing them to screen (C3). To process an interrupt, represented by the constant break, it passes the list [nl, b, r, e, a, k, nl] to screen. It also discards any buffered characters: this is achieved by recursing with a reference to the input stream Cs, not Cs1, as its second argument.

In the absence of interrupts, the kb process ultimately reduces twice for each character typed: once to echo it, and once to communicate it to a requesting process. If characters are typed faster than they are requested, kb will tend to reduce more frequently using the second clause than the third. The guard primitive var can be used to establish priority between the clauses. (Recall that a call var(X) succeeds if its argument is currently a variable.) For example, adding a guard var(Cs) to clause C4 ensures that user requests are not serviced if pending input (characters or interrupts) has not been processed.

7.2 PROVIDING ACCESS TO SERVICES

User-level programs must be able to communicate with the nucleus to request access to services. These *system calls* should not be able to compromise the correct execution of either the nucleus or other user-level programs. This section shows how this communication can be provided securely using kernel facilities.

A simple way of supporting communication with an OS is to provide a *supervisor call* instruction which causes a context switch to a privileged supervisor program. The supervisor processes the request, then returns control to the user program. Unfortunately, this approach is inappropriate in multiprocessors, as the service requested may be located on another processor. It is unacceptable to block the requesting processor while the request is serviced. An alternative message-based approach permits user processes to send messages to OS processes. A user process blocks until a reply is received; however, if the kernel supports lightweight processes, other processes in the same task can continue executing.

Recall that the task management facilities introduced in Chapter 4 use exception messages to report error conditions in tasks. These messages are placed on a status stream which can be monitored by other processes. Exception messages can also be used to provide an elegant and secure message-based implementation of system calls. Each user-level program is executed as a separate task and system calls are translated into exceptions. A nucleus process called a *supervisor* is associated with each task. The supervisor monitors the task's status stream, detects exceptions representing system calls and either processes these itself or forwards them to services. Meanwhile, other processes in the task can continue executing.

Figure 7.2 illustrates the relationship between a task and its supervisor. The task is pictured as a user-level computation, while the supervisor is shown as part of the nucleus. However, this distinction is conceptual, not physical: if all user-level programs are written in a high-level language such as FP, and programs communicate with the nucleus using exceptions, then both can safely execute in the same address space. No hardware support for protection is required.

An FP implementation of this approach to user-nucleus communication compiles requests for services into calls to the kernel primitive raise_exception. A distinctive exception type (say sys) identifies the resulting exceptions as system calls. Thus a system call:

>   send(Service, Request)

when encountered in a user-level program is compiled as:

>   raise_exception(sys, send(Service, Request))

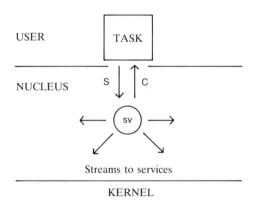

Figure 7.2 An application task and its supervisor (sv).

This system call then generates the following exception message when executed at run-time:

> exception(sys, send(Service, Request), Cont)

A simple task supervisor is presented to introduce basic concepts. This supervisor, assumed to be defined by a procedure supervisor/2, may be invoked in conjunction with a task as follows:

> ..., call(M, P, S, C), supervisor(S, C),...

where call/4 creates the task using the control call presented in Section 4.3, P is the process to be executed by the task, M is the module to be used to execute it and S and C are status and control variables associated with the task by the control call. The supervisor takes as arguments the status and control variables returned by the control call.

Recall that a task's status variable may be instantiated to a stream of exception messages and terminated with constants succeeded or stopped. The supervisor presented here simply ignores exceptions representing system calls (C1), aborts the task if any other exception is signalled (C2), and terminates when the task terminates (C3):

supervisor([exception(sys,_,_) |S], C) ← supervisor(S, C).	% Ignore system calls	(C1)
supervisor([M |S], C) ← M =\= exception(sys,_,_) : C = stop.	% Exception: abort	(C2)
supervisor(succeeded,_).	% Terminate	(C3)

This rudimentary task supervisor can be extended to process system calls in two ways. The supervisor can process them itself: this provides what are termed *local* services. Alternatively, the supervisor can forward them to *remote* services such as the disk and code services described in Section 7.1.

7.2.1 Local services

A system call that permits user programs to register exception handlers is used to illustrate how local services are constructed. An *exception handler* is a procedure to be invoked in a user task when specified types of exception occur. The system call is named e_handler; a call to e_handler has the general form:

> e_handler(Type, Module, Procedure)

It names a Procedure (defined in Module) that is to serve as the handler for exceptions of a specified Type. For example, the system call:

> e_handler(undefined, M, undef_handler)

requests that the procedure undef_handler (as defined in module M) be registered as the handler for exceptions of type undefined. (This exception type indicates a call to an undefined procedure.) Once an exception handler has been registered, processes in the user task that cause exceptions of the specified type are replaced by calls to the exception handler. The type of exception and the process that caused the exception are provided as arguments to the exception handler process.

Program 7.4 implements a task supervisor that supports the system call e_handler as a local service. This program refines the supervisor provided previously by adding an extra argument to maintain a list of exception handlers, initially empty (C1), and extra clauses to deal with exceptions (C5, C6). It detects exceptions representing e_handler system calls and records exception handlers (C2). It replaces other exceptions with a call to a previously recorded exception handler, if one exists (C6), and halts execution if no exception handler can be found (C5). The procedure elookup(T,Hs,M,N) returns a module M and procedure name N if the list Hs contains an exception type T, or a tuple notfound(T) otherwise. The procedure terminates when its task terminates (C4).

The primitive =.. is used in this program to convert between lists and structured terms (C6). A call to =.. suspends if both its arguments are variables. Otherwise the call succeeds if its two arguments can be unified with a structured term $A_0(A_1, \ldots, A_n)$ and a list $[A_0, A_1, \ldots, A_n]$ respectively, and fails otherwise. =.. is used here to construct a call $N(T, P)$ from a procedure name N and arguments T and P.

Note also the use of the code management primitive @ in clause C6. Recall that this kernel primitive initiates execution of a given process using a supplied module. The call M@Proc, returned to the user-level task using the continuation variable Cont, initiates execution of the newly-constructed exception handler process Proc in module M.

```
supervisor(S, C) ← supervisor(S, C, [ ]).          %                                    (C1)

supervisor([exception(sys, e_handler(T, M, R), Cont) |S], C, Hs) ←        %             (C2)
      Cont = true,                             % e_handler system call: succeeds.
      supervisor(S, C, [{T, M, R} |Hs]).       %    Register error handler.
supervisor([exception(T,P,Cont) |S], C, Hs) ←  % Other exception.                       (C3)
      T =\= sys :                              %    Not a system call, so . . .
      elookup(T, Hs, M, N),                    %    Look for handler.
      exception(S, C, Hs, T, P, Cont, M, N).   %    Process exception.
supervisor(succeeded, _,_).                    % Termination.                            (C4)

exception(_,C,_,_,_,_,_, notfound(_) ) ←       % No handler found.                       (C5)
      C = stop.                                %    Abort task.
exception(S, C, Hs, T, P, Cont, M, N) ←        % Handler found.                          (C6)
      N =\= notfound(_) :                      %
      Proc =.. [N,T,P],                        %    Construct handler call.
      Cont = M@Proc,                           %    Replace exception with call.
      supervisor(S, C, Hs).                    %    Continue.
```

Program 7.4 Task supervisor that supports exception handlers.

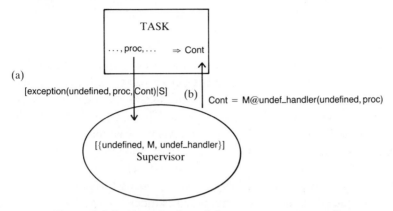

Figure 7.3 Implementation of the e_handler system call.

Figure 7.3 illustrates the execution of this supervisor. Assume that a user-level program has previously registered the error handler undef_handler using a system call e_handler(undefined, M, undef_handler). The supervisor has hence recorded the tuple {undefined, M, undef_handler}. A call to an undefined procedure proc then occurs in the user-level task. An exception message is generated and is intercepted by the task's supervisor (a). This looks up its list of exception handlers and uses the exception message's continuation variable to return a call to the error handler undef_handler to the task (b). The use of the continuation variable to replace an erroneous call with a call to an exception handler illustrates the power of the kernel's exception mechanism.

7.2.2 Remote services

Most system calls are requests to remote services of the type described in Section 7.1. An implementation of remote requests must resolve a number of problems. The overhead associated with remote requests must be minimized. It must be possible to report errors that occur when processing these requests; it may also be necessary to report termination of processing. User programs may wish to sequence the processing of requests to the same or different services. Finally, a service may wish to be informed if a system call that it receives was generated by a task that has already terminated. This may permit it to discard the request without processing it.

Two types of access to remote services are described here: remote procedure call (RPC), and circuit. Both can be supported using the kernel facilities provided. RPC access requires that a user-level program make a system call each time it wishes to access a particular service. A generic RPC system call has the form send(Service, Request) and requests that a supplied Request be passed to a named Service. A task supervisor that receives a system call augments it with a return address and a variable that the supervisor can subsequently use to signal task termination, and then routes it to the named service. This gives a message with the form {Request, Cont, Term} where Cont is the return address (in fact the system call's continuation variable) and Term is a *termination variable*: a unique variable associated with a task by its supervisor. The supervisor guarantees to instantiate this variable when the task terminates; other OS components are assumed not to instantiate it. This permits the service that receives a request to detect if and when the task that generated the request terminates: if the termination variable associated with a request is uninstantiated, then its task is not yet known to have terminated.

Circuit access requires the user-level program to make an initial system call to request a stream or *circuit* to a service. Requests appended to that stream are passed directly to the service without intervention from the supervisor. A generic circuit request has the form send(Service, circuit(Stream)). This is translated by the task supervisor into a request {circuit(Stream), Cont, Term} to Service. The user-level program may instantiate the variable Stream to a stream of requests Stream = [Request1, Request2, ..., RequestN].

These are processed by the service that receives them as if the user-level program had made a sequence of system calls:

send(Service, Request1), send(Service, Request2), ..., send(Service, RequestN).

Closing the stream terminates the circuit. A service may process a request for a circuit in two ways. It may merge the circuit stream with its usual request stream. For example, Program 7.1 may be augmented with an additional clause to handle requests for circuits, as illustrated in Figure 7.4. Recall that the merge procedure produces on its output argument a stream that is some intermingling of its two input arguments, with the order of elements in each input stream preserved.

If the service is stateless or has a fixed state (e.g., a read-only database), there is no need to sequence accesses. A copy of the service may hence be created to process requests on the circuit, as illustrated in Figure 7.5. This avoids any overhead associated with the merge process.

disk(Device, [{circuit(S), _, _}|Rs]) ← merge(S, Rs, Rs1), disk(Device, Rs1).

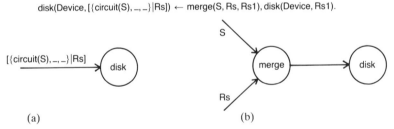

(a)   (b)

Figure 7.4 Circuit access to a disk service. (a) Before. (b) After.

service([{circuit(S), _, _}|Rs]) ← service(S), service(Rs).

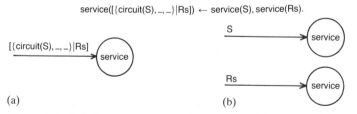

(a)   (b)

Figure 7.5 Circuit access to a stateless service. (a) Before. (b) After.

7.2.3 Errors and termination

A service that receives a request from a user-level task may need to do the following:

- Pass results back to that task.
- Notify the task of errors detected while processing the request.
- Notify the task that processing of the request has terminated.

Both variables in the request itself and the request's continuation variable provide channels that can be used to implement this communication. For example, in the disk service (Program 7.1) a disk block is returned using the Block variable included in a read request.

Services can also use request variables to notify a task of errors detected when processing a system call. For example, the Block variable in Program 7.1's read request could be bound to a special constant error if the supplied address was invalid. However, the task then has the option of ignoring the error condition. Another method is to use a system call's continuation variable for this purpose. Recall that this continuation variable replaces the system call in the user-level task and represents an as yet unspecified process. It can hence be used to define a *continuation* of the original system call. A service receiving the system call can bind its continuation variable to specify that the continuation process is to be a call to the raise_exception primitive:

Cont = raise_exception(Type, Call)

where Type is the type of error the service wishes to signal in the user-level task and Call is the original system call. A further exception is generated in the user-level task, indicating why the original system call could not be processed. The task supervisor can choose to process the call elsewhere, to ignore it, to abort the task, etc.

This error-reporting mechanism cannot be used directly in the case of circuit access. Because a circuit is established by a single system call, only one continuation variable is available for all requests made on the circuit. A solution to this problem is to interpose a filter process between the task making the requests and the service that receives them. The filter associates a new continuation variable with each request received on the circuit

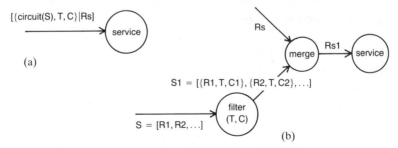

Figure 7.6 Filtering a circuit. (a) Before. (b) After.

and uses these new variables to monitor the progress of the requests. It signals any errors to the user-level task by binding the original continuation variable. This use of a filter process is illustrated in Figure 7.6. In (a), a circuit request {circuit(S),T,C} is received by a service. In (b), a filter has been created. This accepts a stream of requests R1, R2, etc., and forwards a stream of tuples {R1,T,C1}, {R2,T,C2}, etc., to the service. The filter monitors the new variables C1, C2, etc.; if any is bound to an exception message by the service, this is signalled in the user-level task using the original continuation variable, C.

The continuation variable associated with a system call can also be used to notify a task that processing of the system call has terminated. A service that receives a valid system call can instantiate the continuation variable (to true) either *after* processing the system call, or *before* processing the system call (perhaps after some validation).

As a system call's continuation variable represents a suspended process in the user-level task, that process (and hence the task of which it is a part) cannot terminate in the first case until the service has processed the request. In the second case, the system call terminates immediately the call is validated; this corresponds to a spooling of the request.

7.2.4 Discussion

The kernel facilities described in previous chapters permit a simple and secure implementation of system calls. System calls are passed from user-level to nucleus programs as exceptions. Continuation variables are used to signal errors detected during system call processing. This use of the continuation variable for error notification ensures that a user-level program cannot ignore errors, as errors are automatically routed to a task's supervisor.

Two types of access to services have been described: RPC and circuit. The advantages and disadvantages of each are summarized here.

- *Sequencing*. The stream associated with circuit access can be used to explicitly sequence requests. RPCs can only be sequenced by using the results of requests as synchronization tokens to delay the generation (or processing) of subsequent requests.
- *Performance*. Circuit access has set-up and shutdown costs if a filter must be created for validation purposes; RPC does not. However, circuit access does not require routing of requests once a circuit is established. RPC access requires that each request be interpreted and routed by the nucleus.
- *Bottlenecks*. In a multiprocessor, a single circuit may be a bottleneck if a task is distributed over many processors, particularly if requests do not need to be serialized. In contrast, RPC access permits system calls to be handled and routed independently at each node on which the user-level task is executing. This also permits requests for services replicated on several processors to be routed to a 'nearby' processor.
- *Termination and errors*. RPC access associates a continuation variable with each request. This can be used to report termination and errors. A special filter process is required to provide similar functionality when using circuit access.
- *Validation*. As will be seen, circuit access requires additional validation.

It is suggested that RPC access be used when services are accessed rarely or are replicated on many processors. Circuit access is to be preferred when many requests must be made to the same service.

7.3 MAKING SERVICES ROBUST

A service is robust if no other program's behavior can cause it to execute erroneously. This section discusses how services constructed using the techniques presented in Section 7.1 can be made robust. It is assumed that the kernel and compiler ensure that programs can only interact by reading and writing shared logical variables.

User programs use system calls to pass requests to services. The only way that a user program can compromise the correct execution of a service is by generating an invalid system call. System calls consist of a name and a set of arguments. Arguments have output and input components. *Output* components are data to be passed *to* a service; *input* components are return addresses (in FP terms, logical variables) used to receive values *from* a service. For example, a system call read(Addr, Block) made to a disk service (Program 7.1) has name read, output component Addr and input component Block.

The processing of a system call by a service consists of two phases: match and reply. In the match phase, the service accesses the name and output components and computes a reply (if any). In the reply phase, reply values are communicated back to the requestor. An invalid call can cause a service to behave erroneously in both phases. In the match phase, the service can *suspend* because the name or an output component is not available (i.e., it is a variable). This is a *missing data* error: a service should never suspend waiting for user-level program data as it cannot be known when that data will become available. A service can also fail in the match phase, because the name or an output component has an invalid value. This is an *invalid data* error. In the reply phase, errors can occur in a service because an input component is not a valid return address (in FP terms, it already has a value). This is an *invalid address* error.

For example, consider Program 7.1 once again. Table 7.1 lists five potential causes of erroneous behavior due to an invalid RPC system call to this service. (Similar problems are associated with circuit access; these are not considered here). It is assumed that the disk service expects calls of the form read(Addr, Block) where Addr is an integer and Block is a variable, or write(Addr, Block), where Addr is an integer and Block is a valid block.

Table 7.1 Potential causes of disk service failure

Description	Example	Error	Result
1. Incorrect value	read(abc, Y)	1st argument not integer	Error in service
2. Missing value	read(X, Y)	1st argument not bound	Service suspends
3. Unexpected value	read(10, abc)	2nd argument not variable	Error in service
4. Incorrect call	foo(X)	Only read or write valid	Error in service
5. Missing call	X	Call not bound	Service suspends

Examples of erroneous calls illustrate the errors. Errors 1 and 4 are invalid data errors. Errors 2 and 5 are missing data errors. Error 3 is an invalid address error.

Simple validation techniques permit these errors to be avoided. Missing data errors are avoided by not forwarding *partially constructed* system calls (that is, those in which the name or output components are not available) to the service. Invalid data errors are avoided either by validating system calls before they are received by the service or by extending the service with code that detects and accepts invalid formats. Invalid address errors are avoided by:

1. Replacing input components in a request with new variables before processing the request.
2. Creating copy processes to communicate values generated for these new variables to the original input variables, as these values are produced by the service. This ensures that the service never has direct contact with user-level program input variables.
3. Executing copy processes either as part of the user-level program or encapsulated in a separate task. This ensures that an invalid address error does not cause an error in the service.

A *generic* copy procedure may be defined as follows:

```
copy(T, O) ← atomic(T) : O = T.                                          (C1)
copy([H |T], O) ← O = [H1 |T1], copy(H, H1), copy(T, T1).                (C2)
copy(S, O) ← S =\= [_|_], structure(S) : S=..L, copy(L, L1), O =.. L1.   (C3)
```

A call to this procedure suspends until its first argument is available. Constants are then copied from input to output (C1). (The primitive atomic suspends until its argument is bound and then succeeds if it is a constant and fails otherwise.) Lists are copied by copying their head and their tail (C2). Other structures are converted to lists, copied, and then converted back to structures (C3). A more complex copy procedure is required if service output incorporates variables that are to be passed to the user-level program. This copy procedure must be aware of the structure of the input component being copied so that it can pass variable subcomponents immediately instead of waiting for them to be given a value.

These validation techniques can be applied in the user-level programs themselves (*at source*), in services (*at destination*), or in between (*en route*). These three approaches are described and illustrated with examples.

7.3.1 Validation at source

Compile-time transformation of user-level programs can ensure that only valid system calls are generated and hence that only valid requests reach a service. For example, a call:

```
valid_send(disk, read(A, B))
```

can be compiled to a call to a new procedure diskread/2:

diskread(A, B) ← integer(A) : send(disk, read(A, B1)), copy(B1, B).

The integer primitive suspends until its argument is available and then succeeds if it is an integer, and fails otherwise. This avoids missing data and invalid data errors (errors 1 and 2 in Table 7.1). The copy process makes the value of the new output variable B1 available as it is generated, by copying it to B. If an error occurs in copy because B is already bound to a different value, this error is signalled in the user-level program rather than the OS service. Invalid address errors are hence avoided (error 3). Errors 4 and 5 cannot occur in this example as the arguments to the system call send are known at compile-time. Validation at source is not practical if system call arguments can be generated at run-time, as the validation to be performed may depend on argument values.

7.3.2 Validation at destination

Alternatively, the service may itself be made robust. Invalid data errors are dealt with by extending the service with extra code that validates call arguments. Invalid address errors are handled by a copy process which is executed locally as a separate task to permit detection of errors. Missing data errors are not easily handled in this way.

To illustrate this approach, a robust version of the disk service defined by Program 7.1 is presented as Program 7.5. For brevity, this program only supports read requests. Messages generated by task supervisors are assumed to have the form {Request, Term, Cont}, where Term is a termination variable and Cont is the system call's continuation variable. As this tuple is generated by the task supervisor, a trusted nucleus process, the service only needs to validate the Request component.

Program 7.5 copes with invalid data errors (Table 7.1; errors 1 and 4) by testing that arguments are valid (C2) and including clauses to deal with invalid requests (C3, C5). The procedure valid_address(A,R) validates an address A and returns a result R of valid or invalid. The additional clauses signal invalid requests by instantiating the continuation variable Cont to a call to the raise_exception primitive. This causes an exception message exception(badarg, send(Disk, O), NewCont) to be signalled on the status stream of the task that made the request. The string badarg indicates the type of exception. The term send(Disk, O) represents the erroneous call. NewCont is a new continuation variable, which the task's supervisor can use to respond to the exception.

Invalid address errors (error 3) are avoided by calling the relation try/4 (C6), which uses the kernel's TASK facility to encapsulate the copying operation. The call

'TASK'(TR, S, 'GlobalT', copy(Block1, Block))

creates a task that attempts to copy the term Block1 to Block. Any run-time errors are signalled on the status stream S of the task. (Recall that the type *GlobalT* ensures that unification errors are signalled prior to termination of a task: Section 4.2.4.) The result of the unification operation is signalled to the user-level program by instantiating the system call's continuation variable to either true (to indicate success: C7) or to a call to the raise_exception primitive (C8).

```
disk(Device, Requests, Go) ← data(Go) : disk(Device, Requests). % Synchronize.      (C1)

disk(De, [{read(Addr, Block), _, Cont} |Rs]) ←      % Read request received.          (C2)
    valid_address(Addr, Result),                    %     Check address is valid.
    disk_read(De, Addr, Block, Cont, Result, D),    %     Attempt read.
    disk(De, Rs, D).                                %     Process further requests.
disk(De, [{Other, Term, Cont} |Rs]) ←              % Otherwise signal exception.       (C3)
    Other =\= read(_,_) :
    Cont = raise_exception(badarg, send(disk, Other) ),
    disk(De, Rs).

disk_read(De, Addr, Block, Cont, valid, D) ←        % Supplied address is valid.        (C4)
    read(De, Addr, B1), D = Block                   %     Read block using primitive.
    try(B1, Block, Cont, read(Addr, Block)).        %     Perform unification.
disk_read(De, Addr, Block, Cont, invalid, D) ←      % Supplied address is invalid.      (C5)
    Cont = raise_exception(badarg, send(disk, read(Addr, Block)) ),
    D = next.

try(B1, B, Cont, O) ←                               % Attempt to return value.          (C6)
    'TASK'(_, S, 'GlobalT', copy(B1, B) ),          %     Create task for unification.
    result(S, Cont, O).                             %     Check result and bind Cont.

result(succeeded, Cont, O) ← Cont = true.           % Success.                          (C7)
result([_|_], Cont, O) ←                            % Error.                            (C8)
    Cont = raise_exception(badarg, send(disk, O)).
```

Program 7.5 Robust disk service.

7.3.3 Validation en route

Finally, requests can be validated after they are generated by the user-level program and before they are received by the service. A simple example of en route validation is a filter that delays incomplete requests and discards requests generated by tasks that are known to have terminated. Program 7.6 implements a filter that provides this functionality. This consumes a stream of requests and generates a stream of sufficiently instantiated requests, minus any requests generated by terminated tasks. Note that the order of requests on the two streams is not guaranteed to be preserved. This filter can be composed with Program 7.5 to avoid missing data errors (errors 2 and 5 in Table 7.1). Program 7.5 would however have to be modified to accept requests without termination variables, as Program 7.6 strips these variables out.

Program 7.6 calls a procedure data_available/2 for each request received; this is assumed to instantiate its second argument when the request represented by its first

---

```
delay_filter([ {Request, Term, Cont} | Rs], Os) ←        % Request received.        (C1)
        data_available(Request, Done),                   %     Check data is available
        delay({Request, Cont}, Term, Done, Os2),         %     Create delay process.
        merge(Os1, Os2, Os),                             %     Merge output.
        delay_filter(Rs, Os1).                           %     Recurse.

delay(Message, _, Done, Out) ←                           % Forward.                   (C2)
        data(Done) : Out = [Message].
delay(Message, Term, _, Out) ← data(Term) : Out = [ ].   % Task done: discard.        (C3)
```

Program 7.6 Delay filter.

argument is fully constructed. It also creates delay and merge processes. The merge process forwards the output of the delay process to the service (C1). The delay process waits until either data_available's output variable Done or the request's termination variable Term are instantiated. The former event indicates that the request can be forwarded to the service, minus its termination variable (C2). The latter indicates that the task that made the request has terminated: the request is then discarded (C3).

The procedure data_available can easily be extended to check for invalid data errors. Invalid address errors can also be dealt with by a filter of this sort.

7.3.4 Discussion

The three approaches to error avoidance discussed here all apply the same basic techniques to avoid suspension, matching, and unification errors and hence to obtain robust services. Each approach has advantages and disadvantages.

Avoidance at source isolates errors within user-level programs. OS programs can thus be simpler. No filters or termination variables are required to isolate and terminate incomplete requests. In contrast, validation at destination requires potentially complex mechanisms for dealing with partially constructed requests. On the other hand, validation at source requires that the compiler (perhaps a user program) be trusted. The compiler must be aware of all services' request formats; this implies a potentially undesirable degree of global knowledge in an object-oriented system. Also, it is difficult to deal with requests constructed at run-time in this way.

En route validation is conceptually the simplest, as it separates validation of requests from both the generation and processing of system calls. Also, the services themselves need perform no error checking. This simplifies the implementation of services and permits trusted OS components to make requests to services directly, thus incurring no validation overhead. The only disadvantage of en route validation is the potential overhead of processing request streams twice: once en route, to validate requests, and once at the service itself.

For most purposes, en route validation is the simplest and most effective approach. It is used almost exclusively in the system constructed to test the techniques described in this chapter.

7.4 NAMING SERVICES

User programs use names to access resources. Names are generally symbolic: that is, they are mapped by the nucleus onto some other domain (such as the domain of hardware addresses) before a resource is accessed. Naming is related to protection, as restrictions on both possession of names and the mappings applied to them can be used to control access to resources. Names can be resolved at run-time, compile-time, or at intermediate stages such as load-time. Run-time resolution of names (referred to as late binding) is more flexible but also more expensive than compile-time resolution (early binding).

The kernel facilities assumed here provide no direct support for the naming of processes or other computational objects. However, their support for the logical variable as an interprocess communication mechanism provides a limited form of *global address space*: a process possessing a reference to a logical variable can access that variable, wherever it is located. The logical variable in fact provides a sufficient basis for a variety of naming schemes.

Logical variables have been used here to implement service request streams. Logical variables can thus be regarded as ports that provide access to services: possessing a reference to a service's request stream is a *sufficient* condition for accessing that service. If in addition the kernel ensures that user-level programs only manipulate logical variables in ways permitted by the FP language, then a logical variable can only be accessed by processes that possess a reference to it. As references cannot be forged (they can only be copied or equated by unification), possessing a reference to a service's request stream is also a *necessary* condition for accessing a service. Logical variables can hence serve as unforgeable capabilities (Section 2.5) for services. The use of the logical variable as a basis for capability-based protection schemes is explored at length in Miller *et al.* [1987].

The single-assignment property of the logical variable might seem to mean that only a single process can be connected to a port. However, merge processes can be used to multiplex several connections. In principle, this use of merge incurs significant overhead: a binary tree of $N - 1$ merge processes multiplexing N connections requires $O(\log_2 N)$ reductions to forward a single request. However, simple optimizations in an implementation can reduce this overhead to a small constant [Shapiro and Safra, 1986].

In a message passing model, symbolic naming schemes can be implemented using *name servers*: processes that have direct connections to services and which forward requests tagged with symbolic names to these services. This corresponds to late binding of names to services. Early binding is also possible: a program which is known to require access to a particular service can be given a direct stream connection to that service at

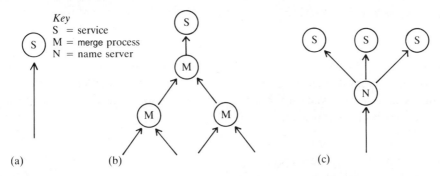

Figure 7.7 (a) A service and its port. (b) Several connections multiplexed to a service. (c) A name server.

compile time. Circuits (Section 7.2.2) provide binding at an intermediate stage.

Figure 7.7 illustrates these ideas by showing a service and its request stream or port; a tree of merge processes, used to multiplex several connections to a single service; and a name server.

Program 7.7 implements a simple name server. This has as arguments a stream of requests, tagged with symbolic names, and a list of {Name,Stream} pairs that defines the naming relation applied by the name server to names in incoming requests.

The name server processes requests received in the form {Destination, Message, Term, Cont} by looking up its list of names for Destination (C2, C3). If it knows of the service, it forwards the request in the form {Message, Term, Cont} (C2). Otherwise, it signals an exception of type unknown_service using the request's continuation variable Cont (C4).

```
names([{To, M, T, Cont} | Rs], Ns) ←          % Message received.                    (C1)
    send(To, M, T, Cont, Ns, Ns1),            %     Attempt to route to destination.
    names(Rs, Ns1).                           %     Recurse.

send(To, M, T, C, [{To1, St} |Ns], Ns1) ←     % Found: forward message.              (C2)
    To == To1 :
        Ns1 = [{To, St1} |Ns], St = [{M, T, C} |St1].
send(To, M, T, C, [{To1, St} |Ns], Ns1) ←     % Recurse.                             (C3)
    To =\= To1 :
        Ns1 = [{To1, St} |Ns1a],
        send(To, M, T, C, Ns, Ns1a).
send(To, M, _, Cont, [ ], Ns1) ←              % Service unknown: exception.          (C4)
    Ns1 = [ ],
    Cont = raise_exception(unknown_service, send(To, M) ).
```

Program 7.7 Name server.

7.5 A SIMPLE OPERATING SYSTEM

The implementation techniques described in this chapter have been incorporated in a simple but usable OS. A subset of this OS is presented here to further illustrate the techniques used to implement systems with the parallel logic programming model. This OS controls a computer system consisting of a processor, a terminal and a disk. Its nucleus permits user-level tasks to do the following:

1. Obtain characters typed at the keyboard.
2. Display characters on the screen.
3. Read and write disk blocks.
4. Read and write named modules.
5. Create new user-level tasks with the same capabilities, which the parent task can monitor and control

Two system calls – send/2 and task/4 – provide access to these facilities. The send/2 system call permits user-level programs to send requests to keyboard, screen, disk and code services. The task/4 system call requests the creation of a new user-level task. The screen service processes requests to display characters at a terminal. The keyboard service processes requests for characters typed at a keyboard. It also echoes characters to the screen service as they are typed. The disk service processes requests to read and write disk blocks. The code service processes requests to load and save named executable modules. It effectively implements a simple file system.

The kernel facilities described in Chapter 4 are assumed. The nucleus is described first. A simple user-level program – a shell – is then presented to show how nucleus services are used by user-level programs.

7.5.1 Nucleus

The structure of the nucleus is presented in Figure 7.8. In essence it consists of *supervisors* that monitor the execution of user-level programs and implement system calls (represented as sv: one is shown); *services* that process requests generated by supervisors on behalf of user-level programs (kb, screen, disk and code); a *name server* that routes requests from supervisors to services (names); *filters* that perform en route validation of requests (F); and *merges* that multiplex request streams (M).

The keyboard service (kb, Program 7.3), code service (code, Program 7.2), disk service (disk, Program 7.1) and name server (names, Program 7.7) have been defined previously. The screen service (not defined), like the disk service, uses kernel facilities to control a physical device. The *merge* processes multiplex requests made directly to the disk with disk requests generated by the code service, and requests made directly to the screen with characters echoed by the keyboard service.

The procedure simple_os/3 in Program 7.8 defines the process network created when the nucleus is initiated. This network is, in fact, that illustrated in Figure 7.8. A call to this procedure might have the form:

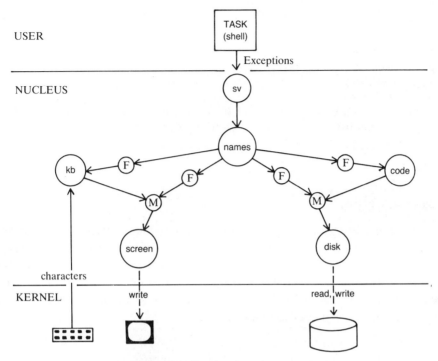

Figure 7.8 Simple operating system.

simple_os(10, ls, shell_prog, shell)

The first argument specifies the size of the cache used by the code service. The second argument is a stream of characters generated by the kernel, representing characters typed at the keyboard. The second and third arguments indicate the module and process to be executed by an initial user-level task. (Note that the second argument, shell_prog, is not a module itself: it *names* a module that the OS is to load and execute.) To initiate this task, the following actions are performed:

```
simple_os(CacheSize, Chars, Name, Process) ←                    % User-level task.
    call(M, Process, Si, [priority(2) |_]),                     % Task supervisor.
    sv(_, So, Term, Ns),                                        % Name server.
    names(Ns, [{kb, Ks}, {screen, Ss2}, {disk, Ds2}, {code, Cs}]),
    kbfilter(Ks, FKs), screenfilter(Ss2, FSs2),                 % Filters for
    diskfilter(Ds2, FDs2), codefilter(Cs, FCs),                 %     validation.
    kb(Chars, FKs, Ss1), screen(Ss),                            % kb + screen.
    code(CacheSize, [code(Name, M) |FCs], Ds1), disk(Ds),       % code + disk.
    merge(Ss1, FSs2, Ss), merge(Ds1, FDs2, Ds).
```

Program 7.8 Operating system bootstrap.

- A message code(Name,M) is sent to the code service to retrieve the named module from disk.
- The control call call/4 defined in Section 4.3 is used to create a task to execute the initial process using this retrieved module.
- A task supervisor sv is created to monitor execution of the new task.

All subsequent computation occurs as a result of system calls made by the initial user-level task or by other user-level tasks created using the task/4 system call. The purpose of the priority message on the control call's control argument in Program 7.8 is made clear subsequently.

7.5.2 Task supervisor

Recall that system calls in user-level tasks are translated into exceptions. These exceptions are processed by a nucleus process associated with a task called a supervisor. A supervisor may process system calls locally or generate requests to services. The supervisor employed here is presented as Program 7.9. It processes two system calls: task/4 and send/2: the first as a local service and the second by forwarding requests to named services. This supervisor takes the following arguments:

1. The task's status stream, generated by the kernel (Si).
2. A filtered status stream, to be generated by the supervisor (So).
3. A termination variable, to be bound by the supervisor when the task terminates (Term).
4. A request stream to the name server, to which the supervisor appends requests for services when processing system calls (Ns).

The filtered stream So is the status stream generated for a task by the kernel, but with exceptions representing send/2 and task/4 system calls removed. It is ignored in the case of the initial user-level task but permits user-level tasks created using the task/4 system call to be monitored by the user-level task that created them.

The task supervisor handles termination by closing the name server stream and instantiating the termination variable (C1, C2). It forwards status messages that do not represent system calls on the filtered status stream (C3). It augments send/2 system calls with the termination variable Term and the system call's continuation variable Cont and forwards them to the name server using the stream Ns (C4).

The last clause, which processes the task/4 system call, is somewhat more complex and deserves careful study. It must create a new task, filter its status stream and process system calls, and ensure that the task/4 system call's continuation variable is bound when the new task terminates. A new task is created using the control call and a new supervisor is created to filter its status stream. The continuation variable of the task/4 system call is retained by the new task supervisor as a termination variable. As the new supervisor instantiates this variable to true only upon termination (C1, C2), this has the effect of making a task/4 system call terminate precisely when its task terminates. The new

sv(succeeded, So, Term, Ns) ←	% Termination.	(C1)
Ns = [ ], So = succeeded, Term = true.		
sv(stopped, So, Term, Ns) ←	% Termination.	(C2)
Ns = [ ], So = stopped, Term = true.		
sv([Other |Si], So, Term, Ns) ←	% Other status message.	(C3)
Other =\ = exception(sys, _,_) :		
So = [Other |So1],	% Forward status message.	
sv(Si, So1, Term, Ns).	% Recurse.	
sv([exception(sys, send(To, Msg), Cont) |Si],	% send system call.	(C4)
So, Term, Ns) ←		
Ns = [{To, Msg, Term, Cont} |Ns1],	% Forward to name server.	
sv(Si, So, Term, Ns1).	% Recurse.	
sv([exception(sys, task(Mo,P,So1,C), Cont) |Si],	% task system call.	(C5)
So, Term, Ns) ←		
call(Mo, P, Si1, [priority(3) |C]),	% Create task.	
sv(Si1, So1, Cont, Ns2),	% Create new task supervisor.	
merge(Ns1, Ns2, Ns),	% Merge name server requests.	
sv(Si, So, Term, Ns1).	% Recurse.	

Program 7.9 Task supervisor.

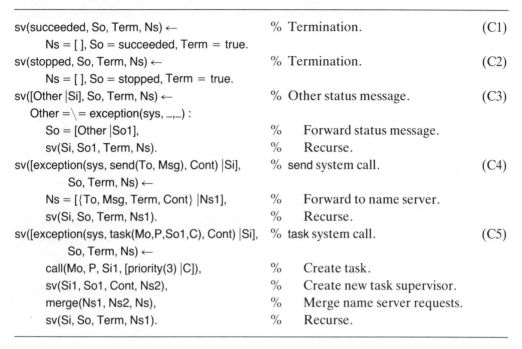

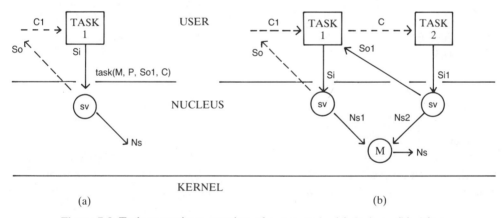

KERNEL
(a)   (b)

Figure 7.9 Task supervisor: creation of a new task. (a) Before. (b) After.

supervisor, like its parent, will generate requests to the name server if it receives send/2 system calls. These requests are merged with requests generated by its parent.

Execution of a task/4 system call in a user-level program thus creates a new task with its own supervisor. This new supervisor filters the new task's status stream, removing system calls; the filtered stream is passed to the user-level program that requested that the task be created. Figure 7.9 illustrates this process, showing the process network before and after the processing of this system call. Note how:

- The new user-level task's status stream Si1 is filtered (by the new sv process) to remove system calls before being passed to its parent task as So1.
- The new supervisor's stream of requests to the name server is merged with that of the parent supervisor.

7.5.3 User-level program

Recall that arguments to the procedure used to create the nucleus, simple_os/4, specify an initial user-level task by providing a process and naming the module that is to be used to execute this process. This task could execute an ordinary user-level program. This would not, however, be very useful, as once this single task had terminated the OS would have to be reinitialized. It is more useful if this initial task executes a program capable of creating many other tasks: for example, a *shell* that reads, interprets, and executes user commands. A simple shell is presented here to illustrate how user-level tasks use the **send/2** and **task/4** system calls to access nucleus services. In this section, system calls are printed in boldface to distinguish them from calls to user-level procedures.

Program 7.10 defines a shell that executes a stream of commands typed at the keyboard. The procedure shell first makes **send/2** system calls to establish circuit

```
shell ←                                    % Shell initialization.              (C1)
    send(kb, circuit(Ks)),                 %    Obtain circuit to keyboard.
    send(code, circuit(Cs)),               %    Obtain circuit to code.
    read(Ks, Rs),                          %    Read commands.
    shell(Rs, Cs, go).                     %    Process commands.

shell([fg(Name, Process) |Rs], Cs, Go) ←   % Foreground command               (C2)
    data(Go) :                             %    Ready to go.
        Cs = [code(Name, M) |Cs1],         %    Get module.
        task(M, Process, S, C),            %    Create task.
        monitor(S, C, Synch),              %    Monitor task's execution.
        shell(Rs, Cs1, Synch).             %    Synch delays next command.
shell([bg(Name, Process) |Rs], Cs, Go) ←   % Background command               (C3)
    data(Go) :                             %    Ready to go.
        Cs = [code(Name, M) |Cs1],         %    Get module.
        task(M, Process, S, C),            %    Create task.
        monitor(S, C, _),                  %    Monitor task's execution.
        shell(Rs, Cs1, go).                %    Synch = go: don't delay.

monitor([_|_], C, Synch) ← C = stop, Synch = go.   % Exception: halt task.    (C4)
monitor(succeeded, _, Synch) ← Synch = go.         % Termination.             (C5)
```

Program 7.10 User-level shell.

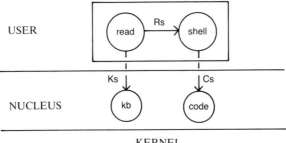

Figure 7.10 Shell process network.

connections to the keyboard and code services, Ks and Cs respectively (C1). These are subsequently used to request characters defining commands and the code these commands are to execute, respectively. Figure 7.10 shows the process network created by a call to shell. The nucleus processes created to trap and process system calls and to validate requests placed on the keyboard and code circuits are not shown. (These are not visible to user-level processes.) The read/2 process (not defined) uses the circuit Ks to request characters from the keyboard, parses these characters and passes terms representing commands to shell/3.

Commands are assumed to have the form fg(Name,Process) or bg(Name,Process), denoting foreground and background commands respectively. The procedure shell/3 uses the **task/4** system call to execute these commands (C2, C3). It uses its circuit to the code service (Cs) to retrieve code as required. It also creates a monitor/3 process for each command. This monitors the execution of the task, aborting its execution if exceptions occur (C4) and binding a synchronization variable Synch when it terminates (C4, C5). The synchronization variable is used in the case of a foreground command to delay the processing of further commands until the command has terminated (C2).

7.5.4 Processor scheduling

The simple OS illustrates the use of task priorities to control the kernel's processor scheduling facilities. Assume that the control call used to create tasks supports a priority(_) control message which sets a task's priority. (This requires that another clause be added to Program 4.2, which defines the control call.) Assume also that the OS is initiated with priority 1 (the highest priority):

```
call(simple_os(10, ls,shell_prog,shell), _, [priority(1) |_])
```

The initial user-level task (the shell) has been scheduled at priority 2 (Program 7.8), while the task supervisor schedules subsequent tasks at priority 3 (Program 7.9, C2).

These priorities specify scheduling policies. They inform the kernel's scheduler that the nucleus is to be allocated processor resources before the initial user task, the shell, which in turn has precedence over other user-level tasks. All user tasks created to execute commands have the same priority and are hence scheduled using a round-robin strategy. Note that the task supervisor presented here does not prevent the shell from increasing the priority of user-level tasks using a priority(1) control message. A small extension to the task supervisor can prevent this by filtering user-level tasks' control streams and validating priority messages.

7.6 SUMMARY

This chapter has shown that the kernel facilities described in previous chapters are sufficient to implement essential services required in an OS nucleus, to provide programs with access to these services, and to protect these services against erroneous or malicious access. It has also presented a body of techniques for designing and implementing operating systems using these facilities. These are summarized here.

- The OS nucleus is implemented as a network of concurrent processes that communicate and synchronize by means of shared logical variables.
- Processes termed services encapsulate both physical and logical resources. Processes that wish to access resources send messages to services. This structure permits accesses to be serialized and controlled when required. Essential services form part of the nucleus; other services may be provided by user-level programs.
- Each user program is encapsulated in a task. Tasks protect the nucleus from errors in user programs and provide a means of monitoring and controlling their execution.
- User programs communicate with the nucleus using system calls, implemented by message-passing using the kernel's exception mechanism. The exception mechanism's continuation variable is used to report errors and termination.
- A nucleus process termed a supervisor is associated with each user-level task. This traps exceptions representing system calls and either processes them locally or translates them into messages to services.
- Requests to remote services are augmented with a termination variable which permits services to detect when a task terminates, and a continuation variable, used to report errors.
- Both remote procedure call and circuit interfaces to services are supported.
- Simple validation techniques that control the sharing of variables between user-level and OS programs provide robust services.
- Naming schemes are implemented by name servers that route streams of tagged messages to their destination.

These techniques have been verified experimentally: a simple but usable system constructed using these techniques has supported large applications. This OS is supported by a kernel implemented by a software emulator and currently executes on a workstation. While the techniques themselves are as machine-independent as the underlying computational model, and are hence applicable to both uniprocessors and multiprocessors, the OS has not yet been ported to a multiprocessor. Issues that must be addressed to develop efficient multiprocessor systems are discussed in Chapter 9.

8

PROGRAMMING ENVIRONMENTS

This chapter is concerned with the design and implementation of programming environments. A programming environment can be viewed as a *user-level program*, to be constructed as a set of services using kernel facilities and basic services provided by an OS nucleus.

USER **Various services**	
NUCLEUS Essential services	
KERNEL Basic facilities	
HARDWARE e.g. Parallel machine	

It is useful for programming environments to support the construction of new tools from old by a process of composition. However, unrestricted side-effects to global state and in particular to file systems often prevent this. A novel approach to programming environment design is presented here that both permits composition of file system-modifying programs, and supports concurrent, atomic transactions on file system components.

An abstract implementation scheme for environments with these characteristics is outlined. A concrete realization of the scheme is also described. This has been constructed as a user-level program using kernel and nucleus facilities described in previous chapters.

8.1 BACKGROUND

The Unix shell illustrates the advantages of a programming environment that permits programmers to construct new tools from old by composition [Ritchie and Thompson, 1974]. Its *pipe* feature permits programs that read and write streams of data to be linked (*composed*) in a pipeline. This allows existing tools to be combined, producing more powerful tools that also read and write streams of data. However, only linear, unidirectional composition is supported and the shell language is distinct from the languages used to program applications. Furthermore, the file system side-effects implicit in many Unix tools limit the extent to which tools can be composed. Programs in a pipeline execute concurrently; the effect of concurrent calls to programs that modify file system state is not well-defined. A final deficiency is that failure of state changing programs can leave file system components in ill-defined states.

Shultis [1983] and McDonald [1987] have described *functional shells* for Unix that support functional composition of programs. These permit more general program composition – for example, several inputs can be passed to a single program – but do not avoid the problem of file system side-effects or failure.

The Logix system is a programming environment for parallel logic programming [Hirsch, 1987]. Logix uses a parallel logic language augmented with system calls as both a shell and an application programming language. A strength of this system is its use of the logical variable as a communication mechanism. This supports general program composition. However, programs that use system calls to request state changes in services cannot be composed, as system calls side-effect the state of nucleus services.

Backus [1978] has proposed a more abstract approach to programming environment design. In his Applicative State Transition systems, the state of a file system containing a functional program is represented as this functional program. A simple shell repeatedly applies functions in this program to the program itself in order to obtain a new program for the next iteration. This permits any state-modifying program to be composed with another. Update only occurs following successful termination of an updating function. This separation of computation and update also ensures that failure does not lead to inconsistent states. Unfortunately, Backus's proposal is not workable as it stands, as it does not show how to represent state efficiently, implement update and support concurrent access to state components.

Bowen [1986] proposes solutions to the problems of representing state and implementing update. In his MetaProlog system, programs are valid language terms and can be constructed using special primitives. For example, a call add_to(Pr1,Cl,Pr2) constructs a program Pr2 that differs from a program Pr1 in incorporating a new clause Cl. Programs are represented in terms of how they differ from other programs: efficient data structures provide rapid access to commonly used programs. However, Bowen does not address the problem of concurrent access to state.

Concurrent access to resources can be controlled using mutual exclusion mechanisms [Hoare, 1974]. The language Argus addresses the problem of concurrent access to file system objects [Weihl and Liskov, 1985]. Its design is intended to support fault tolerant distributed computing. It provides linguistic support for stable objects (which survive crashes) and nested atomic actions (transactions) on these objects. Argus programs perform sequences of actions on objects; the language kernel synchronizes accesses and records changes to objects on stable storage when actions complete. However, Argus programs cannot easily be composed.

This chapter describes an integration of file system state and update into the parallel logic programming model. This integration yields an extended computational model that supports both composition of state-modifying programs and concurrent access to state components. Programming environments that support this model provide a high-level user language that can be used to both describe and compute relations between file system states. Update follows computation of a new state as an atomic transaction. This relational style of programming is shown to permit succinct descriptions of complex state changes.

8.2 DESIGN PRINCIPLES

A number of problems had to be solved to achieve a relational treatment of file system update. These problems, and chosen solutions, are summarized here.

8.2.1 Problems

Representing state and state change. Programs must be able to manipulate representations of file system state if they are to talk explicitly about state and state change. Explicit representation of state permits the definition of procedures such as transform(T, OldState, NewState), that applies a transformation T to a given language term OldState representing a file system state and produces a term representing a NewState. This procedure defines, and can be used to compute, members of the relation: 'States OldState and NewState are related by transformation T'.

The representation of state must be at a suitable level of abstraction for common programming tasks. It must also permit an *efficient* and *succinct* representation of change. A programmer is generally concerned with making quite minor changes to file systems. It should thus not be difficult to construct a new state which differs only in some minor respect from a previous state. This is difficult in computational models that do not support mutable data structures. The problem of efficiently representing the fact that some state differs from another in a single component (without using destructive assignment) has been termed the frame problem [Raphael, 1971].

Implementing state change. A program called with a representation of file system state as an argument can compute a representation of a modified state. For example, if S represents a file system state, a call transform(T,S,S1) may compute a new state S1. This computation of a new state (S1) must be translated into physical changes to the file system represented by the state S.

Self-reference. If a programming system is to be self-contained, programs must be able to access and update their own representations in the file system.

Concurrency. A programming system should support concurrent access to file system state. Concurrency raises both semantic and implementation issues. It is desirable that each program should appear to execute with respect to an unchanging file system. This requires that programs cannot update state components which other concurrently executing programs are accessing. This in turn implies a need for mutual exclusion mechanisms in an implementation, and consequent problems of deadlock detection or avoidance, etc. Similar problems are encountered in distributed databases [Bernstein and Goodman, 1981; Ullman, 1982].

8.2.2 Solutions

The following concepts are applied to solve these problems. Some of these concepts are well-known in metaprogramming, databases, and programming language design. However, their integration in a programming system is new.

Separation of computation and update. Programs are interpreted as defining relations over states. Programs are evaluated with respect to a 'current state'. Computation of a new state by a program results in an atomic transition from the old state to the new state; subsequent programs are evaluated with respect to the new state.

State as a language term. Programs can manipulate states in much the same way as other data types. States can be incorporated in data structures, compared, etc. Primitives are provided that can be applied to states to access components and construct new states.

Incremental description of new states. Programs construct new states by specifying how they differ from other, previously defined states. This avoids frame problems.

Persistent state. The state made accessible to programs corresponds to the contents of a file system. State components can be accessed without concern for their location; new states can be constructed without concern for their longevity. That is, state is *persistent* [Atkinson *et al.*, 1983].

Persistence removes the distinction that most languages make between accessible but volatile primary storage and less accessible but stable secondary storage. Programs in a persistent language simply access *language objects*; these are loaded and saved by the language implementation as required. This means that programs do not need to explicitly manage secondary storage. As it has been suggested that, typically, 30 percent of a program is concerned with moving data to and from disk and converting formats used for disk storage to language structures [Atkinson *et al.*, 1983], this is a significant advantage.

Atomic, serializable transactions. The evaluation of a program with respect to a state, and the replacement of this state by a new state that it computes, is termed a transaction. Transactions can be nested; nested transactions execute concurrently and may compute and commit new states independently. Concurrent transactions are *serializable*

[Bernstein and Goodman, 1981]: that is, for any set of successfully terminating transactions, there exists a sequential ordering of their executions that defines the same state
transition. This permits each transaction to be viewed as executing with respect to an
unchanging state.

State as program. The 'state' made accessible to programs represents a set of programs rather than files, records or strings of characters. A program is a set of statements
(e.g., guarded clauses). It is a basic structural unit and, due to its persistence, may be
compared with both a file in a conventional file system and a module in a conventional
programming language.

Attributes. Conventional file systems normally associate, implicitly or explicitly,
data such as creation date, format, etc., with program files. A representation of state as
a set of programs makes the specification of this information difficult. It can only be
represented as program statements, located either in the program to which it refers or in
some other program. The former approach confuses programs and information about
programs; the latter introduces the problem of relating information to the program which
it concerns. These problems are avoided by permitting labelled terms named attributes
to be associated with state components. An attribute is a {label,value} pair. Thus a
program may have an attribute {created_by,john}, a statement an attribute {description,'A
procedure to sort lists'}, etc.

8.3 A USER LANGUAGE

The concepts introduced in the previous sections are illustrated using a concrete
example. FP+ is a high-level user language derived from FP that incorporates these
concepts. It extends FP in three main ways, as illustrated in Figure 8.1.

FP+'s *state data type* and *state primitives* make file system state accessible in the
language, permitting programs to explicitly define relations over states. *Persistence* con-
ceals the existence of secondary storage from the programmer, permitting file system
management functions to be expressed using FP+ procedures without explicit loading
and saving of file system components. *Atomic, serializable transactions* permit the programmer to ignore the effects of interactions between transactions.

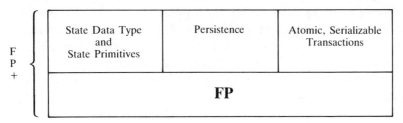

Figure 8.1 FP and FP+

The FP+ language is defined here and its use is illustrated with examples. The implementation of a programming environment that supports FP+ as a user language is described later in the chapter. Note that programs presented in this and the following section are FP+ rather than FP programs. Calls to FP+ primitives are in boldface.

8.3.1 Language definition

A number of preliminary definitions are followed by an informal presentation of FP+'s operational semantics:

- A state consists of a number of programs, each with a unique name.
- A program consists of zero or more procedures and zero or more attributes.
- A procedure is an FP procedure augmented with zero or more attributes.
- An attribute is a pair {T1,T2}, where T1 and T2 are terms. T1 is the name and T2 the value of the attribute.
- A transaction specifies a set of processes and the name of a program in the current state that is to be used to execute these processes.
- A transaction's current state is the state with respect to which it is being evaluated.
- A transaction's next state is the state which is to replace the transaction's current state upon successful termination of the transaction.

A transaction is evaluated in the same way as an FP program, except that FP+ primitives may be called and commitment must be performed upon successful termination. A transaction can use FP+ primitives to perform the following tasks:

- Obtain an encoding of its current state.
- Access descriptions of state components: procedures, attributes, etc. (These are represented as language terms.)
- Construct encodings of new states that differ from the current or other states in specified ways.
- Nominate a next state.
- Execute procedures located in other named programs.

A state is a first-class language object. States can be included in terms and tested for equality.

If a transaction terminates successfully, and has nominated a next state, then *commitment* attempts to replace the current state with this new state. This replacement is performed as an atomic action and either succeeds or is aborted. A transaction hence maps a current state to a next state. Programs can use a transaction primitive to initiate, monitor and control nested transactions. Nested transactions are evaluated with respect to the state as defined at the time they are initiated. They commit independently of their parent transaction.

A *concurrency control* mechanism ensures that all committing transactions are serializable. It may abort a transaction if committing it would violate serializability. The concurrency control mechanism used in the FP+ implementation described later in this chapter applies this constraint on updates:

> A next state computed by a successfully terminating transaction may be committed if it does not modify any program which a concurrently executing (that is, not yet terminated) transaction has already executed or accessed using FP+ primitives.

8.3.2 Example transactions

The syntax:

    ?- <program> : <processes>

is used here to represent a transaction. This specifies that <processes> are to be evaluated using a particular <program>.

Assume the existence of an FP+ procedure plookup(S,N,Ps) which computes a list Ps containing the names of programs in state S that contain a procedure named N. Its implementation uses FP+ primitives to access and analyze components of the state S. It is located in a program tools. The transaction.

    ?- tools: **current**(S), plookup(S, proc/1, X).

executes this program. It calls the primitive **current** to obtain an encoding of the current state and plookup to determine which programs in this state contain procedures named proc/1; the result is returned as X.

Secondly, consider an FP+ procedure transform(T,S,S1) which applies a transformation T to a state S to compute a new state S1. Its implementation uses FP+ primitives to access the state S and to construct the new state S1. The transaction

    ?-tools: **current**(S), transform(<t>, S, S1), **next**(S1).

uses the **current** primitive to obtain an encoding of the current state, calls the procedure transform to apply a transformation <t> to this state to obtain a new state S1 and uses the primitive **next** to indicate that this state is to replace the current state upon successful termination. Successful commitment of this transaction hence results in the updates to file system state required to record the effects of the transformation <t>.

FP+ programs can easily be composed. For example, the transaction

    ?-tools: **current**(S), transform(<t>, S, S1), transform(<t>, S1, S2), **next**(S2).

applies transformation <t> exactly twice to state S to generate a new state S2, and nominates this as the transaction's next state. FP+ also permits self-reference. The transaction

    ?- tools: **current**(S), plookup(S, plookup/3, Ps).

determines which programs contain procedures named plookup/3. The list Ps contains the value 'tools'; if other programs also contain procedures named plookup/3, the list will contain additional elements.

8.3.3 State transitions and concurrency control

If transactions such as:

?-tools: **current**(CState), transform(<t>, CState, NState), **next**(NState).   (T1)
?-tools: **current**(CState), plookup(CState, proc/1, X).   (T2)

terminate, then their evaluation computes a state transition. In the case of a transaction that specifies a valid next state (such as T1), this transition is

T1: CState $\mapsto$ NState

where CState is the current state – the state with respect to which the transaction is evaluated – and NState is the next state it computes. A transaction that is aborted or does not specify a next state (such as T2) computes the identify transition

T2: CState $\mapsto$ CState

An initial transaction can create further, nested transactions. Nested transactions may execute concurrently and, if they access and update disjoint sets of state components, may also compute next states (that is, update the file system) without contention. For example, an initial transaction T may initiate execution of the two transactions T1 and T2 above. These can execute concurrently, unless transaction T1 terminates and attempts to commit changes to a program that has been accessed by transactions T or T2. This causes transaction T1 to be aborted as it violates the concurrency control requirement.

It is important to note that a transaction's 'current state' is not guaranteed to be the state of the file system at the time the transaction executed the **current** primitive. As state may potentially be distributed over many machines, and many transactions may be operating on this state, such a 'global snapshot' is difficult to obtain. What is guaranteed is that all successfully terminating transactions are serializable. This means that for any set of successfully committing transactions, there exists a sequential ordering of their executions that defines the same transition. That is:

$\forall$ E = {T_i: 0 < i $\leqslant$ N}, E: CState $\mapsto$ NState
$\exists$i: [1 .. N] $\xrightarrow{\text{1-1 onto}}$ [1 .. N], $T_{i(1)}$: CState $\mapsto$ S_1, $T_{i(2)}$: $S_1 \mapsto S_2$, ..., $T_{i(N)}$: $S_{N-1} \mapsto$ NState

Thus each transaction in a set of concurrent transactions is evaluated with respect to some unchanging state: for transactions in E, this is one of CState, S_1, S_2, ..., S_{N-1}. The unchanging state may not be the global state at the precise moment the **current** primitive was executed: this is not important. As far as the user is concerned, each transaction evaluates with respect to an unchanging state and computes a member of a relation between file system states.

8.4 PROGRAMMING IN THE USER LANGUAGE

FP+'s extensions to FP are encapsulated in *state access, state generation, transaction*, and *program* primitives. Simple examples illustrate both the use of these primitives and typical applications of the language.

8.4.1 State access

State access primitives permit a transaction to access terms describing state components. They include **programs, dict, definition** and **attribute**. These primitives must be applied to a term representing a state. The **current** primitive can be used to determine the current state.

STATE ACCESS PRIMITIVES
The annotations on arguments indicate whether an argument must be available before the primitive can be evaluated ($\downarrow$) or is generated by the primitive ($\uparrow$):

current(S $\uparrow$)
    S is the current state.
programs(S $\downarrow$, Ps $\uparrow$)
    The list Ps names the programs defined in state S.
dict(S $\downarrow$, P $\downarrow$, Ns $\uparrow$)
    The list Ns names the procedures defined in program P in state S.
definition(S $\downarrow$, P $\downarrow$, N $\downarrow$, D $\uparrow$)
    D is a description of procedure N as defined in program P in state S.
attribute(S $\downarrow$, P $\downarrow$, A $\downarrow$, V $\uparrow$)
    V is the value of the attribute named A associated with program P in state S.

A call to a state access primitive returns an error value if the state component it attempts to access does not exist. Otherwise it returns a description of that state component. The term *description* is used here in a technical sense to denote a metalevel naming of objects [Bowen and Kowalski, 1982]. For example, the primitives **programs** and **dict** return lists of constants corresponding to program and procedure names respectively. **definition** returns a variable-free term describing a procedure. This has the form <clauselist>, and is a list of tuples describing clauses. A clause description has the form {<head>,<guard>,<body>} where <head> is a <process>, and <guard> and <body> are lists of <process>es. A <process> is a string or structured term. The arguments to a <process> are <term>s. A <term> is a constant, which describes itself; a structure v(<name>), which describes a variable named <name>; a structured term t(<termlist>), which describes a tuple with arguments described by a list of <term>s; or a list [<term1>|<term2>], which describes a list structure with head and tail described by <term1> and <term2>. Thus a procedure:

```
on([E1 |L], E, R) ← E1=\= E: on(L, E, R).
on([ ],_,R) ← R = notfound.
```

is described by the following term (text following a % character is a comment):

```
[{ on([v('E1') | v('L')], v('E'), v('R')),        % Clause 1: head.
   [v('E1') == v('E')],                            %    Guard.
   [v('R') = found]},                              %    Body.
 { on ([v('E1') | v('L')], v('E'), v('R')),        % Clause 2: head.
   [v('E1') =\= v('E')],                           %    Guard.
   [on(v('L'), v('E'), v('R'))]},                  %    Body.
 { on([ ], v('_'), v('R')),                        % Clause 3: head.
   [ ], [v('R') = notfound]}                        %    Empty guard; body.
]
```

EXAMPLE: PROGRAM ANALYSIS

State access primitives make it possible to write programs such as interpreters and program analysers that manipulate other programs. For example, consider the problem of locating all procedures with a given name in a file system. This can be achieved by first obtaining a list of programs, and then for each program obtaining a list of procedures and searching for the given name. The FP+ procedure plookup(S,N,As) (Program 8.1)

plookup(S, N, As) ←	% Find procedure N in state S.	(C1)
programs(S, Ps),	% Obtain list of programs.	
plookup(S, Ps, N, As).	% Check them all.	
plookup(S, [P |Ps], N, As) ←	% Is N defined in program P?	(C2)
dict(S, P, Ns),	% Obtain dictionary for P.	
on(Ns, N, R),	% Look for N in dictionary.	
dlookup(As, As1, P, N, R),	% Check whether present.	
plookup(S, Ps, N, As1).	% Recurse: try other programs.	
plookup(_, [ ], _, As) ← As = [ ].	% All programs checked.	(C3)
dlookup(As, As1, P, N, found) ←	% N defined in program P.	(C4)
As = [{P,N} |As1].		
dlookup(As, As1, _, _, notfound) ← As = As1.	% N not defined in program P.	(C5)
on([E1 |Es], E, R) ← E1 == E : R = found.	% E on list if head of list.	(C6)
on([E1 |Es], E, R) ← E1 =\= E :	% E on list if on tail.	(C7)
on(Es, E, R).		
on([ ], _, R) ← R = notfound.	% E not on empty list.	(C8)

Program 8.1 Program analysis in FP+.

does precisely this. It computes a list As of pairs {P1,N},..., {Pn,N} representing the programs P1, ..., Pn in which a procedure N is to be found in state S. A pair {*P,N*} is returned rather than a simple name *P* so as to permit the use of this program in a subsequent transaction.

plookup/3 uses the **programs** primitive to obtain a list of programs Ps defined in a given state S (C1). It then calls the procedure plookup/4, which checks each program P using the **dict** primitive and outputs a pair {P,N} if it contains a procedure named N (C4). Transactions that invoke this program were presented in Section 8.3.2.

8.4.2 State generation

State generation primitives such as **new_program**, **new_definition**, and **new_attribute** are used to construct new states. A new state differs from a previously constructed state in incorporating a new definition for a named state component. Many new states can be computed in the course of a transaction's execution. The **next** primitive is used to nominate the next state that is to replace the current state upon successful termination of the transaction. **next** can be called at most once in a transaction; second and subsequent calls are signalled as exceptions. Commitment of a next state is only attempted if a transaction terminates successfully and if, upon termination, the term specified by a call to **next** is bound to a representation of a valid state.

STATE GENERATION PRIMITIVES

new_program(S ↓ ,P ↓ ,S1 ↑)
> State S1 differs from state S in containing a new (empty) program named P.

new_definition(S ↓ ,P ↓ ,D ↓ ,S1 ↑)
> State S1 differs from state S in containing definition D in program P. D is a term describing a procedure. (The name of the procedure is implicit in this description.)

next(S ↓)
> The state S is to replace the current state upon successful termination, of the transaction in which this call is executed.

EXAMPLE: PROGRAM TRANSFORMATION

State generation primitives permit program transformations to be specified by procedures that compute relations over states. State access primitives are used to obtain descriptions of state components. State generation primitives are used to generate new states that contain transformed versions of these components.

For example, Program 8.2 implements a generic transformation that can be used to apply a supplied transformation to a list of named procedures. The procedure transform(T,S,S1) applies a transformation T to a state S to obtain a new state S1. A transformation is specified by a tuple {Ns,P,A}, which indicates that the procedures named on the list Ns are to be transformed using the procedure named A as defined in the

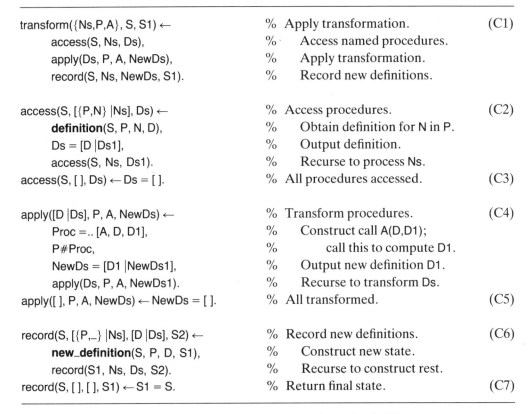

transform({Ns,P,A}, S, S1) ←	% Apply transformation.	(C1)
access(S, Ns, Ds),	% Access named procedures.	
apply(Ds, P, A, NewDs),	% Apply transformation.	
record(S, Ns, NewDs, S1).	% Record new definitions.	
access(S, [{P,N} |Ns], Ds) ←	% Access procedures.	(C2)
definition(S, P, N, D),	% Obtain definition for N in P.	
Ds = [D |Ds1],	% Output definition.	
access(S, Ns, Ds1).	% Recurse to process Ns.	
access(S, [ ], Ds) ← Ds = [ ].	% All procedures accessed.	(C3)
apply([D |Ds], P, A, NewDs) ←	% Transform procedures.	(C4)
Proc =.. [A, D, D1],	% Construct call A(D,D1);	
P#Proc,	% call this to compute D1.	
NewDs = [D1 |NewDs1],	% Output new definition D1.	
apply(Ds, P, A, NewDs1).	% Recurse to transform Ds.	
apply([ ], P, A, NewDs) ← NewDs = [ ].	% All transformed.	(C5)
record(S, [{P,_} |Ns], [D |Ds], S2) ←	% Record new definitions.	(C6)
new_definition(S, P, D, S1),	% Construct new state.	
record(S1, Ns, Ds, S2).	% Recurse to construct rest.	
record(S, [ ], [ ], S1) ← S1 = S.	% Return final state.	(C7)

Program 8.2 A generic program transformation in FP+.

program named P. The transformation is achieved by *accessing* the definitions of the named procedures in the state S, *applying* the given transformation to these definitions, and *recording* the resulting new definitions by constructing a new state S1 that differs from the current state in containing them (C1). These three operations are performed by the procedures access/3, apply/4 and record/4 respectively.

The procedure access(S, Ns, Ds) computes a list Ds of terms describing procedures on a list Ns in a state S. A procedure is named by a pair {P,N}. The list Ds is constructed by retrieving descriptions of the named procedures using the state access primitive **definition**. The procedure apply(Ds,P,A,NewDs), when applied to a list Ds of procedure definitions, computes a list NewDs containing those definitions transformed using the procedure named A in program P. A call to A is constructed for each procedure on the list using the =.. primitive. (This primitive translates a list [N,A$_1$,...,A$_n$] to the structured term N(A$_1$,...,A$_n$).) This call has the form A(D,D1) and is assumed to compute a new procedure definition D1 from the definition D. The FP+ primitive # (to be described) is used to evaluate the newly constructed process using the program named P. Finally, the procedure record(S,Ns,Ds,S1) computes the state S1 from the state S by redefining the procedures on the list Ns with the definitions in the list Ds. The state generation primitive

new_definition is used to construct a series of states containing the new definitions (C6). The final state in this series is returned as the new state (C7).

Assume that the procedures presented here are located in a program named tools. Then, as noted previously, transform can be executed in the transaction:

?- tools: **current**(S), transform(<t>, S, S1), **next**(S1).

where <t> represents a transformation. (An example of a possible transformation is given in the next section.) This transaction attempts to compute a new state S1 in which transformation <t> has been applied to the current state S. It applies the update S ⊢ S1 upon successful termination.

---

abort([{Head, G, B} |Cls], AProc) ←	% Make procedure abortable.	(C1)
AProc = [{NewP, [ ], [ ]} |ACls],	% Create skeleton of new procedure.	
Head =.. [Name |Args],	% Select args to construct new head.	
NewP =.. [Name, stop |NewArgs],	% Construct head of new clause.	
args(Args, NewArgs),	% Construct args of new head (all '_').	
abort_cls([{Head, G, B} |Cls], ACls).	% Transform clauses.	
abort_cls([{H, G, B} |Cls], As) ←	% Transform a list of clauses.	(C2)
As=[{AH,[var(v('_$'))]|G],AB}|As1],	% Output new clause.	
extra_arg(H, AH),	% Add argument '_$' to head.	
abort_ps(B, AB),	% Transform body processes.	
abort_cls(Cls, ACls1).	% Recurse: transform other clauses.	
abort_cls([ ], ACls) ← ACls = [ ].	% Done: all transformed.	(C3)
abort_ps([Proc |Ps], APs) ←	% Transform a list of processes	(C4)
primitive(Proc, R),	% Determine whether a primitive.	
process(Proc, APs, APs1, R),	% Transform if not a primitive.	
abort_ps(Ps, APs1).	% Recurse: transform rest.	
abort_ps([ ], APs) ← APs = [ ].	% Done: all transformed.	(C5)
process(Proc, Ps, Ps1, yes) ← Ps = [Proc |Ps1].		(C6)
process(Proc, Ps, Ps1, no) ← Ps = [AProc |Ps1], extra_arg(Proc, AProc).		(C7)
extra_arg(Proc, AProc) ← Proc =.. [Name |Args], AProc =.. [Name, v('_$') |Args].		(C8)
args([ ], NArgs) ← NArgs = [ ].	% Produce list of variables ('_').	(C9)
args([_ |Args], NArgs) ← NArgs = [v('_') |NArgs1], args(Args, NArgs1).		(C10)

Program 8.3 Program transformation in FP+.

EXAMPLE: A PROGRAM TRANSFORMATION

Transformations to be applied by the generic Program 8.2 should take as input a term representing a procedure and generate as output a term representing a transformed procedure. The procedure abort/2 in Program 8.3 implements such a transformation. This makes an FP+ procedure abortable by adding an extra argument which, when instantiated to a constant stop, causes evaluation to terminate. Note that in the program, the procedure primitive(P,R) is used to determine whether a process P is a call to an FP+ primitive: it binds R to the constant yes if it is and to no if it is not.

To illustrate the transformation, the procedure on/3 is shown untransformed (on the left) and transformed (on the right):

	on(stop,_,_,_).	(1)
on([E1 |L],E,R) ←	on(_$,[E1 |L],E,R) ←	(2)
E1 == E : R = found.	var(_$), E1 == E : R = found.	(3)
on([E1 |L],E,R) ←	on(_$,[E1 |L],E,R) ←	(2)
E1 =\= E : on(L,E,R).	var(_$), E1 =\= E : on(_$,L,E,R).	(2), (3)
on([ ],_,R) ← R = notfound.	on(_$,[ ],_,R) ← var (_$) : R = notfound.	(2), (3)

The annotations, (1), (2), etc, in this program refer to the following list of transformations specified by Program 8.3. Note that it is assumed that application programs do not contain variables named _$.

1. Add an extra clause to the procedure on(stop,_,_,_) (C1).
2. Add an extra argument – the variable _$, represented in the program as v('_$') – to the head of each clause (C2) and to each process in each clause's body which is not a primitive(C4–C7).
3. Add an extra guard test var(_$) to each clause (C2).

Recall that state access primitives provide programs with *descriptions* of procedures, etc. The procedure abort/2 computes a relation over procedure descriptions. If it is called with the following description of the procedure on/3 as input:

```
[{ on([v('E1') | v('L')], v('E'), v('R')),          % Clause 1: head.
    [v('E1') == v('E')],                             %     Guard.
    [v('R') = found]},                               %     Body.
 { on([v('E1') | v('L')], v('E'), v('R')),           % Clause 2: head.
    [v('E1') =\= v('E')],                            %     Guard.
    [on(v('L'), v('E'), v('R'))]},                   %     Body.
 {on([ ], v('_'), v('R')),                           % Clause 3: head.
    [ ], [v('R') = notfound]}                        %     Empty guard; body.
]
```

it generates as output:

```
[{ on(stop, v('_'), v('_'), v('_')), [ ], [ ]},        % Clause 0.              (1)
   { on(v('_$'), [v('E1') | v('L')], v('E'), v('R')),  % Clause 1.              (2)
       [var( v('_$')), v('E1') == v('E')],             %    Guard.              (3)
       [v('R') = found]},                              %    Body.
   { on(v('_$'), [v('E1') | v('L')], v('E'), v('R')),  % Clause 2.              (2)
       [var( v('_$')), v('E1') = \ = v('E')],          %    Guard               (3)
       [on( v('_$'), v('L'), v('E'), v('R'))]},        %    Body.               (2)
   { on( v('_$'),[ ],v('_'), v('R')),                  % Clause 3: head.        (2)
       [var( v('_$'))], [v('R') = notfound]}           %    Guard; body.        (3)
]
```

In this transformed term, additional components are in boldface; annotations refer once again to the list of transformations.

Assume that the procedures in Program 8.3 are located in a program named trans. Then the transaction:

?- tools: **current**(S), plookup(S, on/3, Ns), transform({Ns,trans,abort}, S, S1), **next**(S1).

uses the procedure abort/2 to make all procedures named on/3 in the current state abortable. The call to plookup/3 (Program 8.1) yields a list of programs in which on/3 is defined; transform/3 (Program 8.2) generates a new state in which these are transformed using the procedure abort/2.

8.4.3 Transactions and programs

By default, an FP+ process is evaluated using procedures in the program in which it was called. The **transaction** and **#** primitives permit calls to procedures located in other programs. The **transaction** primitive also supports the creation and management of nested transactions.

THE TRANSACTION AND PROGRAM PRIMITIVES

transaction(P $\downarrow$,N $\downarrow$,R $\uparrow$,C $\downarrow$)

Initiates a transaction to execute process N using the program named P. R and C can be used to monitor and control the transaction in the same way as the status and control streams of the control call presented in Section 4.3. Upon successful termination of process N, an attempt is made to commit a next state, if one has been nominated (using **next**) during its execution. This attempt may fail, due to conflict with another transaction. Commitment failure is signalled by the transaction termination status commit_error. The argument to this message indicates both why commitment failed and the updates that were not performed. If commitment succeeds, the usual termination status (succeeded) is returned.

P $\downarrow$ #N $\downarrow$

Executes process N in program P.

Both these primitives refer implicitly to (and are evaluated with respect to) the current state. The language can easily be extended to permit evaluation of processes using programs defined in new states generated by a transaction; for simplicity, this is not considered here.

EXAMPLE: A SHELL WITH DELEGATION

One application of the **transaction** primitive is the programming of command interpreters. A command interpreter can execute multiple commands as separate transactions. FP+'s concurrency control mechanisms prevent conflict when concurrent commands access the same state components.

The ability to call procedures located in other programs permits the use of programs to structure applications. A program that consists of logically distinct components can be divided into several subprograms. These programs can then be linked either statically using the **#** primitive, or dynamically by delegation mechanisms, to be invoked following calls to undefined procedures. For example, a simple delegation mechanism could seek undefined procedures in an auxiliary program associated with each program. (It is emphasized that this trivial example is proposed only to illustrate programming techniques.) Program 8.4 implements a simple command interpreter or *shell* that supports this mechanism. It is assumed that the name of the auxiliary program associated with a particular program is specified by a program attribute delegate. Thus an attribute {delegate,library} associated with a program my_prog indicates that calls to procedures undefined in my_prog should be evaluated using the program named library.

The shell implemented by Program 8.4 executes each command received on its input stream as a separate transaction using the **transaction** primitive (C1). Commands are represented as tuples {P,N} where P names a program and N represents a process. The **current**, **attribute**, and **dict** primitives are used to obtain a list of procedures defined in the program P's auxiliary program (C2). The procedure monitor then monitors the new transaction's status stream. It detects calls to undefined procedures (signalled by exception messages with type undefined C5) and executes them in the auxiliary program, using **#**, if they are defined in that program (that is, if they are on the list Ns, C7). This delegation is achieved by binding the *continuation variable* associated with the exception. The procedure name(P,N) determines the name of the procedure called by a process P. Otherwise, execution of the transaction is aborted (C8). Other clauses deal with termination (C3, C4).

A range of more sophisticated shells can be programmed in FP+, using the exception message to detect calls to undefined procedures; attributes or procedures to define inheritance structures, etc.; the **dict** primitive to locate procedures in programs; and the **#** primitive to initiate execution of procedures in other programs. Interesting possibilities include the following.

- *Unix-style search path.* A shell can search through a list of programs (rather than a single program, as in the example) to locate procedures not present in the original program. The list of programs to search may be defined by a procedure specified in some program assumed to define a user environment.

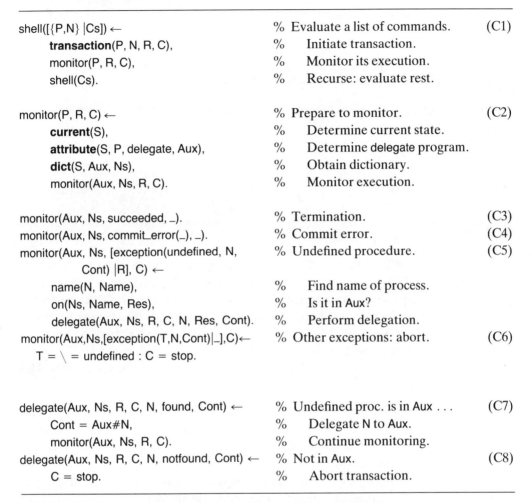

shell([{P,N} |Cs]) ←	% Evaluate a list of commands. (C1)
transaction(P, N, R, C),	% Initiate transaction.
monitor(P, R, C),	% Monitor its execution.
shell(Cs).	% Recurse: evaluate rest.
monitor(P, R, C) ←	% Prepare to monitor. (C2)
current(S),	% Determine current state.
attribute(S, P, delegate, Aux),	% Determine delegate program.
dict(S, Aux, Ns),	% Obtain dictionary.
monitor(Aux, Ns, R, C).	% Monitor execution.
monitor(Aux, Ns, succeeded, _).	% Termination. (C3)
monitor(Aux, Ns, commit_error(_), _).	% Commit error. (C4)
monitor(Aux, Ns, [exception(undefined, N,	% Undefined procedure. (C5)
Cont) |R], C) ←	
name(N, Name),	% Find name of process.
on(Ns, Name, Res),	% Is it in Aux?
delegate(Aux, Ns, R, C, N, Res, Cont).	% Perform delegation.
monitor(Aux,Ns,[exception(T,N,Cont)|_],C)←	% Other exceptions: abort. (C6)
T = \ = undefined : C = stop.	
delegate(Aux, Ns, R, C, N, found, Cont) ←	% Undefined proc. is in Aux . . . (C7)
Cont = Aux#N,	% Delegate N to Aux.
monitor(Aux, Ns, R, C).	% Continue monitoring.
delegate(Aux, Ns, R, C, N, notfound, Cont) ←	% Not in Aux. (C8)
C = stop.	% Abort transaction.

Program 8.4 Inheritance shell in FP+.

- *Conditional delegation.* A shell can execute procedures in an auxiliary program to determine where to seek undefined procedures. For example, a procedure refer(N,P) may be used to compute a program P in which a process N may be evaluated. A range of delegation schemes can be specified in this way.
- *Restarting transactions.* A shell can detect transactions aborted due to concurrency control (signalled by a commit_error termination status) and re-execute them.
- *Directory structure.* A shell may implement its own program access primitives and consult a program defining a 'directory structure' when processing them. Arbitrary directory structures can be defined in this way.
- *Query-the-user.* A shell can prompt the user for definitions for undefined procedures, cache the answers and interpret these answers when attempting to solve subsequent calls to the same procedures. It can also add new definitions to programs upon success-

ful termination of the transaction that required them. Such a query-the-user facility is useful in expert systems and other interactive programs in which the user must contribute to the solution of a problem [Sergot, 1982]. It can also facilitate top-down program development: the user is asked for definitions for undefined procedures as they are encountered in a partially completed program.

This range of possibilities emphasizes the advantages of a high-level user language with FP+'s characteristics.

8.5 AN IMPLEMENTATION SCHEME

An implementation of a programming environment that supports a user language such as FP+ must resolve four problems:

1. *Efficient representation of state*. Transactions can generate many states in the course of evaluation; these must be represented in a space- and time-efficient manner.
2. *Persistence*. Requests to access existing state components and construct new state components must be translated into load and save commands to secondary storage.
3. *Atomic updates*. The state transition defined by a transaction must occur as an atomic action: that is, all or nothing.
4. *Serializability*. Concurrently executing, nested transactions must be serializable. This requires concurrency control mechanisms in an implementation.

An abstract implementation scheme that addresses these problems is presented. This scheme models both linguistic entities and physical resources as processes. These processes encapsulate local data and communicate to implement system features. Figure 8.2 illustrates the type of process network employed by the scheme.

A *transaction manager* (TM) encapsulates the states constructed by a single transaction and processes requests to perform operations on these states. (These requests correspond to calls to state primitives.) A *component manager* (CM) encapsulates a single state component and processes read and write requests generated by transaction managers. As will be seen, component managers implement concurrency control algorithms. The size of component encapsulated in a manager is hence determined by a

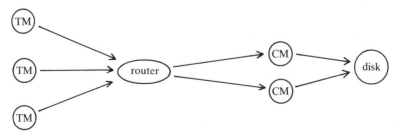

Figure 8.2 Abstract process model.

tradeoff between the run-time cost of a fine grained implementation and the convenience of concurrent accesses to small components. The *router* is a process (or, in a multi-processor system, a network of processes) responsible for communicating requests from transaction managers to component managers. A *disk manager* (disk) encapsulates a secondary storage device. It processes requests such as read_term and write_term generated by component managers.

8.5.1 Efficient representation of state

Calls to state primitives in application programs are translated into messages to the manager of the transaction in which the program is executing. This manager processes the requests with respect to a local data structure termed a *virtual copy*. A virtual copy contains representations of all states constructed by a transaction. The name of this data structure derives from the fact that it represents states in terms of how they differ from the current state. The current state is characterized solely by a lack of modification. The state representations provided to programs (in FP+, following calls to current, new_definition, etc.) are in fact just indices, which the transaction manager uses to access its own representation of these states, recorded in the virtual copy.

To process a call to a *state access* primitive (for example, definition(S,P,N,D)), the transaction manager must locate the state with the supplied index (S) in the virtual copy. Then, that state is searched to determine whether it contains a new definition for the required component. (In the example, the component required is the definition of procedure N in program P.) If it does, the new definition is used; if not, the definition of the component is determined by making a request to the manager of the state component in question. Efficient data structures minimize the time required to locate a definition in the virtual copy.

A call to a *state generation* primitive (for example, new_definition(S,P,D,S1)) is processed by adding a representation of the newly created state to the virtual copy. The representation of a new state can be simply the representation of the state from which it was derived (state S) plus the modification used to generate it ({P,D}). The index of the new state in the virtual copy data structure is returned as S1; the application program can then use S1 to refer to that state in subsequent primitive calls.

The transaction manager also maintains the name of any next state nominated by the transaction. Upon successful termination of the transaction the transaction manager examines the virtual copy to determine whether a next state has been nominated. If so, a commitment procedure is invoked to attempt any updates that it implies.

8.5.2 Persistence

Recall that persistence implies that programs that access and modify state components can do so without concern for their location or longevity. Persistence is supported by component managers. A component manager processes both read and write requests from transaction managers. Transaction managers generate read requests following calls to state access primitives. They generate write requests when a transaction terminates successfully, having nominated a next state which implies modifications to state components.

A component manager's principal task is to correctly service requests from transactions while maintaining a consistent representation of its components on stable storage. It achieves this by generating messages to disk managers to store and retrieve data as required. It may also cache frequently accessed state components in memory to reduce disk traffic.

8.5.3 Atomic update

In the absence of contention, the new state computed by a transaction is used to replace the current state upon successful termination. This update must be performed as an atomic action, 'all or nothing'. The implementation of atomic update involves both transaction managers and component managers. The transaction manager coordinates updates to ensure that they are applied atomically. Component managers perform the actual updates.

Transaction managers use a form of *two-stage commit* [Lampson and Sturgis, 1976] to commit updates. In the first stage of this algorithm, a transaction manager makes a prewrite request to each component manager affected by an update. This requests the component manager to validate its update. Any component manager may refuse its update at this stage; this does not matter, as no state component has been modified. If all affected component managers accept their updates, then write requests are issued to request component managers to actually apply the updates.

8.5.4 Serializability

Concurrently executing transactions must be serializable, so that each transaction is evaluated with respect to an unchanging state. The implementation of serializability is linked with the implementation of atomic update. Recall that a transaction manager caches representations of new states constructed by its transaction. When the transaction terminates, the transaction manager uses a two-stage commit algorithm to coordinate the application of updates to affected state components. Component managers apply a *concurrency control algorithm* at this point to verify that serializability is not violated.

Concurrency control has been extensively studied by the distributed database community. The reader is referred to Bernstein and Goodman [1981] and Papadimitriou [1986] for a detailed discussion of this topic and for a precise definition of serializability and the concurrency control problem. Informally, concurrency control seeks to avoid or detect *conflict*. Transactions in database systems (and in systems such as the programming environments considered here) perform a series of read and write operations to state components. A set of concurrent transactions conflict if the sequence of operations that they perform are such that the same final result cannot be achieved by executing the transactions in some sequential order.

For example, consider the following four (independent) sequences of operations. Each such *history* represents the operations that two transactions T1 and T2 were observed to perform on state components X and Y. read(T,X) signifies a read operation by transaction T on term X and write(T,X) signifies the corresponding write operation:

$H1 = \{$ read(T1,X), write(T2,X), read(T1,X) $\}$

$H2 = \{$ write(T1,X), write(T2,Y), write(T2,X), write(T1,Y) $\}$

$H3 = \{$ read(T1,X), write(T2,X), read(T1,Y) $\}$

$H4 = \{$ write(T1,X), write(T1,Y), write(T2,X), write(T2,Y) $\}$

Conflict occurs in both histories H1 and H2, as in neither case can the execution of T1's operations followed by T2's, nor the reverse, give the same final result. Conflict does not occur in either history H3 or history H4, as in each case the same final result can be achieved by executing first transaction T1 and then T2.

Concurrency control mechanisms either *avoid* conflict by sequencing transactions when necessary, or permit transactions to execute concurrently and seek to *detect* conflict at run-time. As conflict avoidance requires prior knowledge of the behavior of transactions, conflict detection is more commonly used.

Various conflict detection algorithms have been proposed. Those based on *locks* and *timestamps* seek to detect conflict as early as possible by requiring that transactions announce their intention to modify items. *Optimistic* approaches, on the other hand, assume that conflict is rare and therefore only check for conflict immediately prior to committing a transaction [Badal, 1979]. (Commitment is the process which makes updates computed by a transaction permanent and accessible to other transactions.) All approaches resolve conflict by aborting transactions. As long as commitment of updates computed by a transaction is performed as an atomic action, an aborted transaction can be re-executed.

An optimistic conflict detection algorithm checks for conflict immediately prior to commitment of a transaction T. It tests whether, if T is committed, the set of all committed transactions would still be serializable. In general, this requires it to keep a record of all preceding reads and writes. The overhead of maintaining this information militates against optimistic approaches. For example, assume that a transaction T2 is allowed to commit and that T2 writes a term X which an active transaction T1 has previously read. The operation write(T2,X) must be recorded, as if T1 were subsequently to commit, having read term X again, serializability would be violated: this is the conflicting history H1 presented previously.

Nevertheless, an optimistic conflict detection algorithm is used in the implementation scheme presented here. Conflict detection rather than conflict avoidance is used because it is not generally possible to know what programs a transaction will access without executing it. An optimistic algorithm is used because it cannot be known whether a next state computed by a transaction is to be committed until the transaction terminates. There is thus little point in attempting to detect conflict early. The overhead associated with optimistic approaches is avoided by using what may be termed a *non-pre-emptive* conflict resolution algorithm: this aborts a committing transaction if subsequent action of any active transaction *could* lead to conflict. (An active transaction is one that has not yet terminated.) The algorithm aborts committing transactions that would write state components other active transactions have previously read. In the example in the previous paragraph, T2 would be aborted when it attempted to commit. This algorithm only requires information on reads by active transactions, rather than reads and writes by all transactions. This is a significant saving. On the other hand, the algorithm tends to abort more transactions than other concurrency control algorithms. As these transactions may never reread these components, this abortion may be unnecessary.

In database systems, concurrency control may be applied at various levels of granularity. There is a tradeoff between the run-time cost of recording accesses to components and the convenience of concurrent updates to components. In the concrete implementation described in the next section, a fairly large grain size is adopted: read and write operations are defined to occur on programs rather than particular procedures or attributes. The overhead associated with procedure-level concurrency control was deemed excessive.

> A transaction is therefore allowed to commit if and only if the next state it has computed does not modify programs which any other active transaction has accessed using a state access, program, or transaction primitive.

Note that as update is viewed here as the generation of a new state that differs from a previous state in some specified way, the possibility of conflict within a transaction is precluded. Any next state computed by a transaction can only specify a single new definition for any item.

8.6 A CONCRETE IMPLEMENTATION

A realization of the abstract implementation scheme described in the previous section is presented. This is Parlog Programming System (PPS) [Foster, 1986], a programming environment that supports FP+ as a user language. PPS is constructed as a *user-level* program using the kernel facilities and nucleus services described in previous chapters. PPS is effectively a more sophisticated version of the simple shell presented in Section 7.5.3. Like that shell, it uses system calls to access services and create tasks. However, instead of two simple processes it consists of a network of complex processes. These provide run-time support for FP+'s extensions to FP.

The abstract implementation scheme introduces complex concepts such as two-stage commit and concurrency control but does not say how these are implemented. Implementation of these concepts is illustrated here with selected code fragments. Note that programs presented in this section are FP, not FP+, programs. FP is used here as an implementation language for PPS; FP+ is the user language supported by PPS.

In an FP implementation of PPS, the abstract processes introduced in the previous section are implemented as processes as illustrated in Figure 8.3. Shared variables used to implement stream communication between these processes are represented by arrows in the figure. Disk managers provide an interface to a disk service (DISK) in the nucleus.

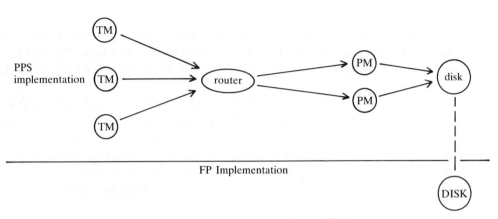

Figure 8.3 FP implementation of PPS.

Recall that the state provided to programmers in PPS consists of a number of programs. Each such program is managed by a single component manager, termed a program manager (PM).

8.6.1 Bootstrap

The process network illustrated in Figure 8.3 must first be created. The procedure boot/2 implements the first stage in this process. This procedure creates three processes: transaction_init, programs_init, and disk_manager, which initiate the first transaction, create the program managers and implement a single disk manager respectively. The bootstrap process also makes a **send/2** system call to request the nucleus to establish a circuit to the disk service.

```
boot(P,N) ←
        transaction_init(Term, M, N, Rs),            % Initial transaction.
        programs_init([ {P,read(code(M),Term)} |Rs], Ts),   % Spawn program managers.
        disk_manager(Ts, Ds),                        % Create disk manager.
        send(disk, circuit(Ds)).                     % Establish circuit to disk.
```

The arguments to the boot/2 procedure represent the process to be executed by the initial transaction (N) and the name of the program that is to be used to evaluate this process (P). The other variables shared by the three new processes (Rs, Ds, Ts, and Term) are subsequently used for interprocess communication. Rs is used to communicate requests from the initial transaction manager to program managers, Ds to communicate requests from program managers to the disk manager, Ts to communicate requests from the disk manager to the disk service, and Term to signal termination of a transaction.

The process transaction_init will create an initial transaction and a manager for this transaction. First however the object code this transaction is to execute (M) must be retrieved from disk. This is achieved by placing a request {P, read(code(M),term)} on the stream consumed by the programs_init process. This request will subsequently be passed to the manager of the program named P, which will in turn generate requests to the disk manager to load the program's module. The variable M will eventually be bound to the object code module.

The following program specifies the programs_init process, which creates one program manager per program in the file system state. The procedure programs_init/2 asks the disk manager for a list of programs located in the initial state (using a request programs(Ns)), spawns a router, and reduces to programs_init/3. This latter procedure recursively spawns a program manager for each program named in the list of programs Ns retrieved from disk. It also constructs a routing table Ps. This is a list of {ProgramName,RequestStream} pairs to be used by the router.

```
programs_init(Rs, Ds) ←            % Create program managers.
    Ds = [programs(Ns) |Ds1],      %     Request list of programs from disk.
    router(Rs, Ps),                %     Spawn router.
    programs_init(Ds1, Ns, Ps).    %     Recursively spawn program managers.

programs_init(Ds, [N |Ns], Ps) ←   % Spawn program managers and create list
    Ps = [{N, P} |Ps1],            %       of {Name,Stream} pairs for router.
    program(P, N, Ds1),            %     Spawn program manager.
    merge(Ds1, Ds2, Ds),           %     Multiplex disk manager requests.
    programs_init(Ds2, Ns, Ps1).   %     Recurse: spawn remainder
programs_init(Ds, [ ], Ps) ← Ps = [ ].  % Done: terminate routing table.
```

8.6.2 Transaction manager

Creating a transaction involves initiating execution of a given process as a separate task and creating a transaction manager to monitor its execution. The procedure trans-action_init/4 uses the **task/4** system call to create a new task. The system call associates a status steam with the task; this stream is subsequently used by the nucleus to signal errors, calls to FP+ primitives, and/or termination. A transaction manager, t_man, monitors the new task's status stream and detects these messages. The t_man process takes as arguments the task's status stream R, its Term variable, and the request stream to the router Rs.

```
transaction_init(Term,M, N, Rs) ←  % Create new transaction.
    task(M, N, R,_),               %     Initiate transaction as a task.
    t_man(R, Term, Rs).            %     Create manager to monitor process.
```

Figure 8.4 illustrates the relationship between a transaction and its manager. A simple manager is presented here. The first clause initializes the transaction's virtual copy to be empty (C1). Each of the three following clauses deals with a different transaction status.

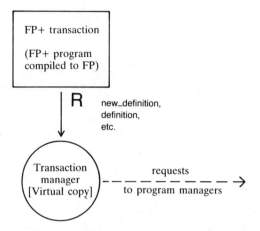

Figure 8.4 An FP+ transaction and its manager.

The first handles calls to FP+ primitives, assumed to be represented by exceptions of type user. A procedure system_call/5 is used to process each such call (C2). This takes as arguments the Term variable, the virtual copy before and after the call (Vc, Vc1), the FP+ call Req and a request stream to the router Rs1. It accesses the virtual copy and communicates with program managers to retrieve state components if required. It may also recursively spawn another transaction manager, following a call to the FP+ **transaction** primitive. The second t_man/4 clause ignores other exceptions, and the third accesses the virtual copy to determine any next state, and calls the procedure t_commit/3 to handle successful termination (C4). This procedure is presented in the section dealing with atomic update.

```
t_man(R, Term, Rs) ← t_man(R, Term, [ ], Rs).                              (C1)
t_man([exception(user,Req,Cont) |R], Term, Vc, Rs) ←   % An FP+ primitive call. (C2)
      system_call(Term, Vc, Req, Rs1, Vc1),             %     Process system call.
      Cont = true,                                      %     No error handling here.
      merge(Rs1, Rs2, Rs),                              %     Multiplex requests.
      t_man(R, Term, Vc1, Rs2).                         %     Recurse.
t_man([exception(Type,_,_) |R], Term, Vc, Rs) ←        % Other exception:         (C3)
      Type =\= user :                                   %     ignore.
      t_man(R, Term, Vc, Rs).                           %     Recurse.
t_man(succeeded, Term, Vc, Rs) ←                        % Termination.            (C4)
      next_state(Vc, Next),                             %     Look for next state.
      t_commit(Term, Next, Rs).                         %     Attempt commit.
```

Compare this program with the task supervisor presented as Program 7.9. The two programs are very similar. Both monitor a task and interpret certain exceptions as requests for services. However, they operate at different levels: the status stream received by a transaction manager has already been filtered by a task supervisor in the nucleus to remove any system calls. The transaction manager then removes exceptions representing calls to FP+ primitives. In principle, it should forward other exceptions on a filtered status stream for consumption by the FP+ program that initiated the task using the **transaction** primitive. For simplicity, the transaction manager presented here does not do this.

8.6.3 Program manager

Recall that a program manager processes requests to read and write program components (received on its first argument, the stream Rs), and that it achieves this by generating requests to disk to load and store terms (using its third argument, the stream Ds). A simple program manager is presented here. This first initializes itself by obtaining the disk address of its program's contents. (In the PPS implementation, it also initializes a cache used to retain terms read from disk. For simplicity, this cache is not presented here.)

```
program(Rs, N, Ds) ←            % Initialize program manager.
    Ds = [program(N, A) |Ds1],   %    Retrieve program address A.
    p_man(Rs, A, Ds1, [ ]).      %    Initiate program manager.
```

The following two clauses process read and update requests and implement the program manager proper. A read request has the form read(Req,Term) and is processed by a procedure read_request/3. This generates requests to disk managers to retrieve program components. Update requests are processed by a procedure p_commit/4. This is presented in the next section.

```
p_man([read(Req,Term) |Rs], A, Ds, Ts) ←        % Read request received.
    read_request(Req, A, Ds1),                    %    Process read request.
    merge(Ds1, Ds2, Ds),                          %    Multiplex requests to disk.
    p_man(Rs, A, Ds2, [Term |Ts]).               %    Recurse.
p_man([update(Us,Com,Term,Ack) |Rs],A, Ds,Ts)←  % Update request received.
    p_commit(Ts, Ts1, Ds1,                        %    Attempt commit.
        update(Us,Com,Term,Ack)),
    merge(Ds1, Ds2, Ds),                          %    Multiplex requests to disk.
    p_man(Rs, A, Ds2, Ts1).                       %    Recurse.
```

8.6.4 Two-stage commit

The commitment of a transaction's updates involves the cooperation of the transaction's manager and the managers of the programs affected by the update. The transaction manager uses two-stage commit to synchronize updates performed by program managers.

so that update of all programs occurs as an atomic action. An FP implementation of two-stage commit consists of commitment procedures for both the transaction and program managers. These are presented here.

A transaction manager invokes its commitment procedure, t_commit/3 (C1–C6 below), when its transaction terminates successfully having nominated a valid next state. The arguments to this procedure are the transaction's termination variable T, the next state as represented in the virtual copy (State) and a stream to the name server (Rs). The procedure determines what updates are required and generates update messages to request the program managers concerned to perform the updates. These have the form {ProgName,UpdateReq}. The router delivers the update requests to the named program. The procedure updates(State,Ps) is used to determine the list Ps of {Program,Updates} pairs implied by a state State.

```
t_commit(T, State, Rs) ←          % Commit updates recorded in State.    (C1)
    updates(State, Ps),           %     Compute updates required.
    phase1(Ps,Commit,T,Acks,Rs),  %     Phase 1 of 2-stage commit.
    phase2(Commit, Acks, T).      %     Phase 2 of 2-stage commit.


phase1([{P, Us} |Ps], Commit,     % Request programs to apply updates.    (C2)
        T,A,R) ←
    A = [Ack |Acks],              %     Build list of ack variables.
    R = [{P, update(Us, Commit,   %     Generate request.
        T,Ack)} |R1],
    phase1(Ps, Commit, T, Acks, R1).%   Recurse: request other programs.
phase1([ ],_,_,A,R,) ← A = [ ], R = [ ].   %                              (C3)


phase2(Commit, [true |Acks], T) ← % Wait for result.                      (C4)
    phase2(Commit, Acks, T).
phase2(Commit, [false |_], T) ←   % Error.                                (C5)
    Commit = false, T = commit_error.
phase2(Commit, [ ], T) ←          % Update can proceed.                   (C6)
    Commit = true, T = succeeded.
```

A program manager invokes its commitment procedure, p_commit/4 (C7–C16), when it receives an update request. This procedure's arguments are a list of termination variables, before and after commitment (Ts, Ts1, used for concurrency control; see the next section), a request stream to a disk manager Ds, and the update request generated by the transaction manager.

```
p_commit(Ts, Ts1, Ds,             % Update request.                      (C7)
        update(Us, Commit, T, Ack)) ←
    valid_updates(Us, R1),        %     Are updates valid?
    inactive(T, Ts, R2),          %     Concurrency control?
```

```
p_commit2(Ts, Ts1, Ds, Us, Commit,     %      Apply updates if ok.
    Ack, R1, R2).


p_commit2(_, Ts1, Ds, Us, Commit, Ack,  % Ok to apply updates.              (C8)
    valid, inactive) ←
    Ack = true, Ts1 = [ ],              %      Signal that updates ok.
    program2(Ds, Us, Commit).           %      Wait for write.
p_commit2(Ts, Ts1, Ds,_,_,Ack, invalid,_) ←  % Updates invalid.             (C9)
    Ack = false, Ts1 = Ts, Ds = [ ].    %      Signal cannot apply updates.
p_commit2(Ts, Ts1, Ds,_,_,Ack,_, active) ←   % Transactions active.        (C10)
    Ack = false, Ts1 = Ts, Ds = [ ].    %      Signal cannot apply updates.


program2 (Ds,Us,true) ←                 % Wait for 'commit' signal:        (C11)
    perform_updates(Us, Ds).            %      Commit=true: proceed.
program2 (Ds,Us,false) ← Ds = [ ].      % Commit=false: abandon.           (C12)


inactive(T,[T1 |Ts],R) ← data(T1):     % Terminated if bound.             (C13)
    inactive(T,Ts,R).
inactive(T,[T1 |_],R) ← var(T1), T =\= T1 :  % Not terminated if variable. (C14)
    R = active.
inactive(T,[T1 |Ts],R) ← T == T1:      % Ignore committing task.          (C15)
    inactive(T,Ts,R).
inactive(T,[ ],R) ← R = inactive.      % All terminated                   (C16)
```

Figure 8.5 illustrates how a transaction manager (TM) and the managers of programs (PM) affected by commitment of a next state communicate to implement two-stage commit. A transaction has terminated and nominated a next state that involves updates to three programs. The transaction manager then executes the procedure t_commit/3. In

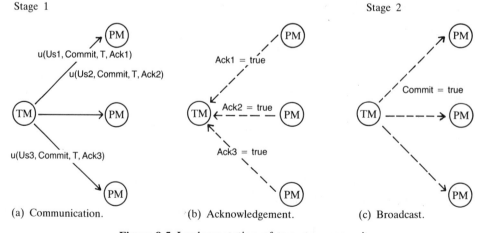

Figure 8.5 Implementation of two-stage commit.

Figure 8.5(a) the transaction manager communicates the updates Us1, Us2 and Us3 to the program managers, along with a Commit variable, unique acknowledgement variables Ack1, Ack2 and Ack3 and the transaction's termination variable T (C2, C3). This is the prewrite phase of the two-stage commit algorithm.

Each program manager receiving an update message calls p_commit, which validates the updates and (as described in the next section) uses inactive/2 to check that concurrency control constraints are satisfied (C7). It either allows (C8) or disallows (C9, C10) the update, and binds its acknowledgement variable to true or false respectively.

In Figure 8.5(b) all program managers allow their updates and bind their acknowledgement variables to true. In (c) the transaction manager, which has been waiting for the acknowledgement variables to be bound (C4–C6), detects that all have been bound to true, and binds the variable Commit (included in the initial update messages to each program manager) to true to signal that the update can proceed (C6). This informs the program managers that they can proceed to update the programs (C11). This is the write phase of the two-stage commit algorithm.

If, on the other hand, any of the acknowledgement variables is bound to false, the transaction manager binds Commit to false (C4). The program managers then discard the updates and no updates occur (C12). In each case, the transaction manager binds the transaction's termination variable to indicate the result of the transaction: succeeded (C6) or commit_error (C5).

The implementation of two-stage commit presented in this section ignores the possibility of system failure during commitment. If stable storage can be assumed, extension to incorporate a recovery mechanism that ensures that commitment is also atomic in the face of hardware failure [Bernstein *et al.*, 1983] is straightforward.

8.6.5 Concurrency control

As noted previously, concurrency control is applied at the level of programs in the PPS implementation. Each program manager keeps a record of all transactions that have accessed its components. Then, when it receives an update request, it checks whether any of these transactions are still active (that is, have not terminated). If so, the update is disallowed.

The PPS implementation uses logical variables to both identify transactions and signal their termination, and hence avoids a need for explicit name servers and termination messages. This is achieved as follows. A unique *termination variable* is associated with each transaction; the global address space maintained by kernel facilities permits these variables to serve as unique identifiers, even in a multiprocessor. A transaction manager includes this variable in each message that it generates. In addition, it guarantees to bind the variable when its transaction terminates. Any process that possesses a reference to a termination variable is hence able to detect termination of the associated transaction by checking whether it has a value.

Program managers keep a record of all transactions that have accessed their components by retaining references to termination variables. They can then use the procedure inactive/2 above to apply the concurrency control constraint. This procedure verifies that a list of termination variables are either instantiated, indicating termination (C13), or identical to the termination variable of the committing transaction (C15). This indicates that all other transactions that have accessed a program have terminated. The primitive var is used to determine whether a particular variable is currently instantiated.

8.6.6 Deadlock and starvation

For simplicity, the preceding presentation ignores the problem of deadlock. Upon receiving an update request from a transaction manager, a program manager invokes p_commit/4 to execute the two-stage commit and concurrency control algorithms. The program manager processes no further messages until p_commit/4 terminates. However, if two transactions that update the same programs attempt to commit at about the same time, the situation can arise where one of each transaction's update requests is delayed, as illustrated in Figure 8.6. update requests have been generated by two transactions, T1 and T2, to programs A and B. Program A receives T2's update message; program B receives T1's. The other update messages remain unreceived, and will remain unreceived, as neither program will accept further messages until update is completed or aborted. Yet neither transaction manager can complete or abort its update until it has received a response to both its messages. This is deadlock.

The solution to this problem employs a programming technique also used in the implementation of the keyboard service in Chapter 7. A program manager attempting to commit an update must, while waiting for the transaction manager to indicate whether it should proceed, concurrently scan ahead on its input stream and abort any pending update requests encountered by binding their acknowledgement variable to false.

The concurrency control algorithm used in PPS may abort successfully terminating transactions if contention is detected. An aborted transaction can always be re-executed. However, other concurrent transactions can conspire to prevent a transaction that is executed repeatedly from ever committing. This is starvation. Starvation has not yet proved to be a problem in PPS. If required, techniques from distributed databases can be applied to ensure that all successfully terminating transactions eventually succeed in committing [Bernstein and Goodman, 1981].

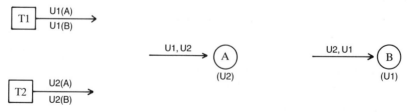

Figure 8.6 Deadlock in the implementation of two-stage commit.

8.7 IMPLEMENTATION NOTES

The program fragments presented in the previous section are simplified components of a PPS implementation. This currently runs on a workstation using nucleus services similar to those described in the previous chapter. Both PPS and the nucleus are executed by an emulator that provides the kernel facilities described in Chapter 4. Despite the overhead inherent in emulating rather than directly executing kernel mechanisms, the FP+ language supported by PPS has been successfully used to develop several applications, including a program analysis package, an execution tracer, a browser system, and a variety of shells and program development tools. The program analyzer is somewhat slow, but the other programs execute at acceptable speeds. This performance has been achieved by optimizing the PPS implementation to cache program components retrieved from disk. Caching is performed in both transaction and program managers, and is most effective in programs such as the execution tracer which access the same state components repeatedly. Program analysis does not benefit from caching; this accounts for its poor performance.

Experience with PPS prompts the following conclusions:

- Providing implicit access to file system state via persistent data significantly reduces the size and complexity of many applications. (This observation has also been made by Atkinson *et al.* [1983], pioneers in persistent programming.)
- The ability to compose state changing programs is of great benefit. In particular, it encourages reuse of program components. Indeed, re-use has been found to be the norm when developing tools in PPS.
- The overhead associated with persistent data and atomic transactions is not important in many applications, particularly at a shell programming level. When performance is critical, a mechanism for bypassing these facilities is required.

8.8 SUMMARY

This chapter has presented a novel approach to programming environment design that supports a relational treatment of program update in a concurrent environment. Statements in a high-level user language define and can be used to compute relations over file system states. File system update is defined to occur as an atomic transition if and only if a program successfully computes a new state. Programs that specify updates can be composed and executed concurrently. The user language in a programming environment with these characteristics, PPS, has been used to illustrate these concepts.

The approach requires that programming environments support separation of computation and update, program access to state, persistence, incremental description of new states and atomic, serializable transactions. An abstract implementation scheme that provides an integrated treatment of these issues has been presented. This scheme models both linguistic entities such as transactions and state components, and physical resources such as secondary storage, as concurrent, communicating processes. The functionality required in the principal process types has been described in detail. Transaction managers implement program access to state and component managers implement persistence. Both cooperate to implement atomic update and serializability.

This implementation scheme has been applied in a uniprocessor implementation of PPS. This system is implemented as a user-level program using services similar to those described in the previous chapter. Its user language has been used to build a variety of programming tools. It is suggested that this exercise confirms the utility of kernel facilities in that they are shown to be capable of supporting a sophisticated and usable programming system.

9

OTHER ISSUES

This chapter addresses OS design issues not dealt with in the main body of the book. It shows how the techniques presented in previous chapters can be applied on *multi-processors*. It also describes mechanisms intended to support more sophisticated *processor scheduling* algorithms. This material has not been implemented or evaluated experimentally; it is presented as potentially useful ideas rather than proven techniques.

9.1 MULTIPROCESSOR OPERATING SYSTEMS

The kernel facilities described in previous chapters support a global address space. A uniprocessor OS developed using these facilities can hence be ported to a multiprocessor without modification. OS processes are located on different processors; variables shared by these processes allow them to communicate as if they were located on a single processor (albeit more slowly). However, if an OS is to exploit the power of a particular parallel computer, issues such as bottlenecks, communication overheads, the location of services, bootstrapping, and global scheduling must be considered. A multiprocessor version of the simple OS described in Chapter 7 is used to illustrate a discussion of these issues.

Figure 9.1 represents four nodes, labelled n1–n4, of a multiprocessor OS nucleus. This OS is implemented by a program quite similar to Program 7.8. There are four principal differences:

1. Services are distributed over the different processors.
2. The name server is duplicated at each processor.
3. Identical *mapping servers* (named node1, node2, node3, node4, etc.) are located one per processor.
4. There is a new *distributor service* (dist).

As before, a single user-level task is created initially. The task supervisor that controls

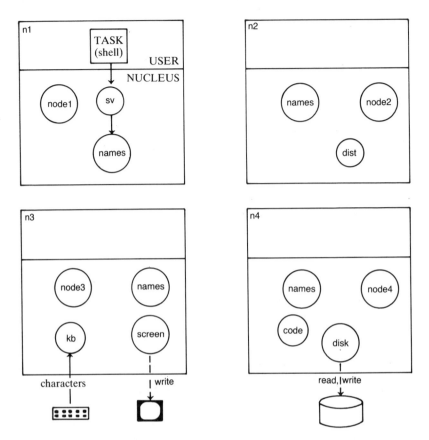

Figure 9.1 Multiprocessor operating system.

this initial task has stream connections to a local name server. Each name server can access every service. For simplicity, stream connections between name servers and services, the filter processes that validate requests and the merge processes that multiplex request streams (all illustrated in Figure 7.8) are not shown here.

9.1.1 Replicating and distributing services

A uniprocessor OS is unlikely to perform well if ported unmodified to a multiprocessor. Two potential sources of inefficiency are bottlenecks, due to too frequent accesses to centralized structures, and excessive interprocessor communication. These problems can be avoided by *distributing* and/or *replicating* services. For example, a centralized name server is likely to constitute a bottleneck and furthermore will result in many unnecessary interprocessor communications. The OS illustrated in Figure 9.1 hence replicates the name server at each processor. This permits services located on the same processor as a task to be accessed directly. It may be impractical in a large multiprocessor to maintain a consistent list of services on every processor. An alternative is to provide a hierarchical network of name servers. A request for a particular service is then communicated through this network until the named service is found.

The code service (code) is a candidate for distribution. Recall that this provides a simple file system, permitting user-level tasks to read and write named code modules. If this service is centralized, potentially large terms must be copied between processors each time a program is executed. A solution to this problem is to provide a code cache at each processor. This caches modules retrieved from the code service, hence distributing code service functionality. However, code caches must be kept consistent in the face of updates.

9.1.2 Locating physical services

Recall that physical services invoke kernel mechanisms to access or modify the state of physical devices. It may be assumed that these primitive operations access hardware directly. Physical services must therefore be positioned on the processors to which the devices they control are connected. This is illustrated in Figure 9.1: the screen and disk services are located on the processors on which the terminal and disk drive are located.

9.1.3 Bootstrapping and process mapping

In order to bootstrap the OS illustrated in Figure 9.1, it must be possible to create processes on particular processors. This can easily be achieved if an initialization procedure creates a single mapping server process on each processor plus a central bootstrap process, provided with streams to the mapping servers. In Figure 9.1, mapping servers node1, node2, node3, and node4 plus a further bootstrap process (not shown) are assumed to be created at initialization.

A *configuration file* associated with a system as a whole or with individual processors can be used to specify the initial process network. This file is read by a bootstrap program, which creates the network using the mapping servers. For example, the following configuration statement specifies a part of the nucleus represented by Figure 9.1. Each *processor* : *process* pair specifies the location of a single process; shared variables define communication channels:

```
n1:sv(Ns), n1:names(Ns,[{kb,Kb},{dist,Dist}]), n1:mserver(Ms1),
n2:dist(Dist,[{n1,Ms1},{n2, Ms2}]), n2:mserver(Ms2),
n3:kb(Kb)
```

9.1.4 Global scheduling

The global scheduling problem is commonly stated to be that of computing a one-to-one mapping of tasks to processors [Wang and Morris, 1985]. This assumes that tasks cannot exploit internal parallelism to execute faster in a multiprocessor. If tasks are composed of many lightweight processes, a many-to-one mapping of processors to tasks may be more natural, particularly on massively parallel machines. This introduces a further dimension to the scheduling problem. It may be convenient to allocate disjoint sets of processors to tasks. The priority of a task can then be expressed in terms of how many processors it is allocated. However, few programs can exploit an unlimited number of processors. In addition, while some programs can execute well on a smaller than expected number of processors, others require a particular number to run effectively. A programmer may hence wish to specify preferences about the number of processors a task requires. A multiprocessor OS must allocate processors subject to task priorities, programmer preferences and the number of processors available.

Processor allocation can be handled by a distributor service. This service is represented in Figure 9.1 as a single process which handles requests to create multiprocessor tasks. A request specifies a program to be executed and may indicate what resources are required. The distributor keeps track of free processors and can hence allocate them to new tasks. This use of a distributor process has already been illustrated in Section 4.7. In a large multiprocessor, the use of a centralized distributor is likely to be a bottleneck. Its functionality can readily be distributed by making subdistributors responsible for allocating some portion of all processors. One approach to distribution is to arrange subdistributors in a hierarchy: if a request for processors cannot be satisfied locally, it is forwarded up the tree [Wittie and van Tilborg, 1980].

New system calls are required to provide application programs with the ability to create multiprocessor tasks. For example, a call dtask(M,Ps,S,C) can request multiprocessor execution of a set of processes Ps. This system call is implemented in the same way as the uniprocessor system call task/4 (Section 7.5.2) except that the new task is created by sending a message to the distributor rather than by direct use of kernel task management facilities.

9.2 GLOBAL SCHEDULING WITHIN A TASK

Shapiro [1984b] and Hudak [1986] have proposed dynamic processor scheduling schemes supported by programmer-supplied process mapping annotations. These annotations permit programmers to specify that particular processes are to be mapped to particular processors when executed. Taylor *et al.* [1987a] show that programs with mapping annotations can be preprocessed into programs without such annotations. The derived programs implement process mapping using interprocess communication.

These approaches can work well when a programmer has a good understanding of an algorithm's structure and behavior or when communication costs are low. In other circumstances, studies suggest that *load balancing* schemes, which redistribute processes in response to changing load, can give better performance [Sato *et al.*, 1987b]. This is because load balancing schemes only migrate processes when load becomes unbalanced. In consequence, they tend to migrate fewer processes, which in turn tends to reduce interprocessor communication. This improves performance if communication is expensive.

Sato *et al.* incorporate load-balancing mechanisms in the kernel of a parallel logic programming system. Unfortunately, this complicates kernel implementation. An alternative approach to the implementation of load-balancing algorithms is proposed here. This does not require additional kernel mechanisms but instead exploits existing task management facilities. In particular, it uses the notion of task quiescence to detect when a processor is idle (and hence requires processes from other processors), and implements process mapping using interprocess communication.

Dynamic scheduling can be implemented by a network of manager processes, one per processor (Section 4.7.2). A manager has a single input stream and one or more output streams. Each manager encapsulates a number of application processes and forwards process mapping requests (*mappings*) generated by these processes on output streams to other managers. A manager creates a process for each mapping that it receives on its input stream.

Load balancing can be implemented by a similar network of *load balancing managers*. Each load balancing manager encapsulates a process mapping manager in a task and filters its input and output streams. It does not forward mappings generated by the process mapping manager, but instead retains them within a process list. It only distributes these mappings when requested by other load balancing managers. This retention

---

```
lbmanager(M, In, Out) ←                              % Load balancing manager.   (C1)
    call(M, manager(To, Fr), S, C),                  %     Initiate process manager.
    lbmanager(In, To, S, Fr, Out, [ ]).              %     Monitor its execution.

lbmanager(In, To, S, [P |Fr], Out, Ps) ←             % Mapping request.           (C2)
    lbmanager(In, To, S, Fr, Out, [P |Ps]).          %     Add to process list.
lbmanager(In, To, [quiescent(_) |S], Fr, Out, [P |Ps]) ←   % Task idle.           (C3)
    To = [P |To1],                                   %     Select process.
    lbmanager(In, To1, S, Fr, Out, Ps).
lbmanager(In, To, [quiescent(_) |S], Fr, Out, [ ]) ←  % Idle but empty cache.     (C4)
    wait(W,To1), Out = [W |Out1],
        merge(To1, To2, To),
    lbmanager(In, To2, S, Fr, Out1, [ ]).            %     Request work.
lbmanager([W |In], To, S, Fr, Out, [P |Ps]) ←        % Request for work.          (C5)
    W = P,                                           %     Grant request
    lbmanager(In, To, S, Fr, Out, Ps).
lbmanager([W |In], To, S, Fr, Out, [ ]) ←            % Request for work.          (C6)
    Out = [W |Out1],                                 %     Cache empty: forward
    lbmanager(in, To, S, Fr, Out1, [ ]).
wait(W, Out) ← data(W) : Out = [W].                  % Wait for request           (C7)
```

Program 9.1 Load balancing manager.

of processes permits the manager to return processes represented by cached mappings to its local task if the kernel signals that this is quiescent. A mapping generated by an application process is hence now interpreted as 'this is a candidate for migration' rather than 'this is to be migrated'.

Program 9.1 illustrates the approach. The procedure lbmanager/3 takes a module containing manager code and two streams In and Out as arguments. The streams are presumed to be connected to other lbmanager processes in a circuit. A call to lbmanager/3 initiates execution of a process mapping manager as a separate task and creates a load balancing manager lbmanager/6 (C1). lbmanager/6 arguments are: streams defining a circuit (In and Out), the process mapping manager's input and output streams (To and From), the task's status stream S and an initially empty process list.

The load balancing manager must respond to the following:

1. *Mappings generated by local processes.* These are added to the cache (C2).
2. *Quiescence in the local task.* If the cache is nonempty, a process is added to the task (C3), otherwise, a request is injected into the circuit (C4).
3. *Requests from other managers.* These are granted if the local cache is nonempty (C5) and forwarded otherwise (C6).

A request injected into the circuit consists simply of a variable. A wait process is created (C4) that waits for this request to be granted and then passes it to the task (C7). A manager receiving a request variable on the circuit instantiates it to a mapping, thus migrating the process represented by that mapping, if its process list is not empty (C5); otherwise it forwards it (C6). Requests are thus generated when processors are idle and circulate around the circuit until they are serviced. No requests are generated and no migration occurs when processors are busy. To simplify presentation, Program 9.1 does not deal with status messages other than quiescent(_).

Figure 9.2 illustrates the execution of this program on a two-processor ring. M1 and M2 are load balancing managers monitoring a task. In (a), two process mapping requests – f and g – are generated in M1's task. (The annotation @mg is used here to signify that a

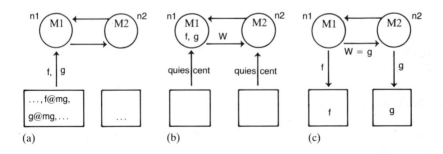

Figure 9.2 Load-balancing. (a) f, g migratable. (b) f, g in process list; M1 and M2 need work. (c) g migrated to M2.

process is a candidate for migration). Manager M1 places these in its process list. In (b), both tasks become idle. M2 generates a message W to request M1 for work and in (c), is given the process g, which it starts executing. Meanwhile, M1 starts executing the process f.

9.3 LOCAL SCHEDULING

The facilities described in Chapter 4 provide programmers with some degree of control over the kernel's local scheduling policies. Programmers associate priorities with tasks; the kernel schedules tasks according to their priority, used a fixed algorithm. An alternative, more flexible approach would permit an OS programmer to provide a scheduler program. This approach is explored here. Kernel facilities that support the approach are presented, and an implementation scheme for these facilities is described.

9.3.1 Kernel facilities

A scheduler can naturally be implemented as a process in a process-oriented OS. This process is effectively part of the nucleus: it executes a high-level program, and uses kernel facilities to schedule tasks for execution. The scheduler process is invoked by the kernel at bootstrap time, and is given a *scheduler event stream* as an argument. Each time a new task is created, a suspended task is resumed, or a task timeslice ends, a message representing the task in question is sent to the scheduler process on this stream. The scheduler maintains the tasks represented by such messages in a scheduling structure. The scheduler process is itself scheduled for execution each time it is sent a message, at which point it selects a task from its scheduling structure and initiates its execution. The scheduler must of course be careful not to lose task records, as a lost task can never be scheduled. A new primitive, RUN, supports the writing of schedulers:

- 'RUN'(TR?, TSlice?, Done ↑): instructs the kernel to execute the task with task record TR for a period TSlice and binds the variable Done to the constant ok when completed.

  A call to the RUN primitive causes the kernel to execute the specified task for the specified timeslice or until the task no longer requires processor resources. In the former case it appends the task record to the scheduler's input stream; in both cases it switches to executing the scheduler. The kernel thus alternates between executing the scheduler and executing other tasks nominated by the scheduler.

9.3.2 A simple scheduler

A simple example is used to illustrate this approach to local scheduling. Assume that an OS is normally initiated by a call to a procedure os_init. To use a programmer-supplied scheduler, it is instead invoked with a call to the procedure init/1:

```
init(Es) ←
    scheduler(Es),                    % Initiate scheduler
    'TASK'(_, _, 'Local', os_init).   % Initiate task to execute OS proper.
```

where Es is the kernel-generated scheduler event stream. The initial task created to execute init/1 creates a new task to execute the rest of the OS, while it itself continues to execute a procedure scheduler/1. This is the programmer-supplied scheduler.

A programmer-supplied scheduler can maintain any convenient scheduling structure. As task records are accessible to the programmer, programs can be written that examine their fields. This makes it possible to verify that tasks have not been aborted and to determine their priority.

Program 9.2 implements a very simple scheduler that maintains a queue of pending tasks which it schedules using a round-robin algorithm. The timeslice allocated to a task is determined by the task's priority, which is assumed to be a nonnegative integer. The procedure scheduler/1 is initially invoked with the scheduler event stream as its

---

```
scheduler(Es) ← scheduler(Es, [ ], ok).        % Initially empty queue.            (C1)

scheduler(Es, Ts, ok) ←                                                             (C2)
    events(Es, Es1, Ts, Ts1),          % Add new tasks to queue.
    sched(Ts1, Ts2, Task, Time),       % Select a task from queue.
    scheduler(Es1, Ts2, Task, Time).   % Schedule task.

scheduler(Es, Ts, Task, Time) ←        % Switch to new task.                        (C3)
    'RUN'(Task, Time, Done), scheduler(Es, Ts, Done).

events(Es, Es1, [Task |Ts], Os) ←      % Find end of queue.                         (C4)
    Os = [Task |Ts1],
    events(Es, Es1, Ts, Ts1).
events([Task |Es], Es1, [ ], Os) ←     % Add new events to queue.                   (C5)
    Os = [Task |Ts1],
    events(Es, Es1, [ ], Ts1).
events(Es, Es1, Ts, Os) ←              % No more pending events.                    (C6)
    var(Es) : Es1 = Es, Os = Ts.

sched([Task | Ts], Ts1, Task1, Time) ← % Select 1st task in queue.                  (C7)
    Ts1 = Ts, Task1 = Task,
    priority(Task, Time).

priority(TR, PR) ← arg(1,TR,PR).       % Select priority from task record.          (C8)
```

Program 9.2 A programmer-supplied scheduler.

argument. scheduler/3 then executes as a recursive process. Each time it is executed, it first adds any new tasks signalled on the scheduler event stream to the tail of its queue (C4–C6). It then selects the first task on this queue (C7) and requests the kernel to execute it (C3). The procedure priority/2 uses a primitive arg to access the first argument of a task record, which is assumed to contain the task's priority (C8). The priority is used as the task's timeslice.

9.3.3 Implementation

Recall that the eFPM abstract machine described in Section 5.4 incorporates a fixed processor scheduling algorithm. An implementation scheme for the kernel facilities just described is presented as a set of modifications to the eFPM. The principal modifications concern the actions to be performed when a task switch occurs. Recall that a task switch occurs when: (1) a task timeslice ends; (2) the current task no longer requires processor resources; or (3) a higher-priority task requires processor resources. In the eFPM, a built-in scheduler is invoked at this time. In the modified eFPM, the scheduler task is made the current task. The third criterion for a task switch becomes any task that was previously inactive requires processor resources.

The architecture of the modified eFPM discards the general registers TF and TB and introduces two new general registers, SCH and SES.

SCH   Scheduler, points to the task record of the scheduler task.
SES   Scheduler Event Stream, points to the uninstantiated tail of the scheduler event stream.

These new registers support task scheduling. The SCH register permits the scheduler to be invoked when a task switch occurs. The SES register permits the kernel to communicate the task records of new and rescheduled tasks to the scheduler.

Figure 9.3 represents the data structures of the eFPM immediately prior to a task switch. Four tasks are represented in this figure. One of these, labelled T3, is the current task; its fields are buffered in the task registers. T2 is quiescent: its active queue is empty. T0 is the scheduler task; its single process (P) is the scheduler. The scheduler possesses a reference to the scheduler event stream, which contains a single task (T1). The scheduler will process this task as soon as the task switch occurs. The task T1 is referenced by a list structure; the tail of this list references the uninstantiated tail of the scheduler event stream, the variable V. This is also referenced by the SES register.

The new scheduler also requires changes to the implementation of the task management primitives introduced in Chapter 4. The TASK, PRIORITY, and CONTINUE primitives all add the task record to which they are applied to the scheduler event stream and cause an immediate task switch. The primitive RUN, which can only be executed by the scheduler, is defined as follows:

■ 'RUN'(TR, TSlice, Done): first copies the contents of the task registers to the scheduler's task record. It then records TSlice in the task register SL, loads the other task registers

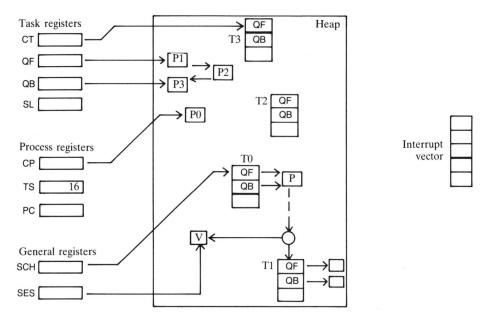

Figure 9.3 Modified eFPM architecture.

from task record TR, sets the current task register CT to TR, selects a process from task TR's active queue and starts to execute it. The variable Done is bound to the constant ok.

9.3.4 Discussion

The alternative approach to task scheduling described here is attractive for two reasons. First, it requires only simple kernel mechanisms, as no scheduler is built in to the kernel. Second, it is flexible: programmers can provide a range of scheduling algorithms. These may be expected to be less efficient than equivalent algorithms implemented entirely in the kernel, as the scheduler must perform some small number of reductions each time a task switch occurs. This inefficiency is not important if a significant number of reductions is performed between task switchs. However, it may become expensive to use tasks to perform very simple operations.

10

CONCLUSION

10.1 SUMMARY

This book has investigated the application of three simple concepts to OS design. Two of these concepts – dynamic lightweight processes and the logical variable – find a natural expression in the parallel logic programming model. The third, tasks, is an extension to this model introduced to support systems programming. The result is a simple yet powerful computational formalism which can be implemented efficiently on a variety of computer architectures. This formalism has been shown to permit simple and effective solutions to OS design problems.

A set of kernel facilities is described in Chapter 4. These facilities provide solutions to problems of concurrency, communication, synchronization, shared resources, nondeterminism, protection, and task management. Implementation techniques for these facilities are described in Chapter 5. These support uniprocessor process management, the global address space implied by the logical variable, and the kernel's task management facilities. Experimental studies confirm the efficiency of these techniques.

In Chapter 7, it is shown that essential services required in an OS nucleus can be implemented using kernel facilities. Lightweight processes, tasks, and the logical variable are used to implement basic services, to provide access to these services, and to protect services against illicit or erroneous access. The result is an object-oriented OS that does not require centralized structures for its implementation. The logical variable provides the basis for simple but effective protection and naming schemes. These techniques are shown in Chapter 9 to extend naturally to multiprocessors.

An excellent test of an OS is the ease with which sizeable applications can be constructed using its facilities. Chapter 8 describes the design and implementation of a sophisticated programming environment using the facilities and services provided by the kernel and nucleus. This environment supports persistent data and atomic transactions on this data. The material in this chapter stresses the advantages of the relational style of programming supported by parallel logic languages: the environment supports a relational user language which permits concise specifications of complex file system updates.

The parallel logic programming model provides a set of valuable conceptual tools for structuring complex concurrent systems. Specifications expressed in parallel logic languages can be executed, providing rapid prototyping capabilities. Efficient implementation techniques make it feasible to use parallel logic languages as implementation languages for concurrent and multiprocessor systems. In fact, they have already been used for this purpose to good effect, for example:

- *Programming environments.* Multiprocessors containing hundreds of processors are already commercially available. The kernel facilities described here can be used to support portable programming environments that assist application programmers to program these machines. This is essentially the approach taken in the Strand programming environment.

- *Process control.* Telecommunications researchers have used parallel logic languages to implement control programs for telephony switches [Armstrong and Virding, 1989]. Benefits reported include increased programmer productivity and ease of maintenance.

- *Bilingual systems.* Parallel logic languages are good at expressing communication and synchronization. Low-level languages such as C currently offer better performance. A bilingual parallel programming style, in which computationally intensive activities are programmed in low-level languages and communication and synchronization in a parallel logic language, has been used to build high performance parallel programs in engineering and biology [Butler *et al.*, 1986, 1989].

- *Symbolic computers.* Specialized symbolic computers, designed to execute languages such as Lisp or FP at high speeds, require a symbolic systems programming language. For example, McCabe *et al.* [1987] proposed an architecture for parallel symbolic computing that links together sixty-four or more symbolic language processors using a high-speed switching network. The design used a parallel logic language as the systems programming language.

The parallel programming language FP has been used as a framework for this investigation. Other languages in the parallel logic programming family, such as FCP, KL1 and Strand, could also have been used: the techniques developed still apply. Many of the results can also be applied in formalisms with similar characteristics: in particular in functional and object-oriented programming.

10.2 RELATED RESEARCH

Given the current level of interest in logic programming and parallel machines, it is not surprising that considerable research in the use of parallel logic languages for systems programming has proceeded concurrently with that reported herein. This work has been referenced in previous chapters where appropriate. This section provides a summary of the most closely related research.

10.2.1 Logix

Ehud Shapiro's group at the Weizmann Institute in Israel has investigated the application of parallel logic languages to systems programming. A major project in this area has been the development of Logix, a multitasking, single-user programming environment implemented in Flat Concurrent Prolog.

Flat Concurrent Prolog (FCP) [Mierowsky et al., 1985], a flat variant of the language Concurrent Prolog [Shapiro, 1986], was the first flat parallel logic programming language. Like FP, FCP is based on guarded clauses, concurrent evaluation, logical variables and dataflow synchronization. It differs from FP in two principal respects. The first is its support for *atomic unification*. In FCP, unification rather than matching is used to determine whether a clause can be used to reduce a process; a clause can hence bind process variables during head and guard evaluation. To avoid problems due to incorrect bindings (which may occur if a clause try binds variables and subsequently fails), such bindings can only be made accessible to other processes if the clause that generates them is selected for reduction. Head unification and guard evaluation must thus be performed as an atomic operation. FP, in contrast, only allows process variables to be bound *after* a clause try has completed. Prior to reduction, clauses are restricted to testing process arguments. Thus incorrect bindings cannot arise.

The second major difference between FCP and FP is its process synchronization mechanism. In FP, dataflow constraints are specified statically in procedure definitions. In contrast, FCP supports dynamic dataflow: references to variables can be specified at run-time to have a *read-only* property; processes that attempt to bind variables through such references suspend until another process binds the variable. Read-only references are represented in programs by a ? annotation. For example, consider the FCP processes producer(X), consumer(X?). Both producer and consumer may attempt to generate bindings for X. However, as consumer is given a read-only reference to X, it suspends until producer instantiates X.

Both atomic unification and dynamic dataflow permit elegant programming techniques. For example, the read-only variable can be used to protect an operating system service against unexpected instantiation of shared variables [Miller et al., 1987]; this protection must be programmed explicitly in FP (Section 7.3). However, these language features complicate implementation. As indicated in Chapter 6, semantic differences between FP and FCP lead to significant differences in performance. It is hence unclear whether these language features are appropriate in an OS kernel.

Though FCP is more complex than FP, the FCP implementation used as a kernel for the Logix system is in other respects simpler than the kernel described in Chapter 4. This is because it provides no support for tasks. Instead, certain task management facilities are implemented using program transformation techniques [Hirsch et al., 1987]. Several levels of control are implemented in this way. System programs are typically executed untransformed and hence uncontrolled: this is the most efficient; however, failure of an untransformed program terminates the entire system. User programs may be transformed so as to provide control functions similar to those provided by the task management functions described in Chapter 4, on a module-by-module basis. The lack of support for tasks simplifies kernel design. However, as studies reported in Chapter 6 show, program transformation provides a less efficient implementation of task management functions than the kernel mechanisms described here. In addition, it does not appear possible to solve all OS design problems without explicit support for tasks in the OS kernel.

The Logix system [Hirsch, 1987] can be regarded as intermediate in scope between the nucleus described in Chapter 7 and the programming environment, PPS, described in Chapter 8. Like the FP nucleus, Logix provides task management and basic services such as terminal and disk I/O. However, issues such as processor scheduling have not been addressed at the time of writing. Like PPS, it provides the programmer with an augmented user language. The user language supported by Logix is FCP plus modules and a remote procedure call mechanism. This is not as rich as the FP+ language supported by PPS, which provides persistent data and atomic, serializable transactions.

Logix's treatment of secondary storage is rather different from that of PPS. Users manipulate programs located in Unix files, which may be compiled and loaded as Logix modules. In contrast, PPS's implementation of FP+'s persistent state effectively provides its own integrated file system. Programs (modules) can be modified from within PPS using FP+ primitives. An advantage of the Logix approach is that existing Unix tools can be applied to programs.

10.2.2 SIMPOS and PIMOS

The Japanese Fifth Generation Computer Systems Project [Kawanobe, 1984] aims to develop powerful computer systems based on logic programming languages. The research goals of this project include the development of programming systems for such machines. These programming systems are themselves to be implemented in logic programming languages.

One of the products of the first stage of this project was a sequential Prolog machine (PSI). This featured a sophisticated OS (SIMPOS) [Takagi *et al.*, 1984] implemented in a high-level language, ESP [Chikayama, 1983]. Although it has logic programming components, ESP makes extensive use of side-effecting primitives. This means that SIMPOS cannot easily be ported to parallel machines.

More recently, research at the Institute for New Generation Computer Technology (ICOT) on parallel inference machines [Uchida, 1987] has motivated the definition of the parallel logic programming language KL1 (Kernel Language version 1) [Furukawa *et al.*, 1984]. This language is intended to serve as the principal systems programming language for these machines. Its design was strongly influenced by Parlog and Concurrent Prolog.

KL1 is defined to consist of three components: a user language, KL1-u, implemented on top of a core language, KL1-c, augmented with pragmas for process mapping, process priorities, etc. (KL1-p). At the time of writing, KL1-c is the flat form of the parallel logic language Guarded Horn Clauses [Ueda, 1986] plus a task management primitive termed Sho-en. Flat Guarded Horn Clauses is essentially equivalent to FP, as Takeuchi and

Furukawa [1986] point out, and the Sho-en primitive provides many of the task management functions described in Chapter 4.

KL1 is to be used to implement PIMOS, an OS for the parallel inference machines currently being developed at ICOT [Sato *et al.*, 1987a]. PIMOS is intended to be a single-user, multitasking OS that will enable users to run applications on these machines. I/O functions are to be provided by a front-end machine such as PSI. PIMOS will no doubt have certain similarities to the OS described in this book. However, it appears that a rather different approach is to be taken to the implementation of lower-level functions such as multiprocessor task management. These will be implemented in the language kernel rather than in KL1. This provides a more efficient implementation of these facilities, but results in a more complex and less flexible kernel.

10.3 FUTURE RESEARCH

There is considerable scope for further research in areas related to the use of parallel logic programming for specifying and implementing concurrent systems.

- *Kernel design.* Kernel facilities described herein support task scheduling and quiescence detection. These functions are necessary for systems programming but are not required in many other applications. Kernel implementation is simplified if these functions are not supported. Two other kernel features, namely FP's general unification, and nonstrict tests, lead to complexity in an implementation but provide little advantage to the programmer. These considerations have led to the design of a language that is even simpler than FP, Strand [Foster and Taylor, 1989]. Strand does not support nonstrict tests, provides variable assignment rather than general unification, and only supports termination and error detection as task management functions. Further research may permit further simplifications to Strand, or may encourage reintroduction of certain features presented in this work.
- *Kernel implementation.* An important area for future research is efficient implementation of kernel facilities. Memory management is a particularly important problem that has received scant attention to date.
- *Formal semantics.* A formal semantics for parallel logic programs is required if concurrent systems are to be verified with respect to global properties such as termination and liveness. Some preliminary work in this area has been performed but much remains to be done [Gerth *et al.*, 1988].
- *Distributed systems.* It is unclear whether the parallel logic programming model is appropriate for distributed systems [Sloman and Kramer, 1986]. High communication costs in these systems militate against the use of the logical variable as a communication mechanism. Unreliable components and communications must be dealt with in the kernel. Further research is required to determine whether efficient and effective solutions to these problems exist within the parallel logic programming model.

APPENDIX I

A TUTORIAL INTRODUCTION TO FLAT PARLOG

This appendix uses simple examples to introduce the Flat Parlog (FP) language. It assumes familiarity with the concepts and syntax presented in the language overview in Section 3.1.

I.1 PRODUCERS AND CONSUMERS

Consider the following program:

```
producer(Xs) ← Xs = [hi |Xs1], producers(Xs1).
consumer([ ]).
consumer([hi |Xs]) ← consumer(Xs).
```

This consists of three *clauses* defining two procedures, producer/1 and consumer/1. The implies operator ← divides clauses into a *head* and a *body*. Both heads and bodies consist of processes. Process arguments are *variables* (represented by strings beginning with a capital letter: e.g., Xs) or nonvariable terms such as *constants* (e.g., hi) or *lists*. The syntax [H |T] represents a list with head H and tail T.

The following statement specifies a computation containing two processes. Subsequent sections examine how this computation is evaluated. The processes are seen to implement a producer/consumer pair:

```
producer(Xs), consumer(Xs)
```

I.1.1 Process reduction

Computation proceeds by repeatedly selecting processes and attempting to reduce them using clauses in an associated program. Assume that the process consumer(Xs) is selected for reduction. Each clause in the consumer procedure represents a *rewrite rule* that can be used to reduce this process. Reduction replaces a process by a clause's body processes. Nonvariable head arguments in a clause represent *preconditions* that must be satisfied before that clause can be applied. A precondition is a test that can succeed or fail, depending on the value of the corresponding process argument, or *suspend* if lack of data does not permit it to proceed. This use of data availability to constrain process reduction is termed *dataflow synchronization*.

The first consumer/1 clause can be used to reduce a consumer process if the process's first (and only) argument is the empty list ([ ]). The second clause can be used if its argument is a list [E |Xs1], where E and Xs1 represent any term. As the consumer process considered here (consumer(Xs)) has an unbound variable as its argument, it cannot be reduced using either clause. Another process must be selected.

Assume that the process producer(Xs) is now selected for reduction. The single clause in its procedure specifies no preconditions, so this process can be reduced immediately to two new processes, Xs = [hi |Xs1] and producer(Xs1). This gives a new computation state containing three processes:

Xs = [hi |Xs1], producer(Xs1), consumer(Xs)

The recursive call to producer can be interpreted as a continuation of the same process with modified state: its argument is now the new variable Xs1. The process Xs = [hi |Xs1] is a *unification process*: it invokes FP's unification primitive, =.

I.1.2 Stream communication

Either the producer or unification process may now be selected for reduction. Assume that the unification process Xs = [hi |Xs1] is selected. This instantiates the variable Xs to a list with the constant hi as its head and the variable Xs1 as its tail. As the consumer process also possesses a reference to the variable Xs, this has the effect of communicating this value to consumer. The new computation state contains two processes:

producer(Xs1), consumer([hi |Xs1])

Either of these processes can be selected for reduction. Assume that the producer process is selected again. This can again be reduced to two new processes; clause variables are effectively renamed at each reduction, so the process producer(Xs1) is reduced to Xs1 = [hi |Xs2] and producer(Xs2), where Xs2 is a new variable. If the unification process is evaluated immediately, this gives the following computation state:

producer(Xs2), consumer([hi, hi |Xs2])

The argument to the consumer process is now a list containing two elements plus a variable tail. Assume that consumer is selected for reduction. The first clause of the consumer procedure cannot be used to reduce this process, as the process's argument is a list and this clause requires the empty list. The second clause can be used to reduce the process, however, to a recursive call to consumer: consumer([hi |Xs2]). The consumer process has effectively received the message hi generated by producer. In this example, the incoming message is simply discarded: normally, another process would be created to process it.

This example illustrates a fundamental parallel logic programming technique: *stream communication*. Recall that producer and consumer originally share a single variable: Xs. This variable has the single assignment property – it can be assigned only a single value – yet it is used to communicate a stream of values between the two processes. This is achieved by instantiating the variable to a partial data structure (a list) containing a message and a further variable (Xs1). The new variable is then used to communicate further messages in the same way.

I.1.3 Guards

A disadvantage of the program just described is that it will never terminate: producer will generate hi messages forever. Fortunately, the producer procedure can easily be extended to generate only a fixed number of messages. The modified procedure is given here. This defines a process that generates N hi messages and then terminates, at the same time closing the communication stream:

```
producer(Xs, N) ← N > 0 : Xs = [E |Xs1], N1 is N − 1, producer(Xs1, N1).
producer(Xs, N) ← N ≤ 0 : Xs = [ ].
```

The extended definition for producer incorporates an additional argument N, which signifies the number of messages still to send. In addition, the first clause is given a guard process $N > 0$ to prevent its application once the specified number of messages has been sent. A *guard* in a parallel logic program is a set of preconditions separated from a clause body by a *commit operator*, ':'. The new second clause terminates evaluation when $N \leq 0$. It is assumed that the initial call to producer specifies a message count. For example:

```
producer(Xs, 5), consumer(Xs)
```

If a producer process's message count is greater than zero ($N > 0$), the first clause is used to create two new processes: Xs = [E |Xs1] and N1 is N − 1. A recursive call creates a new producer with a message count N1. The value N1 is computed by the process N1 is N − 1.

The process producer(Xs, 5) eventually reduces to producer(Xs5, 0), having generated five messages. The latter process is reduced using the second clause to give a final process Xs5 = [ ]. This terminates both the producer process and the stream of messages, giving a final value for the initial variable Xs = [hi, hi, hi, hi, hi]. This list of five elements is consumed by consumer, which reduces five times using its second clause to give the process consumer([ ]). This process is reduced using the first clause for consumer; as this clause creates no further processes, consumer also terminates.

I.1.4 Incomplete messages

FP's operational model guarantees that any process capable of being reduced will eventually be reduced. This means that in the preceding computation consumer will eventually consume all messages generated by producer. However, producer can generate up to N messages before this occurs. To avoid flooding memory with unconsumed messages, the program is extended so that producer waits for an acknowledgement for each message that it generates:

```
producer(Xs, N) ← producer(Xs, N, go).

producer(Xs, N, go) ← N > 0 :
        Xs = [{hi, Sync} |Xs1], N1 is N − 1, producer(Xs1, N1, Sync).
producer(Xs, N, _) ← N ≤ 0 : Xs = [ ].

consumer([{hi, Sync} |Xs]) ← Sync = go, consumer(Xs).
consumer([ ]).
```

The producer procedure has an additional third argument and its second clause specifies an additional precondition: the third argument must be the constant go. The first clause initializes this argument to go, permitting an initial communication. The message generated is now a tuple {hi, Sync}. (The syntax $\{T_1, \ldots T_N\}$ represents a tuple with arguments $T_1, \ldots, T_N$.) The second component of this tuple is a new variable. This variable is also given to the recursive call to producer as the third argument. This means that the producer process cannot reduce further until this variable is instantiated to the constant go.

The new consumer procedure expects to receive messages with the form {hi, Sync} rather than simple hi. It binds the Sync component of messages to the constant go when it receives them. This informs producer, which is waiting for Sync to be assigned a value, that a message has been received and that it can hence proceed to generate a further communication.

This example illustrates a second important parallel logic programming technique, known as *incomplete messages* [Shapiro, 1986] or back communication. The message passed from producer to consumer is incomplete: it contains a variable component. The consumer uses this variable to communicate a value back to the producer.

I.2 MERGERS AND DISTRIBUTORS

Two further examples illustrate the use of FP to specify more complex communication and process structures.

I.2.1 Nondeterministic choice

Each clause in a procedure specifies a different way of reducing a process. In the example considered previously, clauses have been mutually exclusive. But this need not be the case. Consider the following merge procedure. Its two clauses specify nonexclusive preconditions: the first clause requires that a merge process's first argument be a list, and the second clause requires that the second argument be a list.

merge([X |Xs], Ys, Zs) ← Zs = [X |Zs1], merge(Xs, Ys, Zs1).
merge(Xs, [Y |Ys], Zs) ← Zs = [Y |Zs1], merge(Xs, Ys, Zs1).

A merge process which only has its second argument bound to a list can only be reduced using the second clause of the merge procedure. If only the first argument is so bound only the first clause can be used. If both arguments are available, either clause can be used. A merge process tends to select items from its two input streams as they become available in real time.

The ability to represent time-dependent or nondeterministic choice is important in systems programming applications. Consider the problem of passing a stream of items generated by two producers to a consumer as they become available. This can be achieved using a merge process, as specified by the following statement:

producer(Os1), producer(Os2), merge(Os1, Os2, Os), consumer(Os)

This statement defines the process network illustrated in Figure I.1. The circles in this figure represent processes. The arrows linking the processes represent the communication streams Os1, Os2 and Os; the direction of these arrows signifies the direction of communication. If producer and consumer use incomplete messages to synchronize their activities, as described previously, then further communications also occur from consumer to the producer processes.

I.2.2 Stream distribution

Analogous to a merger is a distributor that passes requests received on a single stream to one of a number of destinations. The messages received by a distributor can usefully be labelled terms with the form {Name, Message}; the distributor passes each message to the named destination. A simple distributor that passes messages received on its first argument to destinations named 1 and 2 is specified as follows:

distributor([{1, E} |Is], Os1, Os2) ← Os1 = [E |Os1a], distributor(Is, Os1a, Os2).
distributor([{2, E} |Is], Os1, Os2) ← Os2 = [E |Os2a], distributor(Is, Os1, Os2a).

The first clause outputs messages labelled 1 on the distributor's second argument; the second clause outputs messages labelled 2 on the distributor's third argument. This

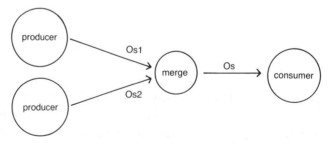

Figure I.1 Merge process network.

program can be used to pass suitably labelled messages (generated by a labelling producer, producer_l) to one of two consumers, as specified by the following statement:

    producer_l(Is), distributor(Is, Os1, Os2), consumer(Os1), consumer(Os2).

I.3 QUICKSORT

The programs presented previously have specified process networks that consist of an
essentially fixed number of processes. A more complex example shows how recursively
defined procedures can specify networks containing arbitrary numbers of processes.
The following program implements the quicksort sorting algorithm. It comprises three
procedures: qsort/2, partition/4 and append/3.

```
qsort([ ], S) ← S = [ ].
qsort([E |L], S) ← partition(E, L, L1, L2), qsort(L1, S1), qsort(L2, S2), append(S1, [E |S2], S).
partition(E, [ ], L1, L2) ← L1 = [ ], L2 = [ ].
partition(E, [N |Ls], L, L2) ← N < E : L = [N |L1], partition(E, Ls, L1, L2).
partition(E, [N |Ls], L1, L) ← N ≥ E : L = [N |L2], partition(E, Ls, L1, L2).
append([ ], Y, O) ← O = Y.
append([E |X], Y, O) ← O = [E |Z], append(X, Y, Z).
```

The qsort procedure specifies the top level of the quicksort algorithm. Its first argument is assumed to be an unsorted list; its second argument is to be bound to a sorted
version of this list. Its first clause deals with the base case – an empty list – by returning an
empty list. The second clause sorts a list with head E and tail L by creating four processes.
The first, partition, partitions the list L about the element E to obtain two sublists. The two
qsort processes sort these sublists, and the append process concatenates the sorted sublists
to produce the output list. The variables shared by these processes are used for interprocess communication.

  To understand how this program works, consider the process qsort([3, 2, 1, 4], S). This
is initially reduced using the second clause for qsort to create a network of four processes,
as illustrated in Figure I.2. The arrows in this figure represent the shared variables used
for interprocess communication.

  These new processes execute concurrently. The first element of the input list, 3, is
chosen as the pivot element. The partition process reduces once for each remaining
element, outputting it on either its third or fourth argument. The first qsort process hence
receives the sublist [2, 1]; the second receives the sublist [4]. Recursive calls to qsort
replace these qsort process by further processes that generate sorted sublists [1, 2] and
[4]. These are passed to the append process, which eventually binds the variable S in the
original process to the sorted list [1, 2, 3, 4]. Evaluation of the process qsort([3, 2, 1, 4], S)
hence generates a large number of communicating processes.

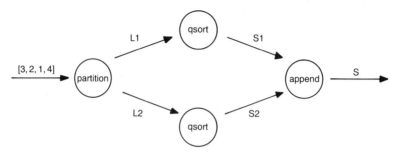

Figure I.2 Quicksort process network.

The quicksort program also serves to illustrate the *declarative* or *relational* interpretation of parallel logic programs. Each clause in this program can be read declaratively as a logical sentence about lists. For example, the second clause of the procedure append/3 reads: appending a term Y to a list [E |X] gives the term [E |Z] if appending Y to X gives Z. The first clause reads: appending a term to the empty list gives that term. Each procedure also defines a relation; for example, the append/3 procedure defines the relation append(X, Y, Z): appending the term Y to the list X gives the list Z.

I.4 TWO PROGRAMMING TECHNIQUES

This final section presents two important parallel logic programming techniques. Both are concerned with cooperative construction of data structures; one is used to permit efficient concatenation of lists, and the other to detect termination in process networks.

I.4.1 Difference list

The append processes used to concatenate sorted sublists in the quicksort program are a source of inefficiency both in time and space: the same list elements are copied repeatedly to no purpose. This unnecessary copying can be avoided using difference lists [Clark and Tärnlund, 1977]. A revised quicksort program which uses difference lists follows.

```
qsort(L, S) ← qsort(L, S, [ ]).

qsort([ ], S1, S2) ← S1 = S2.
qsort([E |L], S1, S3) ← partition(E, L, L1, L2), qsort(L1, S1, [E |S2]), qsort(L2, S2, S3).

partition(E, [ ], L1, L2) ← L1 = [ ], L2 = [ ].
partition(E, [N |Ls], L, L2) ← N < E : L = [N |L1], partition(E, Ls, L1, L2).
partition(E, [N |Ls], L1, L) ← N ≥ E : L = [N |L2], partition(E, Ls, L1, L2).
```

The partition procedure is as before; only the qsort procedure has changed. When an input list is partitioned, each qsort/3 process created is given a portion of the output list to fill in with a sorted sublist. This portion is expressed as a list head and tail. A qsort process binds the supplied head to a list containing the items that it has sorted and binds the variable tail of this list to the supplied tail. The supplied tail will be instantiated to the remainder of the sorted list by another process. The entire sorted list is thus constructed cooperatively and asynchronously by a number of qsort processes. The list constructed by a particular process is the *difference* between the lists referenced by the supplied head and tail. The procedure qsort/2 initializes the output list by defining its tail to be the empty list.

I.4.2 Short circuit

It is sometimes useful to be able to detect termination of a set of processes. This can be achieved using a programming technique known as the short circuit [Takeuchi, 1983]. A set of processes in which termination is to be detected are linked in a circuit using shared variables. Each process shares a variable with the process on its left and another variable with the process on its right. When a process terminates, it binds its two variables, thus closing its portion of the circuit. If one side of the circuit is bound to a nonvariable term, then this term will become visible at the other end only when all processes have terminated. A simple example is used to illustrate this technique. The quicksort procedure is shown transformed to incorporate a short circuit. Each procedure is augmented with two additional variables. The first clause passes in the value done to the left-hand side of the circuit; the variable Done in the initial call will be bound to this value when all qsort and partition processes created to sort a list have terminated. Note how the short circuit is split and threaded through the partition and qsort processes created in the recursive call to qsort (using variables M1 and M2), and is closed in the terminating clauses for qsort and partition.

```
qsort(L, S, Done) ← qsort(L, S, [ ], done, Done).

qsort([ ], S1, S2, L, R) ← S1 = S2, R = L.
qsort([E |Ls], S1, S3, L, R) ←
      partition(E, Ls, L1, L2, L, M1),
      qsort(L1, S1, [E |S2], M1, M2), qsort(L2, S2, S3, M2, R).

partition(E, [ ], L1, L2, L, R) ← L1 = [ ], L2 = [ ], R = L.
partition(E, [N |Ls], L, L2, M, R) ← N < E : L = [N |L1], partition(E, Ls, L1, L2, M, R).
partition(E, [N |Ls], L1, L, M, R) ← N ≥ E : L = [N |L2], partition(E, Ls, L1, L2, M, R).
```

I.5 SUMMARY

Several examples have been used to illustrate the principles of parallel logic programming in FP. Four fundamental programming techniques have been presented. These, and simple task management mechanisms introduced in Chapter 4, are all that are required to understand the programs presented in this book.

- *Stream communication*. Incremental construction and consumption of bindings for shared variables permits streams of data to be communicated between processes.
- *Incomplete messages*. Variables in messages provide implicit return address for subsequent communication.
- *Difference lists*. Representing lists as the difference between a head and a tail permits processes to cooperate in constructing a list of data items without copying.
- *Short circuit*. Shared variables permit termination detection in a set of processes: each process closes its portion of a circuit when it terminates.

The examples also illustrate the program development methodology encouraged by parallel logic languages. Programs are naturally structured in an object-oriented style: a procedure defines a process (object) that handles messages received from other processes. This permits individual processes to be defined and tested in isolation. More complex programs are constructed by combining processes to form process networks. The functionality of individual processes is extended by progressively refining their definition.

APPENDIX II

FLAT PARLOG OPERATIONAL MODEL

This appendix presents a more formal definition of FP's operational model than that employed in Chapter 3. This definition is adapted from similar definitions for the related languages FCP [Gerth *et al.*, 1988; Taylor, 1989] and Strand [Foster and Taylor, 1989]. It consists of a number of preliminary definitions, transition rules for the language and definitions of successful, failed and deadlocked computations.

II.1 DEFINITIONS

Match. A match algorithm is employed to compare a clause head with a process. This algorithm, defined by Table II.1, is applied left to right textually and depth first in term structures. It returns a set of bindings θ, false or suspend.

Guard execution. A clause guard is a sequence of predefined test predicates which are executed from left to right textually. Test predicates evaluate to one of true, false or suspend. If all predicates evaluate to true, the guard evaluates to true. If any predicate evaluates to suspend or false, guard execution terminates and evaluates to suspend or false respectively.

State. The state of a computation is a multiset of processes. Each process $p \in S$ either is or is not a ùnification process of the form $X = Y$.

Table II.1 The match algorithm

process T1 clause T2	Variable	Constant	Structure
Variable	T2 := T1	T2 := T1	T2 := T1
Constant	suspend	if T1 ! = T2 false	false
Structure	suspend	false	match args

II.2 TRANSITIONS

A transition rule specifies a mapping between states. Execution of a program P may include the following transitions.

1. Reduction

$$<p_1, \ldots, p_i, \ldots, p_n> \rightarrow <p_1, \ldots, B\theta, \ldots, p_n>$$
if $p_i \neq (X = Y) \wedge match(p_i, H) = \theta \wedge G\theta = true$

   where $C' = H \leftarrow G : B$ is a fresh copy of a clause $C \in P$. Note that if B is the empty body then no processes are added to the new state.

2. Binding

$$<p_1, \ldots, p_i, \ldots, p_n> \rightarrow <p_1, \ldots, p_n> [X/Y]$$
if $p_i = (X = Y)$ and X is a variable; or $p_i = (Y = X)$ and Y is a variable.

3. Unification

$$<p_1, \ldots, X = Y, \ldots, p_n> \rightarrow <p_1, \ldots, PS, \ldots, p_n>$$
if X and Y are tuples of the same arity; or X and Y are identical constants

   where $PS = \{X_1 = Y_1, \ldots, X_N = Y_N\}$ if X and Y are tuples of arity N; or the empty set $\{\ \}$ if X and Y are constants.

4. Failure

$$S \rightarrow <failure>$$
if $\exists p = (X = Y) \in S$ and X and Y are tuples of different arity, or different constants, or a tuple and a constant; or $\exists p \neq (X = Y) \in S \wedge \forall C = H \leftarrow G : B \in P$, $(match(p, H) = false \vee (match(p, H) = \theta \wedge G\theta = false))$

5. Suspend

$$S \rightarrow <suspend>$$
if $\forall p \in S, p \neq (X = Y) \wedge \forall C = H \leftarrow G : B \in P$, $(match(p, H) = suspend \vee (match(p, H) = \theta \wedge G\theta = suspend))$

II.3 COMPUTATIONS

A computation is a sequence of transitions which ends in a terminal state (that is, one in which no further rules can be applied). A computation which ends in the state $<\{\ \}>$ is called a successful computation. A computation which ends in the state $<failure>$ is called a failed computation. A computation which ends in the state $<suspend>$ is called a deadlocked computation.

APPENDIX III

FLAT PARLOG MODULE FORMAT

Modules in the Flat Parlog language are first class language objects. This means that they can be included in terms and passed between processors in the same way as other terms. This appendix describes how modules are represented in the Flat Parlog Machine (FPM).

As illustrated in Figure III.1, a module consists of five main components: Header, Exports, Code, SymbolTable, and Symbols. A Header identifies the term as a module and specifies the length of the Exports and Code components (ModSize), the number of entries in the SymbolTable (SymbolCount) and the size of the Symbols component

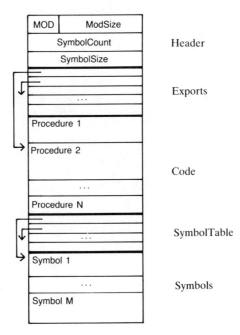

Figure III.1 Flat Parlog module format.

(SymbolSize). The Exports component contains one entry for each exported procedure; each entry consists of a pointer to the object code for its procedure. FP's @ primitive uses this table to find the code for a named procedure. (Recall that a call Module@Process initiates execution of a named process using code in a given module.) The Code component contains encoded FPM instructions representing the module's procedures. Finally, the SymbolTable contains a set of absolute references to symbols contained in the Symbols component. FPM instructions in the Code component that refer to symbols take a relative offset to SymbolTable entries as arguments. The relative offsets permit modules to be relocated during garbage collection or when copying modules between processors; the level of indirection provided by the SymbolTable permits strings and modules to be garbage collected independently.

REFERENCES

Abramsky, S. 1982. A simple proof theory for non-determinate recursive programs. Research report, Queen Mary College, Computer Systems Laboratory.

Agha G. 1986. *Actors: A Model of Concurrent Computation in Distributed Systems*. Cambridge, Mass.: MIT Press.

Almes, G. T., Black, A. P., Lazowska, E. D. and Noe, J. D. 1985. The Eden system: a technical review, *IEEE Trans. Softw. Engng* SE-11: 43–59.

Andrews, G. R. and Schneider, F. B. 1983. Concepts and notations for concurrent programming, *Computing Surveys*, **15**: 3–43.

Armstrong, J. and Virding, R. 1989. Programming telephony, *Strand: New Concepts in Parallel Programming*, Foster, I. T. and Taylor, S. *op. cit.*

Arvind and Brock, J. D. 1982. Streams and managers, *Operating Systems Engineering*. Springer-Verlag LNCS-143: 452–65.

Atkinson, M. P., Bailey, P. J., Chisholm, K. J., Cockshott, W. P. and Morrison, R. 1983. An approach to persistent programming, *Computer Journal*, **26**: 360–65.

Augustsson, L. 1985. Compiling pattern matching, *Conf. on Functional Programming Languages and Computer Architecture*. Springer-Verlag LNCS-201.

Backus, J. 1978. Can programming be liberated from the von Neumann style? A functional style and its algebra of processes, *CACM* **21**: 613–41.

Badal, D. Z. 1979. Correctness of concurrency control and implications in distributed databases, *Proc. COMPSAC '79 Conf.*, Chicago.

Berglund, E. J. 1986. An introduction to the V-system, *IEEE Micro* **6**(4): 35–52.

Bernstein, P. A. and Goodman, N. 1981. Concurrency control in distributed databases, *ACM Computing Surveys*, **13**: 185–221.

Bernstein, P. A., Goodman, N. and Hadzilacos, V. 1983. Recovery algorithms for database systems, *Information Processing 83: Proc. IFIP 9th World Computer Congress*, 799–807. Amsterdam: North-Holland.

Birrell, A. D. and Nelson, B. J. 1984. Implementing remote procedure calls, *ACM Trans. Comput. Systems* **2**: 39–59.

Bowen, K. A. 1986. Meta-level programming and knowledge representation, *New Generation Computing* **3**: 359–83.

Bowen, K. A. and Kowalski, R. A. 1982. Amalgamating language and metalanguage in logic programming, *Logic Programming*, pp. 153–72. New York: Academic Press.

Brinch Hansen, P. 1972. Structured multiprogramming, *CACM* **15**: 574–8.

Brinch Hansen, P. 1975. The programming language Concurrent Pascal, *IEEE Trans. Softw.*

Engng **SE-1**: 199–207.

Brinch Hansen, P. 1976. The SOLO operating system, *Softw. P. and E.* **6**: 141–9.

Brinch Hansen, P. 1987. Joyce – a programming language for distributed systems, *Softw. P. and E.*, **17**: 29–50.

Bruynooghe, M. 1986. Compile time garbage collection, *Proc. IFIP TC2 Conf. on Program Specification and Transformation*, Bad Toelz.

Butler, R., Lusk, E., McCune, W. and Overbeek, R. 1986. Parallel logic programming for numeric applications, *Proc. 3rd Int. Logic Programming Conf.*, Springer-Verlag LNCS-225.

Butler, R. *et al.* 1989. Aligning genetic sequences, *Strand: New Concepts in Parallel Programming*, Foster, I. T. and Taylor, S. *op. cit.*

Cheriton, D., Malcolm, M. A., Melen, L. S. and Sager, G. R. 1979. Thoth: a portable real-time operating system, *CACM* **22**: 105–115.

Chikayama, T. 1983. ESP – Extended Self-contained Prolog – as a preliminary kernel language of fifth generation computers, *New Generation Computing*, **1**: 11–24.

Chu, D. A. and McCabe, F. G. 1988. Swift: a new symbolic processor, *Logic Programming*: *Proc. 5th Int. Conf. and Symp.* 1415–28. Cambridge, Mass.: MIT Press.

Clark, K. L. and Gregory, S. 1981. A relational language for parallel programming, *Proc. 1981 ACM Conf. on Functional Programming Languages and Computer Architectures*, 171–8.

Clark, K. L. and Gregory, S. 1984. Notes on systems programming in Parlog, *Proc. Int. Conf. on 5th Generation Computer Systems*, 299–306. Amsterdam: North-Holland.

Clark, K. L. and Gregory, S. 1986. Parlog: parallel programming in logic, *ACM Trans. Program. Lang. Syst.* **8**: 1–49.

Clark, K. L. and Tärnlund, S-A. 1977. A first order theory of data and programs, *Information Processing 77*: *Proc. IFIP Congress 77*, 939–44. Amsterdam: Elsevier/North-Holland.

Cohen, J. 1981. Garbage collection of linked data structures, *ACM Computing Surveys*, **13**: 341–67.

Cohen, E. and Jefferson, D. 1975. Protection in the Hydra operating system, *Proc. 5th Symp. Operating System Principles*, 141–60.

Conway, M. E. 1963. A multiprocessor system design, *Proc. AFIPS Fall Jt Computer Conf.*, 139–46. Baltimore: Spartan Books.

Crammond, J. A. 1988. Parallel Implementation of Committed-choice Languages. PhD thesis, Herriot-Watt University, Edinburgh.

Crammond, J. A. and Miller, C. 1984. An architecture for parallel logic languages, *Proc. 2nd Int. Logic Programming Conf.*, Uppsala, Sweden, 183–94.

Dahl, O-J. 1968. Simula 67 Common Base Language. Technical report, Norwegian Computing Centre, Oslo.

Dennis, J. B. and van Horn, E. C. 1966. Programming semantics for multiprogramming computations, *CACM* **9**: 143–55.

Dijkstra, E. W. 1968a. The structure of the 'THE'-multiprogramming system, *CACM* **11**: 341–6.

Dijkstra, E. W. 1968b. Cooperating sequential processes, *Programming Languages*. New York: Academic Press.

Dijkstra, E. W. 1975. Guarded commands, nondeterminacy and formal derivation of programs, *CACM* **18**: 453–7.

Dijkstra, E. W., Feijen, W. H. J. and van Gasteren, A. J. M. 1983. Derivation of a termination detection algorithm for distributed computations, *Information Processing Letters* **16**: 217–9.

Douglis, F. and Ousterhout, J. 1987. Process migration in the Sprite operating system, *7th Int. Conf. on Distr. Comp. Syst.*, Berlin, 18–23.

Foster, I. T. 1986. Parlog Programming System: user guide and reference manual. Research report, Dept of Computing, Imperial College, London.

Foster, I. T. 1987a. Logic operating systems: design issues. *Logic Programming*: *Proc. 4th Int. Conf.*, 910–26. Cambridge, Mass: MIT Press.

uters **C-34**: 204–217.

D. H. D. 1977. Implementing Prolog – compiling predicate logic programs.
rch reports 39 and 40, University of Edinburgh.

D. H. D. 1983. An abstract Prolog instruction set. Technical report 309, Art
igence Center, SRI International.

W. and Liskov, B. 1985. Implementation of resilient, atomic data types, *ACM Tran*
ram. Lang. Syst. **7**: 244–69.

N. 1977. Design and implementation of Modula, *Softw. P and E* **7**: 67–84.

L. D. and van Tilborg, A. M. 1980. MICROS, a distributed operating system for Micro
configurable network computer, *IEEE Trans. Computers* **C-29**: 1133–44.

W. A., *et al.* 1975. Overview of the Hydra operating system, *Proc. 5th Symp. Opera*
tem Principles, Austin, Texas, 122–31.

W. A., Levin, R. and Harbison, S. P. 1981. *HYDRA/C.mmp: An Experimental Compu*
tem. New York: McGraw-Hill.

Foster, I. T. 1987b. Efficient metacontrol in parallel logic languages. Research report PAR 87/18. Dept of Computing, Imperial College, London.

Foster, I. T. 1988a. Parallel implementation of Parlog, *Proc. 1988 Int. Conf. on Parallel Processing*, 9–16. Pennsylvania State University Press.

Foster, I. T. 1988b. A declarative state transition system. *Journal of Logic Programming* (forthcoming), and Research Report PAR 88/9, Dept of Computing, Imperial College, London.

Foster, I. T. 1988c. A multicomputer garbage collector for a single-assignment language. Preprint MCS-P81-0689, Argonne National Laboratory.

Foster, I. T. 1989. Implementation of a declarative state transition system, *Softw. P. and E.*, **19**: 351–70.

Foster, I. T. and Taylor, S. 1988. Flat Parlog: a basis for comparison. *Int. J. Parallel Programming* **16**(2).

Foster, I. T. and Taylor, S. 1989. *Strand: New Concepts in Parallel Programming*. Prentice Hall, Englewood Cliffs, New Jersey.

Foster, I. T., Gregory, S., Ringwood, G. A. and Satoh, K. 1986. A sequential implementation of Parlog, *Proc. 3rd Int. Logic Programming Conf.*, Springer-Verlag LNCS-225, 149–56.

Francez, N. 1980. Distributed termination, *ACM Trans. Program. Lang. Syst.* **2**: 42–55.

Friedman, D. P. and Wise, D. S. 1976. CONS should not evaluate its arguments. *Automata, Languages and Programming*, 257–84. Edinburgh: Edinburgh University Press.

Friedman, D. P. and Wise, D. S. 1980. An indeterminate constructor for applicative programming, *Proc. 7th ACM Symp. on Principles of Programming Languages*. New York: Springer-Verlag.

Furukawa, K., Kunifuji, S., Takeuchi, A. and Ueda, K. 1984. The conceptual specification of the Kernel Language version 1. Technical report TR-054, ICOT, Tokyo.

Gerth, R., Codish, M., Lichtenstein, Y. and Shapiro, E. 1988. Fully abstract denotational semantics for FCP, *Proc. Symp. on Logic in Computer Science*.

Goodenough, J. B. 1975. Exception handling: issues and a proposed notation, *CACM* **18**: 683–96.

Gregory, S. 1987. *Parallel Logic Programming in Parlog*. Reading, Mass.: Addison-Wesley.

Gregory, S., Foster, I. T., Burt, A. D. and Ringwood, G. A. 1989. An abstract machine for the implementation of Parlog on uniprocessors, *New Generation Computing*, **6**: 389–420.

Halstead, R. H. and Loaiza, J. R. 1985. Exception handling in Multilisp, *Proc. 1985 Int. Conf. on Parallel Processing*, 822–30. Pennsylvania State University Press.

Henderson, P. 1980. *Functional Programming: Application and Implementation*. Hemel Hempstead: Prentice Hall.

Henderson, P. 1982. Purely functional operating systems, *Functional Programming and its Applications*. Cambridge: Cambridge University Press.

Henderson, P. and Morris, J. H. 1976. A lazy evaluator, *Proc. 3rd ACM Symp. on Principles of Programming Language*, Atlanta, Georgia.

Hewitt, C. E. 1977. Viewing control structures as patterns of passing messages, *J. Artificial Intelligence* **8**: 323–64.

Hirsch, M. 1987. The Logix System. MSc thesis. Weizmann Institute, Rehovot.

Hirsch, M., Silverman, W. and Shapiro, E. 1987. Layers of protection and control in the Logix system, *Concurrent Prolog, Collected Papers*. Cambridge, Mass.: MIT Press.

Hoare, C. A. R. 1974. Monitors: an operating system structuring concept, *CACM* **17**: 549–57.

Hoare, C. A. R. 1978. Communicating Sequential Processes, *CACM* **21**: 666–77.

Houri, A. and Shapiro, E. 1987. A sequential abstract machine for Flat Concurrent Prolog, *Concurrent Prolog, Collected Papers*. Cambridge, Mass.: MIT Press.

Hudak, P. 1986. Para-functional programming, *IEEE Computing* **19**(8): 60–70.

Hudak, P. and Goldberg, B. 1985. Distributed execution of functional programs using serial combinators, *IEEE Trans. on Computers* **C-34**: 881–91.

Ichiyoshi, N., Miyazaki, T. and Taki, K. 1987. A distributed implementation of Flat GHC on the

Multi-PSI, *Logic Programming: Proc. 4th Int. Conf.*, 257–75. Cambridge, Mass.: MIT Press.

Ichiyoshi, N., Rokusawa, K., Nakajima, K. and Inamura, Y. 1988. A new external reference management and distributed unification for KL1, *Proc Int. Conf. on 5th Generation Computer Systems*, *Tokyo*. Amsterdam: North-Holland.

Inmos Limited, 1984. *occam Programming Manual*. Hemel Hempstead: Prentice-Hall International.

Jones, A. K. 1978. The object model: a conceptual tool for structuring software, *Operating Systems: An Advanced Course*. New York: Springer-Verlag.

Jones, S. B. 1984. A range of operating systems written in a purely functional style. Technical monograph PRG-42, Oxford University Computing Laboratory.

Joseph, M., Prasad, V. R. and Natarajan, K. T. 1984. *A Multiprocessor Operating System*. Hemel Hempstead: Prentice Hall International.

Kahn, G. and MacQueen, D. B. 1977. Coroutines and networks of parallel processes, *Proc. IFIP 77*, 993–8. Amsterdam: North-Holland.

Kawanobe, K. 1984. Current status and future plans of the Fifth Generation Computer Systems project, *Proc. Int. Conf. on 5th Generation Computer Systems*, *Tokyo*, 3–17. Amsterdam: North-Holland.

Kliger, S. 1987. Towards a native-code compiler for Flat Concurrent Prolog. MSc thesis, Weizmann Institute, Rehovot.

Kowalski, R. A. 1974. Predicate logic as programming language, *Information Processing 74*; *Proc. IFIP Congress*, 569–74. Amsterdam: North-Holland.

Kowalski, R. A. 1979. *Logic for Problem Solving*, New York: North-Holland.

Krasner, G. 1983. *Smalltalk-80, Bits of History, Words of Advice*. New York: Addison-Wesley.

Kusalik, A. J. 1986. Specification and initialization of a logic computer system, *New Generation Computing* 4: 189–209.

Lampson, B. W. and Sturgis, H. 1976. Crash recovery in a distributed data storage system. Technical report, Computer Science Laboratory, Xerox PARC, Palo Alto, Calif.

McCabe, F. G., Foster, I. T., Clark, K. L., Cheung, P. and Knowles, G. 1987. The X machine – a proposal for design and construction. Research report, Dept of Computing, Imperial College, London.

McDonald, C. S. 1987. fsh – a functional Unix command interpreter, *Softw. P. and E.* 17: 685–700.

May, D. and Shepherd, R. 1984. The transputer implementation of occam, *Proc. Int. Conf. on 5th Generation Computer Systems*, *Tokyo* Amsterdam: North-Holland.

Mierowsky, C., Taylor, S., Shapiro, E., Levy, J. and Safra, M. 1985. The design and implementation of Flat Concurrent Prolog. Technical report CS85-09, Weizmann Institute, Rehovot.

Miller, M. S., Bobrow, D., Tribble, E. D. and Levy, J. 1987. Logical secrets, *Logic Programming: Proc. 4th Int. Conf.* 704–728. Cambridge, Mass.: MIT Press.

Ousterhout, J. K. 1982. Scheduling techniques for concurrent systems, *Proc. 3rd Int. Conf. on Distributed Computer Systems*, Fort Lauderdale, Florida, 22–30.

Papadimitriou, C. 1986. *The Theory of Database Concurrency Control*. Rockville, Maryland: Computer Science Press.

Parnas, D. L. 1972. On the criteria to be used in decomposing systems into modules, *CACM* 15: 1053–8.

Peterson, J. L. and Silberschatz, A. 1983. *Operating System Concepts*. Reading, Mass.: Addison-Wesley.

Pnueli, A. 1986. Applications of temporal logic to the specification and verification of reactive systems: a survey of current trends, *Current Trends in Concurrency*, Springer-Verlag LNCS-224, 510–84.

Powell, M. L. and Miller, B. P. 1983. Process migration in DEMOS/MP, *Proc. 8th Symp. Operating Systems Principles*, 110–19. New York: ACM SIGOPS.

Raphael, B. 1971. The frame problem in problem solving sy... *Heuristic Programming*, 159–69. Edinburgh: Edinburgh Uni...

Richards, M. 1971. The portability of the BCPL compiler, *Softw...*

Ritchie, D. M. and Thompson, K. 1974. The Unix time-sharing...

Saltzer, J. H. 1974. Protection and the control of information... 388–402.

Sato, H., Chikayama, T., Sugino, E. and Taki, K. 1987a. Outlines... *Convention IPS Japan*. (In Japanese)

Sato, M., Shimizu, H., Matsumoto, A., Rokusawa, K. and Goto, A. for PIM cluster with shared memory, *Logic Programming: P.* Cambridge, Mass.: MIT Press.

Seitz, C. L. 1985. The cosmic cube, *CACM* 28: 22–33.

Sergot M. J. 1982. A query-the-user facility for logic programming, *Ne... Computing*. Chichester: Ellis Horwood.

Shapiro, E. 1984a. Systems programming in Concurrent Prolog, *Proc.... ciples of Programming Languages*, 93–105. New York: ACM.

Shapiro, E. 1984b. Systolic programming: a paradigm for parallel proces... *5th Generation Computer Systems*, *Tokyo*, 458–71. Amsterdam: Nor...

Shapiro, E. 1986. Concurrent Prolog: a progress report, *Fundamentals (... Springer-Verlag LNCS-232: 277–313.

Shapiro, E. and Safra, M. 1986. Multiway merge with constant delay in C... *Generation Computing* 4: 211–216.

Shultis, J. 1983. A functional shell, *ACM SIGPLAN Notices* 18: 202–11.

Sloman, M. and Kramer, J. 1986. *Distributed Systems and Computer Netw...* stead: Prentice Hall.

Takagi, S., Yokoi, T., Uchida, S., Kurokawa, T., Hattori, T., Chikayama...

Tsuji, J. 1984. Overall design of SIMPOS, *Proc. 2nd Int. Logic Programm... Sweden*, 1–12.

Takeuchi, A. 1983. How to solve it in Concurrent Prolog. Unpublished note,...

Takeuchi, A. and Furukawa, K. 1986. Parallel logic programming languages, *P... Programming Conf.*, Springer-Verlag LNCS-225, 242–54.

Tanenbaum, A. S. and van Renesse, R. 1985. Distributed operating systems, *C... 17: 419–70.

Tanenbaum, A. S., Mullender, S. J. and van Renesse, R. 1986. Using sparse... distributed operating system, *Proc. 6th Int. Conf. on Distributed Computer Syste... IEEE.

Taylor, S. 1989. *Parallel Logic Programming Techniques*, Englewood Cliffs, New J... Hall.

Taylor, S., Av-Ron, E. and Shapiro, E. 1987a. A layered method for process and cod... *New Generation Computing* 5: 185–205.

Taylor, S., Safra, S. and Shapiro, E. 1987b. A parallel implementation of Flat Concu... *Int. J. Parallel Processing* 15: 245–75.

Tick, E. and Warren, D. H. D. 1984. Towards a pipelined Prolog processor, *New... Computing* 2: 323–345.

Uchida, S. 1987. Inference machines in FGCS project, *Proc. VLSI '87*, IFIP TC-10, V...

Ueda, K. 1986. Guarded Horn Clauses, EngD thesis, University of Tokyo.

Ullman, J. 1982. *Principles of Database Systems*, Rockville, Maryland; Computer Scien...

van Roy, P., Demoen, D. and Willems, Y. D. 1987. Improving the execution speed of Pr... modes, clause selection and determinism, *Proc. Int. Joint Conf. on Theory and Pr... Software Development*, Springer-Verlag LNCS-251, 111–25.

Wang, Y. and Morris, R. 1985. Load sharing in distributed computer systems, *IEEE...*

Comp...

Warren,... resea...

Warren,... Intel...

Weihl,... *Pro...*

Wirth,...

Wittie,... a r...

Wulf,... *Sy...*

Wulf,... *Sy...*

INDEX

scheduling, 22, 35, *see also* global scheduling, local scheduling
scheduling structure, 56, 58, 71
semantics of parallel logic programs, 32, 171, 181
semaphores, 11, 26
send/2 system call, 118
separation of computation and update, 128
separation of policy and mechanism, 23
Sequential Parlog Machine (SPM), 56, 60, 82
serializability, 128, 144
services, 97
    error handling in, 109
    implementation of, 97
    location of, 159
    possible actions, 98
    providing access to, 17, 103
    making robust, 111
    replication of, 110, 158
shared memory computers, 3, 17, 57, 67
shared resources, 17
shell, 122, 125, 140
short circuit, *see* programming techniques
Simula, 12
single assignment property, 16, 116
    and distributed implementation, 63
    and garbage collection, 79
Smalltalk, 36
SOLO, 8, 17
starvation, 154
state (in FP+), 127–9
    implementation of, 143
    transitions, 132
status messages, 38
    active, 40
    commit_error, 139
    exception, 37, 38, 65
    quiescent, 39
    stopped, 37, 38
    succeeded, 37, 38
status variable (in control call), 34, 36
Strand, 28, 89, 171
streams, *see* programming techniques
suspension structures, 12, 58
suspension table, 59, 60
symmetric unification algorithms, 74, 92
synchronization, 11, 17,
    in parallel logic programming, 16
synchronous communication, 13, 19, 68
system calls, 103, 120, 160

tail recursion, 57, 58, 70
task, 8, 22, 35
task management, 5, 22, 32, 35
    on multiprocessors, 43, 51, 74, 92
    on uniprocessors, 36, 69, 83
    performance, 83, 92
    and supervisors, 44, 48, 94, 104
task management primitives, 37
    @, 37
    CALL, 37, 72
    CONTINUE, 37, 72, 165
    PRIORITY, 50, 72, 165
    raise_exception, 37, 39, 109
    RUN, 163, 165
    STOP, 37, 38, 72, 94
    SUSPEND, 37, 72
    TASK, 37, 39, 72, 113, 165
task queue, 70
task record, 36, 37, 70
task registers, 71
task switch, 70, 73, 87
task types supported by kernel, 39
task/4 system call, 118
termination detection, 22
    kernel support for, 74
    implementation of, 45
    in parallel logic programs, 34
    in services, 109
test operations in FP, 62
Thoth, 17
timeslice
    for process, 58
    for task, 73, 164
transactions in FP+, 130, 139
transformation of programs, 135
    for control, 40, 83, 138, 169
transition rules for FP, 182
transputer, 19
two-stage commit, 144, 150

unification in FP, 28, 62
    failure of, 38
Unix, 5, 9, 24, 125, 140
user-level, *see* operating system structure

validation of system calls, 112
variable, *see* logical variable
varieties of process, 8
virtual copy, 143
virtual memory, 25
V kernel, 17, 24